Floss & Stan's

"Why are my leaves turning
yellow and falling off?"

Answer Book

Books by the Dworkins

THE APARTMENT GARDENER
BAKE YOUR OWN BREAD
BLEND IT SPLENDID
THE GOOD GOODIES

Floss & Stan's
"Why are my leaves turning yellow and falling off?"
Answer Book

🖋 🖋 🖋 🖋

Floss and Stan Dworkin

A Sunrise Book

E. P. DUTTON · NEW YORK

For information contact: E. P. Dutton,
2 Park Avenue, New York, N.Y. 10016

LIBRARY OF CONGRESS CATALOGING IN PUBLICATION DATA
Dworkin, Floss.
  Floss & Stan's "Why are my leaves turning
yellow and falling off?" Answer Book
    "A Sunrise book."   Includes index.
    1. House plants—Miscellanea. 2. Indoor gardening
—Miscellanea. 3. Container gardening—Miscellanea.
I. Dworkin, Stan, joint author. II. Title.
III. Title: Floss & Stan's "Why are my leaves turning yellow
and falling off?" Answer Book
SB419.D87   635.9′65   77-25098
ISBN: 0-87690-267-0

Published simultaneously in Canada by Clarke,
Irwin & Company Limited, Toronto and Vancouver
Designed by Ann Gold
Production Manager: Stuart Horowitz

10 9 8 7 6 5 4 3 2 1

First Edition

Contents

𝒯 𝒯 𝒯 𝒯

Preface

We didn't grow up green. Neither of us had a houseplant in sight when we were growing up. Neither of us studied horticulture in school. We studied plant books in the New York Public Library, and we studied plants at the greenhouses of the Brooklyn Botanic Garden and the New York Botanical Garden and on our own windowsills.

We can't even say we were self-educated in horticulture (though a great deal of what we know comes from the practical growing experience we have had, from the thousands and thousands of plants we have grown—and the many we have killed), because we have picked the brains of too many professional gardeners, plant-society members, botanists, taxonomists, plant pathologists, entomologists, and county agents—and we have been asked too many questions to consider ourselves *self*-educated.

We have always learned from questions: questions you have asked us and questions we've been forced to ask ourselves.

Our first job answering plant questions came years ago from the Horticultural Society of New York. We were paid $17 a day (for the two of us) for answering plant questions on the telephone on those days when the horticulturist was out or busy. We got that job by making pests of ourselves and asking questions. Their only fear was that we would recommend some poison spray that would kill (person, pet, or plants). Little did they know that even then we were very small on poison sprays.

The next summer we got the job of telephone horticulturists full-time. We worked out of our apartment, answering literally hundreds of phone calls (some of those callers kept our number for years). Our wages went up, and we were to keep a written record of the questions we were asked and turn it in after the summer. The sum was princely (we were broke and anything was princely), and we kept a good record. In fact, some of the questions asked that summer are in this book.

That was a really educational summer. We learned that problems "went around": that is, that plants could have epidemics, too. When a supplier brought a large number of a particular plant onto the market, we learned about that, too, because the questions would pour in. And we learned that it wasn't enough to be smart or well read or even to have the experience of growing the particular plants; we had to communicate the answer, too, to make clear the difference between "tolerating shade" and "demanding shade," for example.

And we learned that as our experiences were different and led to different conclusions from the books we read and the lecturers we listened to, so, also, were the experiences of the people who called us different from ours, and solutions to problems had to be fit to their needs.

When we finally began to teach and lecture, we couldn't find the gardening book we wanted to use, so we wrote *The Apartment Gardener,* which has given us a good deal of satisfaction and made us many friends since.

While *The Apartment Gardener* was being published, we got ourselves an hour-long radio program on WRVR-FM. We went after it because we felt New York needed a gardening program, and we got it because we were willing to start out working for nothing. They did let us call it "The Apartment Gardeners," after our book. Stan thought it might last for thirteen weeks; we've been on WRVR for five years. And the program stays exciting for us because it is a live call-in show.

Answering questions on the spot puts us on the spot, but when we need it we get help from our listeners in New York, New Jersey, southern Connecticut, and a little bit of Pennsylvania. We don't give out our home phone number anymore, but we do stay in the studio after the show to speak to those listeners who can't get through while we're on the air.

As for television, we were lucky. Three years ago, WNBC-TV was expanding its local news program to two hours and was looking for features. Gene Shalit—a man as terrific off camera as he is funny on—arranged a guest spot for us that served as an audition. The producers liked it, audience response was positive, and "The Garden Spot" became a part of *NewsCenter 4*.

We have always been lucky. Starting when we met each other, we have always been lucky.

During our first year on television we offered mail-out culture sheets, detailing the material we presented in our five-minute spots. And when we were doing two spots a week, we were getting some 2,000 letters a week. Which is insanity. We had to handle the mail ourselves (we wound up hiring a secretary), and a great many of the letters required personal answers. We stopped doing it because it was too expensive, in terms of dollars (even though NBC paid for the printing and postage) and time. We didn't write a book that year—we hardly *read* a book that year.

The rest of the questions in this book are largely from our radio callers and television correspondents.

We've met a lot of super people in television: talented, bright, helpful. That's one of the reasons we like it and stay. Another is that it has given us more excuse than ever to visit gardens and meet gardeners.

The truth is, we're being paid to do what we want to do.

One day in the spring of 1977 we filmed a feature piece for *NewsCenter 4* about community gardens. As we were packing up to leave, the organizer of the garden told us that we were the spiritual "parents" of that garden. In 1976 she had heard a guest on our radio show (a county agent) discuss community gardens and give a phone number where he could be reached for help. She called and they started to plan. When community participants were needed, she sent a request to us and we announced it over the radio. And workers came on down. Now that Lower East Side garden is an exemplar, and that reel of film we shot is making the rounds of other counties to stimulate other community gardens.

Now that feels good.

✔ ✔ ✔ ✔

Emergency Care—
What to Do Till the
Plant Doctor Comes

Paste this page on your refrigerator door, right next to fire department, police, and other emergency numbers.

It is not uncommon for plants to go into shock: new plants because of the dramatic change in environment or because of being bounced around in a truck; established plants because of repotting or over- or underwatering; newly propagated plants because of being taken out of the high-humidity propagation box.

All of these are massive insults to the roots and to the plant's circulatory system. You can help the plant along in its own recovery. You can take the pressure off those roots and that circulatory system by creating a high-humidity environment around the plant.

How? By putting it into a plastic bag. Big plants can go into a plastic cleaner's bag. Huge plants can go under a clear-plastic drop-cloth. The clear airtight plastic bag holds in the moisture but also permits in light. If the plant *can* recover, it will recover this way.

When the plant has recovered—you can tell because it looks perked up, with firm leaves held erect—punch a few small holes in the bag every day, to permit in a little of that cruel dry air of reality. When the bag is in tatters, the plant should be acclimated and ready to take its normal place.

How to Use This Book

You can use this book to get rid of almost any insect. Simply open the book, place the insect on the page, then slam the book closed. Squash! The bug is dead.

Or, you can look into the section BUGS: FRIENDLY AND UN-, either for a specific pest or to browse until you come to familiar symptoms.

Environmental problems are difficult to diagnose for yourself, and so you may not know what the cause is, just the problem. Again, browse through those sections on WATERING, FEEDING, LIGHT, etc., until you find a group of symptoms that sounds right. Trust your intuition. Many times we find that a questioner half-suspects the problem quite accurately.

If you're looking for the care of a specific plant (or you have a problem with a specific plant), you may find what you want to know in Part I: PLANT FAMILIES. If you don't find the specific plant there, look at what we've said about the *family*, anyhow. You may get some ideas about growing your plant from growing its close relatives.

More plants are discussed under specific growing conditions, such as TERRARIUMS, HERBS, and BALCONY, TERRACE, ROOFTOP. Again, the section may give you a hint, even if the particular plant is not there.

There is also some information about the general needs of plants, their soil mixes and watering, their light requirements, in the introduction to each plant family.

Keep track of your successes; don't feel guilty about your failures. Every gardener kills a few on the way to learning. Just water your survivors.

☞ ☞ ☞ ☞

Growing:
The Short Course

This is the short course on growing houseplants (one afternoon a week, ½ credit). If you want the long course (five mornings plus a Saturday lab, 4 credits toward the advanced degree) and more detail, see the various cultural notes in Part II; they expand upon the topics below but are in alphabetical order.

LIGHT

A good rule of thumb for growing plants in natural light is to give them as much sun as you can, without burning the leaves. If you have to burn a leaf to find out, it's worth it.

Even plants that will tolerate shade will do better in bright light (though not sun, necessarily).

If your plants are leaning toward the light, they are not getting enough.

Under fluorescent lighting, grow as close to the tubes as you can, without burning the leaves. If leaves grow pale, it may be a TEMPERATURE PROBLEM (which see), not too-strong light.

SOIL

Plants in pots have drainage problems and for the most part must be given a soil that drains well and one that dries (however slightly) between waterings. Even plants that demand a lot of water need some air at their roots: not air pockets, but tiny fluffy spaces between the soil particles.

Plants are not really big feeders, so their soil mixes need not be the breakfast of champions. Texture is more important than nutritional content.

You can use a commercial potting mix, but such mixes are richer than necessary and they are too heavy. Lighten them by adding one part of coarse perlite to three parts of commercial soil mix.

HUMIDITY

Low humidity is a slow killer of plants. A small hygrometer will give you a ballpark figure: if it shows a relative humidity below 25 percent, you and your plants are in trouble.

In the winter, the heat goes on and the humidity plummets—and if you want to keep your plants healthy and your own nose from running, humidify.

Grouping plants together helps. Plants give off water vapor, and some of it will go to a close neighbor.

Pebble trays on your radiators and windowsills help—if you keep them filled with water at all times.

Humidifiers are a great help, but in a large house or apartment you may need more than one.

One of our friends has solved the problem—for his plants if not for himself—by putting all of his hundreds of prize-worthy plants into one room. That former pantry, now a fluorescent-light garden, is easily humidified with a single humidifier. That still left him with the heat problem caused by all those lights—but an exhaust fan took care of that.

WATERING

Water all your plants well, until water comes out the hole in the bottom. After a half-hour, throw away any excess water left in the saucer. If your pot has no hole—shame.

Virtually any water can be used for watering plants, so long as it does not contain alcohol or bleach or ammonia or a similar caustic.

If your tap water is full of chlorine or fluorine, leave it in an open pail overnight: some will evaporate.

Cold water is bad for plants and warm water is good for plants.

FEEDING

Feed less. No more than half the strength the manufacturer touts and half as often.

Mix up your feeding: don't be loyal to one food. Variety is better for your plants.

Read the labels.

BUG JUICE

We don't spray much in the way of poisons. And then only as the last-ditch line of defense. In our living quarters, where we have to breathe, we don't spray at all.

We have used ladybugs indoors with great success.

PINCHING, PRUNING, GROOMING

Plants must have their weak growth, their dying parts, their yellowed leaves removed. This grooming makes plants healthier, stimulates new stronger growth, gets rid of parts which are a drain on the plant, and allows the light to reach the good parts.

Buggy parts can be cut off and some of your worst troubles thrown away.

Plants need support. Most of them get it from their roots. But if a normally upright-growing plant is not being supported sufficiently by its roots, you are going to have to stake it: put in a support to which you can gently tie the plant. The best time to stake is when you repot. But it is better to put a stake into a pot of soil and roots than to allow the plant to flop around. That can break the stem.

Pinching promotes branching, but it's optional.

TEMPERATURE

While there are plants to fit almost every temperature niche from the subarctic to the equatorial, houseplant growers usually do best with tropical plants. Their temperature preferences are similar enough to people's (around 70°F.) so they are compatible.

Plants that can take a hard freeze usually make poor houseplants (miniature rose is an exception), and plants that must have cool temperatures to thrive seldom do well as houseplants for the average grower.

Many orchids need a 15° temperature drop at night to set bud. Camellias, gardenias, and some others need a 10° night drop. That can be a problem. Most plants, though, don't give a damn.

For best growth, lower your thermostat a few degrees. If you need a light sweater, you will be amazed at how well your houseplants do.

Virtually all plants react to season in some way, even in our thermostatically controlled buildings. Some slow their growth in the winter. Some die down to the soil and go completely dormant. A plant with South African ancestry may go dormant in the summer. Even plants that are completely removed from daylight may show a closing-up of their leaves at or near sunset.

Plants are adaptable. On the grand scale, that is how they have stayed around in the world as long as they have—a lot longer than animals. You may not think them adaptable as you throw out your third dead philodendron, but they are.

And their adaptive mechanisms are many and varied: Monstera (split-leaf philo) makes cut leaves in moist air and entire (uncut) leaves in dry air; *Pandanus veitchii* (screw pine) makes leaves with a creamy stripe in bright light but plain green leaves in low light, creating more green to photosynthesize; *Sinningia speciosa* (gloxinia) and many other plants grow bigger in a big pot and smaller in a small pot.

Young plants are better able to adapt to large changes than mature ones. A great many mature plants are sold that have been "spoiled" by the high humidity, bright light, and constant watering of greenhouse life or subtropical or tropical life.

Plants grown in conditions similar to yours have a great chance to thrive for you (is your neighbor upstairs selling off a plant? buy it). Plants grown in the tropics and shipped to your city have less chance.

Plants can't run or fight or switch. They stay in their pots, trying to adapt to your indoor environment: it's the only one they have. Meet them halfway.

Part I ✑ ✑ ✑ ✑
Plant Families

ACANTHACEAE   Acanthus Family

If you have been to Greece, you have seen memorials to the acanthus: the scalloping on the capitals of Corinthian columns depicts acanthus leaves. For most of us, though, members of this family are not quite as enduring as marble. As houseplants, most of them demand a relative humidity in the 40 percent area and constant moisture at their roots in a fluffy, porous soil. Many of them are fascinating, though, with beautifully spotted, streaked, or veined foliage.

Hypoestes sanguinolenta is the pink-polka-dot plant (light green leaves with pink splotches), and the easiest of the Acanthus family to manage as a houseplant, but it requires frequent pinching to keep it from growing leggy. Legginess (loss of lower leaves) is a frequent complaint with this family, especially if they've had erratic watering.

Hemigraphis is a genus with several handsome species, some with waffled leaves. They really need terrarium culture, but will soon grow too large for all but the biggest terrariums.

Two plants in the Acanthus family that will stay compact in your terrarium are *Fittonia verschaffeltii* and *Chamaeranthemum venosum*.

If you grow *Beleperone guttata* (shrimp plant), be sure you keep it well lit, with some direct sun. By the way, those shrimpy-looking things are bracts (adapted leaves), not flowers. The flowers are white and peek out from the bracts.

One little-grown beauty of the Acanthus family is *Jacobinia velutina*. We've neglected ours shamefully—kept it in the same pot for years, allowed it to go too dry—but still it produces 4-inch strawberry-pink flower heads for us in an east window two or three times a year. It must be cut back after flowering to produce new stems for the next flowering. Keep yours well watered.

Why do the lower leaves of my zebra plant turn yellow and fall off?

Because of inadequate culture. A few home growers have luck with *Aphelandra squarrosa* (zebra plant), but they are difficult houseplants for most of us. Zebra plants must have high humidity, constant moisture (though sopping soil may rot them), and strong diffuse light.

If yours gets too leggy, cut off and root the top or air-layer it. Keep the soil moderately moist, and the bottom half of the stem may re-sprout for you. But improve the care you give it, or it will just drop its leaves again.

Can a zebra plant be flowered again?

Yes, but not easily, and not from a tip that has already flowered. Pinch out the tip to encourage branching; keep the humidity high; top-dress, or repot after flowering into very well-drained soil; keep well watered but not sopping wet; feed with 15–30–15 plant food at one-fourth label strength about every three weeks when the plant is in active growth; and give it bright light with some morning sun.

And good luck.

Can I just take a tip cutting of my zebra plant?

Yes, but if your *Aphelandra squarrosa* (zebra plant) has a bunch of leaves at the top and a bare stem, you would do better to air-layer the top.

How much sun does *Jacobinia velutina* need?

This is a truly superior houseplant, flowering best in bright sun, but flowering somewhat in just bright light, too. Cut back after flowering, it will resprout and reflower.

Don't let it get too dry between watering or you will lose leaves—and your flower heads—prematurely.

AIZOACEAE   Carpetweed Family

The Carpetweed family contains some quite advanced (euphemism for bitching difficult) houseplants. Lampranthus (ice plant), for one, seems to rot if you merely stand over it and say "overwater." Seriously, they are vulnerable to overwatering and will not flower unless they get full sun.

I repotted my tiger's-jaw plant and it just *rotted* on me.

Faucaria tigrina is a succulent, and cacti and cactuslike succulents must be *potted dry.* Allow them to go dry for several days (or more with a large plant), then pot into an almost-dry, very well-drained mix, and then don't water for several days to weeks. It sounds cruel, but it keeps them alive.

AMARYLLIDACEAE   Amaryllis Family

Success with amaryllis and other members of this family is too exciting to describe in a plant book.

Tuberose (*Polianthes tuberosa*) is almost foolproof. Pot a single tuber into an 8-inch pot, and put outdoors when danger of frost is past. Water it like a houseplant, and you will be rewarded with creamy-white flowers and a scent that will fill your home (*if* you bring the pot inside—some growers find the scent too strong for comfort). To keep the tubers until the following spring, you'll have to keep them cool and dormant over the winter: like gladioli.

Lycoris squamigera is called resurrection lily or naked lady because the flowers come up in late summer about six weeks after the foliage has disappeared. Give it a large pot and plenty of sun, and you might be able to manage it on a sun porch.

One member of the family without a bulbous root is *Curculigo capitulata,* sometimes miscalled fan palm. It is a delightful and easy houseplant with pleated leaves, requiring even moisture but only moderate light and humidity. It can be propagated easily by separating the offsets that form at the base.

You can also find questions on bulbous members of the Amaryllis family in Part III under INDOORS-OUTDOORS.

I've recently bought for my south window a lovely little plant which was identified as "century plant." How tall will it grow? Does it really bloom only once a century?

Agave americana (century plant) can take twenty years to flower, but we wouldn't worry about that if we were you. It won't flower in your south window, at least not until and unless it grows about 6 feet tall and 5 feet wide. Then (as we've seen in tropical islands) the inflorescence is about 20 feet tall. The parent plant dies after flowering.

Still, it is very attractive, and if the spines don't get you, you'll probably love it.

When will my clivia lose its leaves?

When you kill it. Clivias are evergreen—they have no true dormancy. They only *look* like amaryllis, which do have a dormancy and do lose their leaves.

Will my clivia ever bloom? I've had it for five years and I'm about to give up hope.

Hang in there! Clivias (named after the Duchess of Clive) are terrific in the greenhouse or in those parts of the country where the winters are just cool enough to stimulate bud set: it is a long stretch (several weeks) of cool temperatures which causes these plants to set bud. If you keep them in a warm place over the winter, they won't flower. Even then, they must be *quite* mature (it varies) and crowded in the pot.

I have been given a beautiful amaryllis, just coming into flower. How can I care for it to keep the flower as long as possible, and how can I bring it into flower again next year?

For now, keep it cool and well watered, in as high a relative humidity as you can manage (but don't mist the flower or you will water-spot it). Dry air, dry roots, and high temperature will cause the flower to go faster.

Not that amaryllis flowers last long under the best of circumstances. But the life of the flowers can be extended by snipping off the anthers (they hold the pollen) with a small scissors as soon as each flower opens. Apparently, being pollinated signals the flower that the season is successfully over.

Once the flowers go, allow the stalk to dry out and then cut it off.

Put the plant into as much light and sun as you have and water it normally: that is, allow the soil to go dry down to about $\frac{1}{4}$ inch below the surface before rewatering.

When the weather permits (no danger of freezing), put the plant outdoors, into sun, water it as any houseplant outdoors, and feed it when you feed your other plants (one feeding a month, say) .

In the fall, keep it out until frost touches the leaves (but not the bulbs) . When you bring it inside, allow it to dry in a dim, cool place for about three months—until it resprouts. The next growth that comes up should be the flower bud. Resume watering.

If you want bloom in time for Christmas bring the plant indoors in earliest September, and begin to reduce watering until the soil goes dry.

Can I put a few smallish amaryllis bulbs into one pot?

Don't do it. The hippeastrum (amaryllis) hybrids like to be crowded into their pots, especially when young: pot them with an inch of soil around the bulb (and the top half of the bulb should be above the soil line) .

If they were bulblets about ¾ inch in diameter or less, we might put them into a community pot until they were of blooming size. Amaryllis bulbs may produce flowers when they are as little as 1¼ inches to 1½ inches in diameter, but you can't be sure of bloom until your bulb is fatter than 2½ inches.

Can I grow amaryllis from seed?

Certainly, though they will take three to five years to bloom from seed, that is, if you mean the showy hippeastrum, not the true amaryllis, which are faster. We raised *Amaryllis striata* from seed to flowering completely under a bank of fluorescent lights in two years.

If you gathered the hippeastrum seeds from your own plant, remember that you cannot expect the offspring to look like the hybrid plant.

Start seeds by thrusting them into a pot full of damp long-haired sphagnum moss. Cover the pot with clear plastic and set it in a warm (75°F.) place. Germination is not fast.

Well, here it is, January, and my amaryllis is making big healthy leaves—*but no flower*. This is some kind of ungrateful plant, because I even gave it a new pot this spring.

Stop right there. Amaryllis don't like to be repotted. Repotting can cost you a year's flowering. Don't repot your amaryllis until they break their pots. And then put them into a pot about twice the diameter of the bulb, and do leave the top half of the bulb uncovered.

Next year, and the following year, instead of repotting, top-dress. Scrape out the top inch of soil and put in fresh soil and a bit of bone meal.

APOCYNACEAE   Dogbane Family

We would guess that this is called "dogbane" family because some of its members have poisonous foliage. Many exude a white sap when cut.

The Apocynaceae grow like shrubby weeds in the tropics: nerium (oleander), allamanda (yellow oleander), dipladenia, carissa (Natal plum). But they are not widely grown as houseplants. Which is a shame, because they will make large and handsome potted plants, if kept well pinched and pruned.

Carissa is our favorite of the Apocynaceae. When ripe, the plums make terrific free eating in the tropics, and it will even flower and fruit on a sunny home windowsill.

Grow the tropical members of the family in a well-drained soil, kept evenly moist, but not wet, and mist frequently. Keep an eye out for scale.

Vinca is a hardy member of this same family, and can be grown in a tub on a balcony or terrace, provided the winter sun is not too strong. Vinca can be grown alone, or as a ground cover around a larger shrub.

Is oleander poisonous?

People who write on the subject say yes (though, for anyone writing on poisonous plants, it's in their interest to include as many plants as possible).

But in conversation with the retired head of Bermuda's Department of Agriculture, where oleander is grown extensively as a hedge and specimen plant, we learned that in all his life he'd never heard of a case of oleander poisoning. He says cattle graze right up to the oleander without harm. He also said the leaves *are very bitter,* so it may be that cattle and Bermudians are too smart to eat enough of the plant to hurt them. However, it was a guide from this same Department of Agriculture who, eleven years ago, first warned us that oleander *is* poisonous.

Under normal circumstances, then, oleander is safe to have as a houseplant—but if you have a child who is a determined chewer of even *bitter* things, then perhaps it would be wise to avoid it, just to be safe.

Can I grow an oleander shrub on my sun porch?

Absolutely! Give it bright sun, ample water, and moderate humidity (a minimum of 40 percent). In early spring, prune it a bit to make it shrubbier, and you should have a lovely large flowering shrub.

By the way, given enough sun, your *Nerium oleander* (oleander) could flower year round.

I'm looking for a flowering shrub to make a tender bonsai. What do you suggest?

Carissa grandiflora (Natal plum). The leaves are a lovely green—deep and glossy—the flowers are white and sweet-scented, and the red fruit is tasty. (Yes, it will fruit for you in home conditions.)

Available as outdoor shrubs in frost-free climates, we have found named cultivars such as 'Boxwood,' 'Bonsai,' 'Cascade,' 'Horizontalis,' and others, and they are all great. The cultivars are not as thorny as the wild species, but if these cultivars are not available in your area, take any carissa you can get. If your area has none, get some seed. In fact, seed-grown bonsai are usually better, since you can shape them from the word go.

We got our seed by eating the delicious fruit and spitting.

Surinam cherry (*Eugenia uniflora*), a tropical member of the Myrtle family, also starts very readily from the seed left after eating the tart-sweet fruit, and is easy of culture if you provide enough water.

ARACEAE   Arum Family

Including as it does the simple heartleaf philodendron, the Arum family is one of the most popular houseplant families. But if you generalize care of all Arums by care of that durable, long-suffering plant, you'll mistreat most of them.

Arums are generally water-loving plants, with some, such as colocasia (sometimes called elephant ears) demanding to be constantly wet at their roots, and others, such as pistia (water lettuce) growing on the surface of the water, without soil roots at all.

These are extreme cases, but they do point the way. Aside from the commonest philo, your arums will take more water (and more sun) than you think.

If you can provide the high humidity it must have, alocasia is a beautiful plant, with colored veins and gorgeously leathery leaves.

Acoris is a grasslike plant, and will make a handsome ground cover in a terrarium.

Zantedeschia (calla lily) is quite possible in a pot, if you can water and humidify it. It shows very clearly its Arum family descent by its hooded flowers.

I bought a *Philodendron* 'Friedrich Stedii' at the botanic garden sale. I have it in sun and I water it well and it's growing like crazy, but the new leaves are coming in looking like normal philodendron leaves instead of the Swiss-cheese effect I expected.

Your culture sounds fine, so try this idea for size. When a philoden- dron cutting is taken and rooted for sale, the rooted cutting shows the old mature leaves, but the new leaves that come in are, of course, *juvenile* leaves—which are entire (without holes). Given your culture (which should include rather high humidity along with the sun and water), the new leaves should get holes as they mature—which may take several months—or years.

What is a "self-heading selloum"? I got one as a gift and that's what the label said. And how do I care for it?

"Selloum" is a species of large-leafed philodendron—one of the most popular in cultivation. "Self-heading" means that the leaves come out of the growing tip, rather than from along the stem like a vine.

Philodendron selloum is a self-header and has no vining form.

All the big-leafed philos take roughly the same care: bright light with some direct sun, ample water, and a relative humidity in the 40 percent to 50 percent range. They can grow quite large.

Why won't my fiddle-leaf philo (*Philodendron panduraeforme*) grab hold of its redwood totem? I have to hold it on with rubber bands and string.

Let us ask you a question—honestly, would *you* root into a dry totem? Keep your totem moist and the roots will take hold. Or you can substitute a totem made of long-haired sphagnum moss wrapped in a thick layer around a stick (fishline will hold it on). Keep this moist and your philo should root into it quite readily.

My *Philodendron selloum* isn't doing too well, but it is making an- other little plant right next to it. Can I remove this plant and pot it up separately?

Certainly. An offset of this sort is the best way to propagate your *Philodendron selloum*. Carefully dig down between the parent plant and the offset and separate them with a knife—cutting as little as possible and keeping as many roots as you can on the offset. Pot into rich, well-drained soil.

But why is the parent plant doing poorly? And can you expect the offset to do any better? These large-leafed philodendrons need bright light (with some sun), ample water, and moderate humidity (40 percent or better). Give both plants this kind of treatment and both mother and child should thrive.

I have a miniature philo growing in my bathroom—have you ever heard of such a thing?

If your bathroom is like ours, it is quite dim. And if it is quite-to-rather dim, then what you have is not a miniature, but a normal *Philodendron oxycardium* (heartleaf philodendron) that has been *dwarfed* by poor conditions. Put it into a larger pot and give it more light. If it then stays small-leafed, propagate it like crazy, because you've got something quite valuable.

My velvet-leaf philodendron is doing badly. I grow it on my north window, right next to my regular philo (which is doing fine). The leaves are pale around the edges and droop a lot, and the vines look leggy. What can I do?

You can grow a plant better suited to your situation. *Philodendron andreanum* (velvet-leaf philodendron) requires exacting care: bright light, lots of water, high humidity (50 percent or better), and warm temperatures—almost a terrarium plant (we've grown it in a terrarium, and there it thrives). Try aglaonema (Chinese evergreen) instead.

How can I train my selloum to grow up a trellis?

It won't and you can't. *Philodendron selloum* is a "self-header," which means all the leaves come out of the middle, like an African violet, rather than along the stem, like an ivy.

For a good vining philo how about *P. panduraeforme* (fiddleleaf philodendron). It has a vining habit and can be kept compact with pruning.

I know you say to avoid invalids, but I couldn't say no to this philodendron because it is so unusual. It has a five-pointed leaf and is climbing up a redwood totem (in fact it's hanging over the top). It had lost several of its leaves before I got it, and the remainder are

looking a little pale. The store owner said to keep it on the dry side—but maybe that's what made it look the way it does. Have you any suggestions?

We will refrain from comments about buying sick plants.

If the five points are well separated and slim, you could have *Philodendron* 'Florida,' or *P.* 'Florida compacta,' and it is indeed a handsome plant. And your suspicions about its watering are well founded. The large-leafed philodendrons are big drinkers and need quite bright light with some direct sun (though avoid putting the plant into bright sun too quickly: if it's been grown a while in the dark it could get sunburned). They also require good humidity to do their best.

In order to encourage branching and leaf growth down on the bare stem, cut it off at the top of the totem. Then when it grows past the totem top again—cut it again. This kind of pruning can, with good culture, give you a bushy plant.

My big-leafed philodendron is making these big things that look like roots out of its stem. What are they?

Roots. Aerial roots. If they frighten you, you can cut them off without harming the plant. But they do have a function: they take supplementary water from the moist air.

My two large-leafed philodendrons have begun to go downhill; they are slowly losing their bottom leaves—one leaf at a time turns yellow and falls off. They get morning sun, and I water them when they go dry.

The kind of thing you describe, with the plants losing lower leaves one at a time, sounds like chronic underwatering. It's the symptom of a plant trying to conserve itself, to hang on. It gives up the less efficient oldest leaves and preserves its most important part: the growing tip. Large-leaf philos demand much more water than the small-leafed philos.

I have a Swiss-cheese philodendron that was recently given to me by my mother before she moved, and it's just not doing well. The leaves seem pale and weak. It grew beautifully for my mother. Does it hate me?

That's one of the great things about plants: they hate nobody.

Perhaps the plant did better for mom because she treated it better: more sun, more water, better humidity, no cold drafts.

Or, perhaps the plant is just resentful of being moved. If it was whipped around in the moving, or jarred, it could be showing signs of trauma. Or, it may be just the move itself that has upset the plant's equilibrium. Mist the leaves more; increase the light, if it isn't in a bright place. In general, treat it like some kind of invalid for a while.

Is dumb cane really poisonous?

Definitely, yes. Though people's reaction to dieffenbachia (dumb cane) vary. We know personally someone who was hospitalized after using the same knife on a dieffenbachia and then on an apple. Wash your hands and utensils after working with the plant.

We got a house-warming gift of a large dieffenbachia in a plastic pot. Should we transplant it into a clay pot?

Should you? No. But can you? Yes, if you wish.

Do consider, however, that dieffenbachias are big drinkers and that the plastic pot loses no moisture by evaporation through the sides, as would a clay pot.

We agree that a clay pot is more attractive, but be prepared for more frequent watering.

You say dieffenbachia needs bright sun, but I have a small-leafed dieffenbachia that is making hooded flowers out of direct sun.

We just love questions that start out "You say . . ."

The odds are that your "small-leafed dieffenbachia" is not a dieffenbachia at all but an aglaonema (Chinese evergreen). Dieffenbachias make "rattail" flowers, aglaonemas make "hooded" flowers, and they flower in very little light. There are varieties of the two plants with similar variegations on the leaves, but we've never seen a small-leafed dieffenbachia of flowering size. New on the market is a dwarf dieffenbachia—but even this hybrid doesn't have leaves as small as Chinese evergreen.

How do I water my Chinese evergreen?

Aglaonemas (Chinese evergreens) are easy plants, but from a water-loving family—the arums. Feel the soil: when it is dry $\frac{1}{4}$ inch below the surface, water well.

Large cuttings of aglaonema will grow well for years in a vase of water.

Can I propagate my Chinese evergreen from tip cuttings?

Easily. They'll even root in water.

My anthurium leaves are yellowing. Are they in too much light?

Perhaps—though usually anthuriums in too high light will just go a paler green, rather than yellow. Yellow indicates overwatering, perhaps. Anthuriums want lots of water, and to be kept evenly moist; but if their potting mix is not sufficiently aerated, you can overwater and eventually get root rot. For a potting mix that can be watered a lot without causing rot, mix one-third to a half of your potting mix with long-fibered sphagnum moss cut into small pieces.

Can I grow pothos in a decorative pot without a drainage hole?

Not for long. Unless you are a most careful waterer. With no hole to permit the water to drain out, the roots sit in water and are easy prey to rot.

Pothos (it used to be *Scindapsis aureus* but has undergone a name change to *Epipremnum aureum*) is a member of the Arum family, and aroids are water-lovers, so it will hang in there longer than most plants. But its growth will be weak after a time, and it will not make a good plant.

I had the loveliest devil's ivy—white and green instead of yellow and green—but it never grew and just petered out. I thought devil's ivy was easy to grow.

Most forms are, but your variety of so-called devil's ivy (*Epipremnum aureum* 'Marble Queen') is a good example of a plant that wouldn't be found at all in nature. It has so little chlorophyll-producing potential that it wouldn't survive in the wild.

In cultivation it requires high humidity and very careful watering—with the tendency to rot if overwatered and to lose leaves if underwatered. It needs strong light with some direct sun.

For this much agony, we expect a little more ecstasy.

My monstera is in flower! If it sets fruit, will it be edible? I hear it is delicious.

Congratulations. Yes, it is delicious. That's where it gets its name: *Monstera deliciosa*. In Bermuda it is called "locust and wild honey."

If you get fruit, wait until it is fully ripe: until the individual segments are yellow and ready to fall off of their own accord. Eating the unripe fruit has been likened to chewing on tiny slivers of glass.

My spathiphyllum leaves are turning yellow at their edges and up the center and dying. What could cause that?

Sounds like a poisoning of some kind. Overfertilizing will cause that kind of damage. So will an alcoholic drink dumped on the soil during a party. So will an animal's urinating in the soil. (See PETS 'N' PLANTS.)

If you've been feeding, stop. Water the plant with tap water, overwatering and draining off the excess: this will leach out some of the harmful chemicals in the soil.

Spathiphyllums are such strong growers that you could even bareroot it and plant it in fresh soil.

I bought a large pothos on a totem for $50. When I bought it the leaves were about 8 inches across and partially cut (I'd never seen a pothos with cut leaves before). The new leaves are getting progressively smaller and they are no longer cut. Fifty dollars is a lot to pay for a totem full of ordinary pothos. Is there anything I can do to make the leaves get cut again?

In Florida, you can see *Epipremnum aureum* (golden pothos) with deeply cut leaves 2 feet across climbing up buildings. The form of it we see (and buy) locally is the juvenile form. The plant you bought probably had been raised in the tropics. You would have to provide bright sun, high humidity, and ample water to get it to mature. But even then you're unlikely to get the plant to mature sufficiently to produce large cut leaves.

Sorry, friend.

We have seen the mature leaves in the North, but the plant was years old and growing from the soil beneath the bench in a greenhouse.

I did what you suggested for my monstera, and the new growth is doing quite well. But the old leaves that were damaged by low watering are still brown and yellowing. Is there anything I can do?

Cut them off. Leaves damaged by poor culture won't "heal." They are a drain on the plant and are not carrying their weight. You can remove the entire leaf, or you can trim away the brown and yellow parts.

My caladium did fine all summer, but now its stems are drooping. I water it well, keep it out of direct sun, mist it, etc. Why?

At this time of year [October], it could simply be going dormant. Slow down watering and, as the plant dies back, stop altogether. (But don't allow the soil to go dust-dry.) Keep the pot cool, and wait. When top growth resumes in a few months, water it and bring the pot into a warm place.

By the way, for next spring, caladiums can take direct sun.

Why did my caladium leaves turn yellow and fall off? When I dug up the soil, there was no tuber.

Caladiums go dormant in the fall, at which time their leaves turn yellow one at a time or a few at a time until all are dead. Watering must be reduced at this time, and then stopped completely. If watering is not stopped, the dormant tuber may well rot (as it seems to have done in your case). In the future, after dormancy has been reached, store your tuber in its pot, rather dry, until January or February. Then restart it in a shallow pot or flat of peat moss. When roots develop, pot it up. Keep it warm, watered, and in bright light. Caladiums will take quite a bit of sun, and they prefer an acid soil.

How do I propagate my caladium?

Separate out the offsets that form from the base and pot them individually.

Greenhouse growers can try cutting the tubers into large segments (with a sterile knife) just after they start into new growth in the spring, dusting the cuts with fungicide, then rooting them in a sterile medium. We really hate to recommend the cutting up of tubers: it seems to fail so often.

I grew an elephant-ear caladium in my garden this summer. Can I dig it up and grow it indoors, just as I do my fancy-leafed caladiums?

Elephant ears are not caladiums; they are either alocasia or colocasia—both members of the Arum family, both growing from a tuber. Theoretically, they are possible to grow indoors (certainly, they are not hardy outdoors anywhere but in the tropics).

But you have to provide high humidity, large pots, and constant moisture at the roots. Also, you have to expect that the digging up might send the plant into dormancy. If it does go dormant, just keep it warm, and supply the tuber with a soupçon of water until it resprouts. You are unlikely to get as large leaves indoors as you enjoyed outdoors.

What do dieffenbachias need?

Bright sun, ample water, warm temperatures—and fewer sellers telling people that they are low-light plants.

Here it is, midsummer. The temperatures are warm, the days are long, the air is damp. Yet, I bought a dieffenbachia—very healthy-looking with huge leaves—three weeks ago and it's showing all the signs of shock. How can that be?

You're right. The conditions in your home are as good as they can ever be. But that plant was grown in Florida or Costa Rica or Puerto Rico with more intense sun (the "huge" leaves testify to that), with saturated air, lots of water, and, probably, force feeding.

Your best conditions are so much less than it is used to, that it is indeed going into shock. Give it your brightest sun, frequent misting, and watering when the soil goes dry down to a ¼ inch below the soil surface.

Also, it is just possible that the plant is reacting to rough trucking and not its present environment. In that case, it will want the high humidity and bright sun, but less water. If the surface of the soil is very slow to dry out, this kind of root disturbance is likely. Also try wiggling the stem; if it is indeed wobbly, stake it firmly.

My dieffenbachia sits on a table in my window, and its leaves are bending over because it's touching the ceiling. Now it is making these three small plants from out of the base. Can I take them out and put them into different pots?

Yes, you can. In fact, they probably have a small root system going for them already. Turn the plant out of its pot and loosen each offset gently and carefully, breaking as few roots as possible. Each offset can then be potted into porous soil, and will probably make a decent plant.

But why do that? Why not air-layer the top of the big plant, and then cut the big stem off 2 inches above the soil. Also, cut the leftover stem into 3-inch pieces, allow them to dry for a few hours, and put them into an open or closed prop box (lay them horizontal, halfway into damp sand, perlite, or vermiculite). This will give you the top, and any stem sections that sprout, *and* the three offsets in the original pot: which is probably as much dieffenbachia as any sane person wants. This way, the offsets don't go through the trauma of separation and repotting.

The leaves on my dieffenbachia are coming in smaller, and the stem is getting thin. Do you think I should feed it?

We think you should sun it. Your plant is suffering from lack of sun. Dieffenbachia is a bright-sun plant. When your plant is in a good environment and making active growth, then feed it every few weeks with half-strength fish emulsion.

My dieffenbachia flowered (believe it or not), and now it's looking just awful—droopy and pale. I haven't changed the care. What can I do?

Treat it like an invalid for a while: increase the humidity; reduce the light a bit; be careful not to overwater. We can't tell whether the plant flowered because it was in trouble (some plants will flower when severely injured), or it is in trouble because the flowering took so much out of it.

At any rate, what you describe is not unheard of though rare, and the kind of special care we describe often sets the plant to rights again.

Reports about dieffenbachias flowering come to us in spurts—we'll hear of none for a year, then of several in a single month. We have wondered if these flowerings might be due to a particular air pollutant. There *are* gases that inhibit and stimulate flowering (such as ethylene gas, which destroys flowers on orchids but stimulates bud set on bromeliads).

The leaf tips of my dieffenbachia look "burnt."

Perhaps they are—literally burnt, that is. Dieffenbachias take a good deal of water. Perhaps you are letting yours go chronically dry. A chronic drying may cause your leaf tips to burn. Or the plant may need repotting. Or you may have overfertilized. You'll have to decide which it is.

My dieffenbachia leaves are coming in curled and they don't open fully. It lives in a south window.

Perhaps the south window is too hot. The dieffenbachia needs the sun, but it doesn't care for the kind of heat that can build up behind the glass in a south window. Put a thermometer right where the plant is and find out. It also wants a good deal of water. Feel the soil: if it is dry more than $1/4$ inch below the surface, water well. And mist the leaves frequently with tepid water.

Can I cut the top off my dieffenbachia and just root it?

We have had the tops of dieffenbachias rooting and growing in water for three years, but we won't pot them up. Those "water" roots would never make the transition to soil. Generally speaking, air-layering is a safer bet if you want your "new" plant growing in soil.

If dieffenbachias need sun, as you say, why was mine sold to me as a low-light plant?

Ask the misguided person who sold it to you. Dieffenbachias will stay alive awhile in your sunless room, but not in the healthy way that, say, an aspidistra might. But aspidistras are slow-growing; thus, they are expensive to the retailer and not in good supply. So some stores push what they can get a lot of cheap.

My spathiphyllum spathes turn green and then brown. What causes that?

Nature—that is the way it grows: cream to green to brown. If it is taking less than a couple of weeks to happen, though, perhaps you are watering too little or the situation is too warm.

Why do the leaves of my spathe plant turn brown at their tips?

Underwatering, most likely. Spathiphyllums take lots of water for best growth.

ARALIACEAE   Aralia Family

The Aralia family contains a lot of subtropical shrubs popular because they will grow *large* and, for many people, hugeness is very desirable. We, on the other hand, have always felt that a dozen plants in 4-inch pots were much more interesting than one plant in a 20-inch tub. Also, they are less of an emotional and financial investment, though they probably take more care. If you have one large plant, and something goes wrong with that plant, panic quickly sets in, and we have heard from many panicky single-plant owners.

Once established and growing for a while in the same location, the large Araliaceae can be quite durable and long-lasting plants; but they will tend to repay injury with insult: let them get potbound, and they'll lose leaves; underwater, and they'll lose leaves; move them around, and they'll lose leaves. But there aren't many houseplant families with genera that will grow so *big* and adjust to indoor conditions.

English ivy (*Hedera helix*) is one of the few houseplants that is also a hardy outdoor plant. It has one characteristic we find fascinating: it mutates very readily, even sprouting branches with new forms on old plants. So, if your English ivy suddenly changes leaf shape, it *may* be that you are growing mature leaves (also a different shape from the young leaves), but it may be that you have found something completely different in the world: a new ivy form.

How much light and sun does a schefflera require?

Brassaia actinophylla (schefflera, umbrella tree) does best with quite bright light or some direct sun. We have seen them growing happily outdoors in the tropics in full sun. Growing them in too-low light will cause leaf drop.

Why should the lower leaves of my schefflera be turning yellow and falling off?

Too low-grade an environment, perhaps. Scheffleras (*Brassaia actinophylla*) are durable plants, but they prefer moderate watering and bright light, with some direct sun.

How do I propagate my schefflera?

The safest methods for propagating *Brassaia actinophylla* (schefflera) are air-layering or separating out any offsets that form at the base.

Tip cuttings are uncertain because of the thickness of the stem.

My schefflera leaves are coming in with almost circular holes in them. I have seen no bugs or slug slime trails, and I'm at a loss because otherwise the plant seems perfectly healthy. Can you make a guess?

It sounds like mechanical damage to the leaf buds. When the new leaf bud is forming at the growing tip, it is very delicate, and any slight wound (a person brushing by, a dog's tail hitting it, a paper airplane crashing into it) will cause very tiny weak spots or holes which grow into larger and larger holes as the leaf grows. Of course, there are more exotic possibilities, but if the plant is healthy otherwise, and the leaf is not yellowing and dying, this sort of mechanical damage is a very good bet.

I recently repotted my false aralia. I did the plastic bag thing for a week, but now whole branches are curling at the leaves and falling off!

Those are not branches but compound leaves. (That's a real comfort, isn't it?) *Dizygotheca elegantissima* (false aralia) has a shortcoming which it shares with its close relative, polyscias: it will often react to repotting by dropping its leaves. And, unlike polyscias, it usually does *not* grow back its lower leaves.

Keep the humidity high and the light bright, and it will, let us all hope, reach a balance.

The leaves on my false aralia are shriveling up and falling off. I don't see any bugs, but there are some spider webs.

Sounds like spider mite. Shower the plant well, both under and over the leaves, every day for a week, then every week for a month.

Also, look out for scale on the undersides of the leaves and on the stems. Scale masquerades as the natural spotting of the stems.

Dizygotheca elegantissima (false aralia) is quite susceptible—to everything.

What is good culture for fatshedera?

Fatshedera lizei is a cross between *Fatsia japonica* and *Hedera helix* (English ivy) —both members of the Aralia family.

It is tolerant of moderate light, but it does best in bright light with some direct sun, and it is a big drinker. It has the ivy's susceptibility to spider mite, and the fatsia's tendency to grow as one single stem. It will need pinching and staking as it matures.

If you manage to grow it to a large plant, you will have a beautiful vine, capable of making interesting (if not handsome) flowers.

Why are the leaves of my *Aralia japonica* turning a spotty yellow and falling off? I've looked for bugs. Could it need repotting?

Aralia japonica is no more—its name was changed to *Fatsia japonica* (get out your pen and change the label) .

Need for repotting is one of the easiest things to check with most plants: just water the plant, turn it out of its pot, and look at the roots. If they fill up the soil, you can see that the plant needs repotting.

But there are many other reasons for fatsia leaves to be yellowing and dropping. For instance, they are large drinkers, and they show their displeasure at being allowed to dry by dropping leaves. They want bright light, but not much direct sun. Bright sun may burn the leaves. And they prefer the cooler temperatures of Japanese summers.

They will grow used to warmer temperatures, but they'll never get used to lack of water.

I bought an Algerian ivy the other day and the leaves have gone limp. I put it into a plastic bag, but the soil just stays damp and smells mildewed. What should I do?

It sounds as if your *Hedera canariensis* (Algerian ivy) has root rot. Take the plant back and see if you can get an exchange. If you've had the plant only a few days, the store should still be responsible. If you can't get the store to make an adjustment, take as many cuttings as you can and soak them in tepid water; if they stiffen up, you may be able to propagate them.

My Persian ivy is drying up from the base. It looked so healthy when it was given to me.

Perhaps you are not watering enough. *Hedera colchica* (Persian ivy) is a *big* drinker. And it wants cool temperatures. Treat it right and it can make a lovely houseplant.

Why can't I grow potted ivy? It is forever drying and dying on me. Sometimes it just peters out with no apparent cause of death.

Ivy, which will grow like a weed outdoors, is not the easiest of houseplants. It reacts very badly to heat, but it needs bright light. It must be just about constantly moist. It is prone to spider mite and so should have a regular and frequent hosing down at the sink.

And when ivy is grown indoors it requires a minimum relative humidity of 40 percent to do well.

And it wants a neutral soil (a pH of about 7), whereas most of your other plants want a slightly acid soil (6.5 pH and lower).

Any of these reasons (or more general problems) could cause your failure with ivy. We do know growers who succeed with ivy indoors, but they work at it.

You frequently mention spider mite as a problem with indoor ivy. Does that mean they are otherwise bug-resistant?

No; in our indoor garden, ivy has also had, separately or in combination, mealybug, scale, thrips, and aphids.

We never had one with corn borer.

My California needlepoint ivy is doing poorly; making weak growth and with poor leaf color. Why?

Generally, *Hedera helix* (English ivy, of which yours is a variety) won't make a good houseplant unless you can keep it humid, well watered, and relatively cool. Growth will be weak in high temperatures; leaves will brown in low humidity and drop with infrequent watering. And spider mites (the worst pest of ivy) will cause loss of color. Aside from that, they're great houseplants.

I just bought a lovely large Ming aralia. I put it in my brightest window, and it started to lose its leaves and branches. I moved it to lower light, and the leaves and branches fell even faster. What shall I do?

Stop hassling the poor plant! Put it into a bright place and leave it there. *Polyscias fruticosa* (Ming aralia) and other polyscias will drop leaves if moved. Fortunately, they resprout readily. Until the leaves come back, water carefully so as not to rot the plant, and keep it well misted.

Let its permanent place be a sunny location, then keep it well watered when the leaves come back. And then (as Mother Mary says) *let it be.*

I had a *Polyscias fruticosa* that was doing fine and so I sent for another polyscias, *P. filicifolia,* because I liked the description (they called it lace-leaf aralia). It's doing fine, too. But it looks just like the fruticosa! What's the difference?

We think there is none. This is one of those botanical confusions, where the taxonomists give us minor differences which could be due to culture or climate. We think they are the same plant and will eventually be identified positively as the same.

Can I propagate my Ming aralia from a branch?

Yes, provided that you actually use a branch. *Polyscias fruticosa* (Ming aralia) and other plants of this genus have compound leaves—made up of eleven or so leaflets. These leaflets grow from a leaf stem, which makes them look like a branch with leaves. You can't propagate from that. You need an actual stem with leaves.

At that, air-layering is a lot surer than taking a tip cutting. And, with air-layering, you don't lose your propagation material (if you work with a sterile knife or razor). The worst that happens in air-layering is that the wound you make heals and you have to start again.

Can I grow polyscias in a southern window?

Yes. In tropical and semitropical climates, it is grown outdoors as a hedge, in full sun. In a southern window you only have to be certain that the heat doesn't cook it.

My white aralia has gone very leggy. What can I do?

Air-layer the top of your *Polyscias balfouriana* 'Pennockii' (white aralia) and then cut the plant back to within a few inches of the soil. The stem should resprout.

I bought a plant called "black aralia," but I can't find it in any book.

Not surprising. Neither could we. But we checked around, and it seems that one large (and enterprising) supplier of plants found himself with lots of plants of one kind on his hands—and no common name to help the plant sell: so he made up a common name himself!

As best we can tell, the plant is *Polyscias balfouriana,* which is indeed in the Aralia family.

ARAUCARIACEAE   Araucaria Family

Norfolk Island pine (*Araucaria excelsa*) and monkey-puzzle tree (*A. araucana*) are pretty much the only members of this family grown, and they clearly demonstrate the triumph of hope over experience. Few home growers keep them alive past the seedling stage, and fewer still grow them on to a handsome adult plant.

However: Oh, that a gardener's "reach should exceed his grasp, or what's a heaven for?"

I have no luck with Norfolk Island pines. They go leggy and weak, and the branches turn brown and fall off, no matter what I do. What do they like?

They like to live on Norfolk Island in the South Pacific or on Bermuda or in the moist, warm parts of our own state of Washington. The subtropics aside, they need lots of water, full sun, and high humidity. Your plants sound lacking in all departments.

Look, we all like a challenge, but why not try something a little easier?

My Norfolk Island pine seems to grow so slowly. I mean, it has most of its branches, though it is a little leggy. What can I do to goose it into better growth?

Better? Or just faster? Right now, you are doing as well as anyone growing *Araucaria excelsa* (Norfolk Island pine) indoors. But it does grow slowly. Keep it in bright sun and high humidity with plenty of water. Also give it a roomy pot and a monthly feeding of fish emulsion—and it will do as well as it can for you.

I want to take cuttings of my Norfolk Island pine. Can I get new plants this way?

Araucaria excelsa (Norfolk Island pine) is propagatable from cuttings, but only the tip will give you an upright-growing plant. Side shoots will make side-growing plants. Some semperflorens begonias will also act this way. We have, this year, been growing a marvelous plant, a member of the gardenia family: *Mitriostigma axillare*. Grown from a cutting from an upward-growing stem, the plant tends to be upright. Grown from a side shoot, you get a beautifully pendant plant.

What was the question again? Norfolk Island pine? Did you know they grow to about 200 feet on Norfolk Island?

ASCLEPIADACEAE   Milkweed Family

The Milkweed family contains several excellent houseplants, none of which looks anything like the common milkweed, and most of which are succulents and have odd flowering and/or growth habits.

Ceropegias are a must for anyone looking for an interesting and *durable* houseplant. *Ceropegia woodii* is widely available, but *C. debilis* is very interesting, and almost as foolproof.

Hoyas can grow quite lushly while demanding little care. We have had one in the same 6-inch pot for six years now, and it just flowers and flowers. Some hoyas are fragrant during the day, some at night, but they all have waxy flowers.

Huernia (pronounced either "wernia" or "hernia") looks very much like stapelia (also in this family), and both can make vigorous, if not huge, windowsill plants.

Stephanotis is a viner, with fragrant and waxy flowers; it must be kept somewhat moist and be given something on which to vine.

Is rosary vine a difficult houseplant? I killed mine.

How? We have found *Ceropegia woodii* (rosary vine) an easy and durable houseplant when grown in moderate sun and with moderate watering. It can flower at any time. Propagate it from tip cuttings, leaves, or from the tuberlike growths (propagules) that form along the stems or at the surface of the soil.

Is a rosemary vine a succulent? How do I care for it and propagate it?

We're going to go out on a limb and suggest you have a *rosary* vine (*Ceropegia woodii*) not a *rosemary* vine (which doesn't exist).

Ceropegias are classed among the succulents, but *C. woodii* should be treated as a bright-light-loving houseplant, not a cactus. Keep it in some sun (an east window would do), allow it to go dry down to ½ inch or so beneath the soil surface before watering, and give it a well-drained standard houseplant soil. It should then reward you by making plump leaves, those strange curved flowers, and tuberlike swellings at the nodes and soil line. You can propagate from these tubercles laid upon damp soil, or from individual leaves or tip cuttings in moderate humidity.

My "carrion flower" stapelia opened and it didn't smell of dead meat—why?

Gee, what a shame. Some stapelias *don't* smell like dead meat (and some folks prefer them that way). And then, of course, perhaps you have a huernia and not a stapelia—they look quite similar and take similar care.

The leaves on my *Hoya compacta* are shriveling and falling off. Could you say why? I grow it in bright sun and water it every two weeks.

Why are you thirsting your poor plant? (By the way—we think that your plant is *Hoya carnosa* 'Hummel's compacta,' a twisted form also known as "Hindu rope.") Hoyas are succulents, but even succulents must have ample water when in vigorous growth.

In early summer, when the days are at their longest, the soil of your hoya should go dry down to a depth of no more than ½ inch below the surface. Increase your watering and the leaves may swell again—provided they aren't too badly damaged.

It makes us unhappy to hear of plants being put on a watering *schedule:* they just don't grow that way. Don't be a lazy waterer—feel your soil.

Why won't my variegated wax plant flower?

The variegated forms of *Hoya carnosa* (wax plant) often are very difficult to flower outside a greenhouse. We have had better luck with *Hoya australis* (with silver splotches on the leaves) and the miniature *Hoya bella*.

Hoyas prefer to be somewhat potbound, and they need bright light and some direct sun. Keep yours watered quite well in the warm months and allow it to go somewhat dry between waterings in the dim months.

Also—now don't feel stupid if you've been doing this, lots of folks seem to—hoyas flower on persistent "spurs" which grow a bit longer at each flowering. If you've cut off the spurs, the plant won't reflower.

My Hindu rope plant grows so slowly—why?

Beats us—but *Hoya carnosa* 'Hummel's compacta' (Hindu rope plant) does grow very slowly in home conditions.

Try giving it more sun and a little more water.

The stems of my wax plant end in long whips without leaves. Where am I supposed to get a tip cutting for propagation?

Leaves will eventually grow on those "whips," and you don't need a tip cutting. Hoyas will propagate from a single leaf with the petiole thrust into damp propagating medium (such as sand, perlite, vermiculite, or a Jiffy-7). The leaf will root, then send up a plantlet from the base. When the plantlet is big enough to handle, separate it from the leaf and pot it up.

Or, if you are desperate for a tip cutting, cut off and discard the "whip" and call the resulting end a "tip." Then make your "tip" cutting about 4 inches back from that point.

My wax plant leaves are turning yellow and getting kind of soft, then they fall off when I touch them.

Hoyas need reduced watering in the winter or they can get into root trouble—which is what your problem sounds like: root trouble. Reduce watering, increase light (if possible), and increase the humidity.

And a little prayer wouldn't hurt.

My *Hoya carnosa* 'Tricolor' isn't doing too well. How do I care for it?

A lot of people have trouble with the pink forms of *Hoya carnosa*. It is slower growing and has less chlorophyll, which makes it more difficult. Give it bright sun and now, in winter, only moderate watering.

When the days lengthen again, increase the watering. Still, allow the plant to dry *somewhat* between waterings.

Why is my "Krimson Queen" hoya losing its pink coloring?

Probably it needs more sun.

I bought a wax plant with the name "Krimson Princess." The leaves are red and slightly twisted. I've had it for months and it's done nothing at all. I give it some sun, I allow it to go dry between waterings—I've even tried misting it, but it doesn't grow. Could I perhaps have something wrong with my soil? I use a cactus mix. How would I know if I had nematodes?

Relax! You don't have nematodes. If you did, new growth would come in, but it would be twisted and stunted; and hoyas are quite tolerant of a variety of soils. *Hoya carnosa* (which is the plant from which yours mutated) is not the best hoya for home culture (though it is the most common), and its mutants are even worse: slow to grow and very difficult to flower. They demand more sun and more careful watering than other hoyas. (We like *Hoya australis* as a ready flowerer and vigorous grower.)

Keep your plant in bright sun, don't overwater (don't let it die of thirst, either), and have patience.

Could you tell me why my hoya leaves are yellowing at the tip?

Overwatering or overfeeding are our best (or worst) bets. Remember to reduce the watering of your hoya during the dull months.

BALSAMINACEAE   Balsam or Jewelweed Family

Impatiens (patience plant, impatient plant, patient Lizzie, etc.) is the only genus of this family we grow as a houseplant, but there are several handsome varieties and a host of hybrids, most of them bred from *Impatiens walleriana sultanii*.

Newly introduced, the New Guinea impatiens (*Impatiens hawkerii* 'Exotica' hybrids) show dramatic leaf variegations and large flowers, but several of the growers we've spoken to say they are shy to flower and prone to disease.

The jewelweed, after which the family is named, is one of the most useful hardy weeds we know. Rub some over an area of your body just exposed to poison ivy, and you will not break out. You can recognize jewelweed because its flowers are orange-yellow, spotted, and have the spur characteristic to the Balsam family.

Another characteristic of this family gives impatiens its name. Touch a ripe seed pod of your houseplant impatiens, or a jewelweed, and the pod will burst open and the seeds will fly out. What could be more "impatient" than that?

Why are the leaves of my potted impatiens turning yellow and falling off? It is in an east window, and I feed it regularly.

Well, if it is in trouble, stop feeding it. Stop feeding any plant in trouble.

There are many possibilities: if your east window is blocked, perhaps it's too little sun, or too little water, or too-heavy soil, or too-low humidity, or too much feeding (though that's unlikely), or (and this *is* likely) spider mites.

Pick one reason or several, and correct the situation (give it bright sun, plenty of water, a porous soil, stop feeding, and shower off the mites), then cut the plant back, and allow it to resprout.

All winter long my patience plant has shown these little sugary crystals on the edges of the leaves. Is this some kind of bug I can't see?

No, that's no bug. Those crystals are the plant's way of conserving moisture. And it probably means that either the steam-heated air in your apartment is too dry (in which case, increase your humidity to at least 35 percent) or you're allowing the soil to go too dry (in which case, water more). Impatiens should be watered when the soil is dry down to about $\frac{1}{4}$ inch below the surface.

Though they will survive winter indoors, impatiens suffer from the heat and low humidity.

My impatiens is showing a secretion. Is this natural?

Yes and no. It may be the secretion is in response to too little humidity—impatiens do that. Is that natural?

Or, it may be a honeydew from a piercing insect such as scale. That is natural for the scale, but not for the plant.

I'm growing impatience in a shady window, and it has all the signs of being in too little light. I thought this was a shade-loving plant.

Don't mistake indoor and outdoor needs. Very few plants grow well in indoor shade. Plants such as impatiens or semperflorens begonias or coleus will tolerate shade outdoors, but will need nearly full sun on a windowsill. The difference is the ample *overhead* light that the flower bed gets every day, and the pot on the windowsill never gets.

Can you tell me why my impatiens should be blasting? It gets plenty of sun, but the flowers drop before they open.

If they look healthy when they drop, you may be underwatering: impatiens are big drinkers. If the flowers are brownish when they fall it may be spider mites; look for the webs.

Third and fourth possibilities are too high heat and low humidity. Or any combinations of the above.

BEGONIACEAE   Begonia Family

Begonias are relatively new in cultivation, and so their classification is in flux, with new species frequently discovered in the wild and new hybrids all but pouring out of the hybridizers' greenhouses.

Some are jungle-floor plants, some from drier and brighter regions. Those that are from regions of Mexico that have a dry winter go all-but dormant in the winter, after flowering.

Many have small flowers, though tuberous begonias are among the most spectacular flowering houseplants you can find. Many of the small-flowered varieties have handsomely variegated foliage.

There are begonias available for almost every growing situation. We have seen a species that would grow to adulthood in a teacup, and another that grows to a dozen feet tall.

Why do the lower leaves of my Begonia 'Cleopatra' turn watery and fall off?

Begonia 'Cleopatra' is a rhizomatous begonia (the hairy creeping stem is called a rhizome), and this type of begonia demands careful watering. They must not be kept sopping wet, but also they should not go really dry between waterings. Stick your finger into the soil. When it feels dry down to a depth of about $\frac{1}{2}$ inch (in a 6-inch pot) water well.

Overwatering can cause the plant to rot; underwatering will cause lower leaf loss.

If you have already lost all your leaves, but the rhizome is still plump and firm, you can break off inch-long pieces and propagate the begonia by laying these pieces on damp rooting medium in a moderate-humidity propagation box.

The lower leaves of my angel-wing begonia are falling off. The leaves look sound. I've tried more water and less water, but nothing helps.

Loss of your lower leaves is the agony of growing cane-type begonias. They just seem to do it a lot.

Many plants produce and store in their growing tips a hormone (an auxin) which inhibits the growth of their own lower leaves. You can stimulate lower growth by pinching out that growing tip. If yours is a desperate case, with lots of bare stem, don't be afraid to cut the canes back to within 3 or 4 inches of the soil. Then reduce watering some-what until it resprouts; keep it in bright sun.

The Kussler hybrids seem less prone to leaf loss than some of the older hybrids and species.

In California, the canes seem to hold their leaves better. Could be the cooler evenings.

What is the flowering season for angel-wing begonias?

They have no season; they'll flower any season provided they get enough light (they prefer some direct sun). They'll flower well under fluorescent lights.

My Rieger begonia ('Schwabenland Red') leaves are in poor shape. They are graying and dying.

Many begonias coexist with a particular fungus. The Schwabenland strain seems genetically susceptible to attack from its fungus. We kept ours alive by trimming away the worst parts with a clean manicure scissors.

The Aphrodite series of Rieger hybrids is just as showy and doesn't have this problem.

Tuberous begonias don't do well on my windowsill, though wax begonias do just fine. Is there a special food they need?

No, but they do need special conditions, notably cool nights and high humidity. The best we ever saw were grown on the island of Nan-tucket, off Cape Cod. The island humidity and cool nights, combined with long sunny days, make them beautiful.

They are great on a sun porch, but difficult on a windowsill.

They do require feeding, of course, but any high-middle-number plant food will do (15–30–15, for example) .

My "woolly bear" begonia rotted on me—I dug it up and there were hardly any roots left. Do you think it could have been a bug? Will it spread?

It does not sound like your *Begonia leptotricha* has a bug. How's your soil? If it is heavy (when you water, does the water sit for a long time at the surface or does it drain quickly through?—as it should) *and* you chronically overwater, your begonias will rot. They can take lots of water in a well-drained soil, or going dry in a heavy soil—but not both heavy soil and too much water.

How do I get to grow tuberous begonias like the ones I see at the flower show?

It's not complicated.

Feed well as they grow, with a 15–30–15 food and manure tea; pinch out the stems when young, to encourage branching; pinch out the side flowers (which are females) to allow the showier males at the tips to grow to a bigger size; and move to Luxembourg so the plants can have the cool nights and damp air they need. (This last is optional, if you can provide cool temperatures and humidity another way.)

Does a Rieger begonia bloom continuously?

No, it is seasonal, flowering usually during the winter.

Riegers are highly rated because the flowers are large as begonia flowers go, except, of course, for the tuberous begonias that have really big beautiful flowers. Did you know that Riegers are derived from a semituberous begonia?

My little eyelash begonia seems perfectly healthy, but it never flowers. Do these plants flower?

Certainly—if you treat them right.

The "eyelash" begonias are miniatures with eyelashlike fringes around the outside of the leaves. *Begonia bowerae* 'Nigra-marga' and *Begonia* 'Robert Schatzer' are two of our favorites of the type. These are rhizomatous begonias, which means they grow with a hairy stem more or less parallel to the soil. The leaves come directly out of this "rhizome."

Most of the rhizomatous begonias are long-night plants, which means they require 12 to 14 hours of uninterrupted darkness to flower.

Many of these plants will flower on a normal windowsill, without special treatment, toward the end of or during winter. However, if you have a street light outside that window, the light will disrupt the cycle and no buds will set. Our *Begonia erythrophylla* (beefsteak begonia) flowered for years on our windowsill until they changed the street lights on our block to sodium vapor lamps.

If you grow yours in a room which has a night light, or if you go into the room in the middle of the night and turn the light on, *this* will disrupt the cycle.

Under fluorescent lights, set your timer for 11 hours of day and 13 of night and you'll be fine—as long as the room doesn't get lit up in the middle of the night. If you must disrupt the cycle, do it very early or very late. Research shows this not to have as disastrous an effect as midnight visits do.

I have no luck with the wax begonia called "charm." Does it take special care?

Begonia 'Charm' is a mutation of a semperflorens-type (wax) begonia, that is now called a calla type. It does indeed take special care: higher humidity, more water in a very, very well-drained soil, and better light. It is also more difficult to propagate from tip cuttings (for us, at least) —we suppose because of the small amount of chlorophyll in the leaves.

I recently bought a small plant—*Begonia serratipetala*, which I cannot pronounce (and don't know if I want to). Could you tell me its common name and its care?

Certainly. It is commonly called the "purple-spotted dark-leafed ser-rated-margin lymph plant" (because of the swollen nodes). Isn't that easier to say than *Begonia serratipetala?*

Thank goodness for the many marvelous houseplants, like this one, *without* common names—which all too often are applied to more than one plant or only to that plant in a particular region.

Begonia serratipetala is one of the loveliest begonias you can grow, if you can give it bright sun. Sun keeps it compact and brings out the vibrant colors. This is not a rex begonia, though the colors might mislead you. This is a compact cane type. The specific name *serrati-petala* refers to the almost sawlike shape of the leaf margins.

Keep it well pinched out and allow it to go dry down to about ½ inch below the surface of the soil before rewatering, and it will make you a lovely hanging plant.

Feed with 15–30–15 plant food (at half the label strength) every two weeks while in active growth, and don't be afraid to cut it back.

My shrimp begonia seems to be doing well; it flowers and the leaves look healthy, but the stems droop down. What do I have to feed it to make stronger stems?

Potash (potassium) aids in the formation of strong stems. This is usually present in most soils or can be provided organically by the addition of a tablespoon of fine wood ashes to 4 quarts of potting mix.

But we don't think you have a problem: *Begonia limmingheiana* (shrimp begonia) has a pendant habit and will make a handsome basket plant. If you insist on an upright habit, stake the plant.

How can I grow a rex begonia in my dry apartment?

Put it in a large terrarium lit by two tubes of cool-white fluorescent light. The terrarium will provide the humidity and constant moisture that the rex must have, and the lights will provide warmth and the rather low light intensity that brings out their best coloring.

Without supplementary humidity, rexes are very difficult to manage in an apartment.

I have heard you make mention of miniature begonias, and they sound intriguing. But are they difficult for the amateur?

Miniature begonias are almost impossible to manage under normal home conditions—they are just too demanding. But put them into an open or half-open terrarium (lit by two cool-white fluorescent bulbs) and they are super-easy charmers, delightful in every way. The terrarium provides constant moisture, high (but not 100 percent) humidity, cool but intense light, and the warm temperatures they prefer.

The leaves of my wax begonias curl down. What causes that?

It could be a number of things. First of all, how tightly curled are they? If tightly curled, uncurl some and look for an insect or cocoon. If you find any, cut away any affected leaves and discard them.

Check your temperatures. Persistent heat can cause the leaves to curl down. The leaves do this to conserve moisture.

Finally, continued underwatering can give the leaves a chronic droop which might be taken for a curl.

About six weeks ago, I started some mail-order begonia tubers, and the top growth is only about an inch tall. I give them plenty of light and water—what else can I do?

You didn't say whether you'd started them in a flat or in pots. If they are in a flat, move each one into an individual 4-inch or 5-inch azalea pot (shallow pot).

A little gentle bottom heat will stimulate root growth. Don't let them dry out.

BIGNONIACEAE   Trumpetcreeper Family

This is a family largely of big trees and vines (including campsis—the trumpetcreeper): plants that are not really manageable as houseplants. It includes one of our favorite tropical trees: *Spathodea campanulata* (African tulip tree), which forms dramatic red flowers in masses in the tropics.

Jacaranda stays compact as a pot plant, and will flower (blue) if given enough sun.

On a trip to Canada we recently bought a "jacaranda." How do we care for it?

Jacaranda is a tropical or subtropical tree. Give it a good-size pot; don't let it go dry more than ½ inch below the surface; give it full indoor sun; and in winter give it cool temperatures and maintain a minimum relative humidity of 40 percent.

Can I pinch my jacaranda to get it to branch?

Yes, pinch out the tip. Then when they arrive, pinch out the tips of the new branches.

You probably have *Jacaranda mimosifolia*, which may drop its leaves in the spring.

BROMELIACEAE   Pineapple Family

This is a relatively small family—as plant families go—but it is full of exciting, durable, superior (and prickly) houseplants. Many of them are neglect-proof, and some will give you the most spectacular inflorescence of any houseplant you'll ever grow. If you think we exaggerate, then you haven't grown them.

Mostly, they are tropical and epiphytic (growing upon other plants, not on soil). They dig their roots into pockets of leaf mold in the crotches of trees, and similar situations. However, some of the easiest to flower (cryptanthus—earth star) are terrestrial.

They mostly prefer high humidity, but will adjust to apartment conditions quite well.

Most have their leaves formed into vase shapes, and must have that "vase" kept continuously watered, but some will tolerate quite erratic watering schedules.

They mostly live in jungles, but some grow on desert cacti.

All in all, a most desirable family to get to know.

Generally, the inflorescence of bromeliads lasts quite a while—even months (though some are much shorter-lived than that), but the individual flowers usually live only a single day. Cryptanthus flowers are formed without an inflorescence, but they are formed in profusion. Cryptanthus, however, means hidden flowers, and they must be looked for. They will flower in little light, which can make them very desirable.

There are free bromeliads to be had in the United States. From South Carolina to Florida, Spanish moss (*Tillandsia usneoides*) and other miniature tillandsias grow in the trees, from whence they are blown by the strong winds. We picked some up in Sarasota, Florida, a few years ago, and hung it in our window garden, where, despite neglect, some is still alive. *That* is durability.

Pineapples are the only economically important bromeliad, and you can get a plant free by rooting the top of a pineapple fruit you buy. Twist off the top and then scrape away any flesh that stays, down to the white, where the leaves join. Take your terrestrial bromeliad mix (see below) and stand the pineapple top in it, holding it firmly in place with a piece of heavy wire bent as a clamp or with cloth tape folded so as to keep the gum off the leaves. Water it well, set it in a bright place, and keep it watered. Roots will form, and you will have a handsome plant, suitable for a sunny window, but growing to as much as 3 feet across.

We have seen bromeliads grown and doing very well in every potting mix from furnace clinkers to leaf mold and gravel. They must have excellent drainage, and need little or no real soil. A mixture we have used for years includes equal measures of pea gravel, perlite, medium fir-bark chips, tree-fern fiber, and peat moss.

For terrestrial bromeliads, such as pineapple (ananas) or cryptanthus, we add a measure of soil to the other ingredients.

We use no mix for the miniature tillandsias at all, mounting them on pieces of rough cork bark, or just tying a clump of them together and hanging them from a small piece of wood.

Bromeliads will grow in anything that allows them to drain perfectly. The only problem with using a medium like straight tree-fern fiber which has perfect drainage is that it doesn't have enough weight. Bromeliads often grow to a good size, and may just topple over if their pots are too light.

I would like to build a bromeliad tree—but I don't really know how to start. Can you help?

There are a number of ways to go about putting together a bromeliad tree (a treelike structure on which one mounts bromeliads). The simplest is to use a large piece of driftwood that has been scrubbed clean. Hollow the driftwood's natural pockets further, and stuff them with bromeliad mix. The bromels are then wired into place, with long-hair sphagnum moss wrapped around their bases to hide the workings.

Or, if you're really ambitious, you can make a tree form out of chicken wire. Many segments of coarse cork bark, held on by fishing line, are wrapped around the form to give it the appearance of a real tree. Leave off a piece of cork where you want to place a plant. Now, push the chicken wire to form a small pocket. Line the pocket with long-hair sphagnum moss, stuff in the bromeliad potting mix, and hold the plant in place with more fishing line. A small piece of cork can be placed to cover the bottom of the pocket.

Your tree must be located where it can be hosed down freely and frequently.

Can I grow *Guzmania lingulata* on a bromeliad tree?

Of course, but it is such a prolific bloomer (its common name is "princess' tears") that you'd prefer it at eye level or lower.

The pink flower on my urn plant has dried up—how can I reflower it?

Well, you can't—and then again you can. *Aechmea fasciata* (urn plant) is a bromeliad and, like other bromels, it won't flower again on that growth. In fact, after flowering, the main plant will start to die (don't buy the tombstone yet—it can take three years to die). At the same time, it will start to make offsets (pups) around the base. These pups, when mature, can flower. They can be removed when half the size of the parent plant and fixed firmly into a pot of damp bromeliad mix, or they can be left in the pot. If the pups are removed, more pups will form.

Your aechmea needs bright sun, constant water in the urn, once-a-week watering at the base, moderate humidity, and little food.

Can a bromeliad be forced into flower by being put into a plastic bag with a ripe apple?

Theoretically, yes. An apple gives off ethylene gas, which will blast the buds of many flowering plants but which will force a mature bromeliad into flower. However, we've never known anyone personally to do it.

The New York Bromeliad Society recommends the use of a chemical known as BOH, available under the name Brom-Bloom, for "popping" bromeliads. The chemical is diluted precisely and either put into the empty urn or sprayed onto the leaves (if there is no urn). The flower spike will then take five to eight weeks to rise and open. The inflorescence size will depend on the maturity of the plant.

My *Aechmea fasciata* is drooping and really looking wilty. I have kept the vase full and the soil wet.

Ouch! It sounds as if your plant might be on its way out. Sorry. Aechmeas want to go rather dry at the base between waterings (though the "vase" does want to stay full or nearly so). Keeping the mix wet will encourage rot.

If the base is not yet rotten, allow the medium to dry somewhat before rewatering, and mist the foliage frequently. This misting takes some of the strain off the damaged roots and gives the plant a chance to form new healthy roots.

I have a plant ("Bromeliad Aechmea 'Foster's Favorite' " is what the label says). I would like to have it flower, but it hasn't. You were talking about temperature drop helping to set flowers. How do you do it?

Your plant is *Aechmea* 'Foster's Favorite'; it is a member of the Bromeliad family, but "Bromeliad" is not part of its name. (Mr. Foster had one of these mutate for him, and he named the new one *Aechmea* 'Foster's Favorite Favorite.')

A temperature drop of 10° to 15° at night is vital for most orchids and desirable for many other plants. Plants from equatorial regions—accustomed as they are to constant temperatures—don't need this drop. And one of the things that make bromeliads such great houseplants is that they don't need the drop either.

Your *Aechmea* 'Foster's Favorite' wants only moderate light (with a little sun) to flower, moderate humidity, and accurate watering (keep the small vase full and water the base well once a week). Overwatering the base can rot the plant.

Mostly, bromels must be mature enough to flower (two or three years in your case). They can be "popped" however, by the use of a chemical: Brom-Bloom, made in Holland. Write to The Bromeliad Society, 6153 Hayter Avenue, Lakewood, California 90712, for information about a Bromeliad Society branch near you, where you may get more information.

Bromeliads artificially forced into flower before they are ready will make smaller flowering heads than fully mature plants.

How do I get rid of the white coating on an urn plant?

You don't! That white coating on your *Aechmea fasciata* (the bromeliad most often called "urn plant") is *scurf*, which is the plant's answer to its natural growing conditions. Scurf is made up of cells which absorb water right out of moist air. Leave it alone.

I bought a "matchstick bromeliad." What is its Latin name? And can I expect it to flower for me?

You probably have a variety of *Aechmea nudicaulis,* and when it flowers, you will see why it's called "matchstick." The flowers are blue and look very much like the tips of safety matches.

You can expect it to flower if you give it bright light with some direct sun—a couple of hours a day. Keep the vase filled with water, keep the humidity moderate, and water the base once a week. The inflorescence on this bromeliad doesn't last as long as other aechmeas.

Will *Tillandsia cyanea* flower under fluorescent lights?

Yes—use four tubes of any spectrum, and keep the top of the foliage no farther than 4 inches from the tubes.

I just bought a miniature pineapple plant. How soon can I expect a pineapple, and will it be miniature or full size?

If you get a pineapple from your *Ananas nanus* (miniature pineapple), it will be very miniature indeed—about 3 inches of fruit and not edible, though not poisonous.

You will get fruit only after the plant has flowered and the flowers have been pollinated. The plant will flower when it is mature enough (probably between one and three years old) and if you give it proper culture: bright sun (without the leaves burning), moderate humidity (around 35 percent), and ample water in a perfectly drained soil mix.

Like the premature news of Mark Twain's supposed death, advertisements with claims for lucious fruit from dwarf pineapple have been "exaggerated."

CACTACEAE   Cactus Family

This is a large and complicated family to study, but not complicated to grow.

Cacti are virtually all New World plants that evolved as portions of the world changed from lush jungles to arid deserts. They are slow growers and poor competitors—which is why they grow where hardly anything else wants to. However, with our "protection," so to speak, cacti can do beautifully as houseplants.

If you find yourself laughing bitterly at that last statement, perhaps it's because you haven't noticed that cacti are for the most part very good examples of how a plant changes its growth rate to suit the seasons.

The desert cacti are in rapid growth from spring into the fall. When desert nights get too chilly, and desert days too short, they go into dormancy, from which they awake in the longer and warmer days of early spring. Most growers ignore this cycle and keep their cactus plants hanging on the edge of survival, with constant temperatures year round, despite day length.

Jungle cacti are treated differently. These are plants that require a rich potting medium, of good drainage but high in organic material (desert cacti need excellent drainage, but not a really rich soil), and more water year round. They do extremely well as houseplants if given plenty of bright light and direct sun and allowed to be somewhat cooler in winter than in summer.

What should I feed my cacti and how often?

Very little and very seldom. You can scratch a teaspoon of bone meal into each medium-sized pot; and incorporate bone meal into your cactus mix.

For cacti living in a sunny conservatory or warm sunny climate, more feeding is appropriate: perhaps one feeding a season with quarter-strength 15–30–15 plant food.

My cactus has this white cottony stuff around the bases of its needles. I think it's mealy bug: what should I do?

Mealybug is easily cleaned off cacti with a cotton swab dipped in alcohol and touched to the insects (repeat every week for three or four weeks).

But are you certain that it is mealybug? All cacti have areoles, which are hairy organs around the bases of the needles (or where the needles would be). They are the equivalent of nodes in other plants, the places where new growth, flowers, branches, etc., come from. Mealies scrape off easily, but these areoles do not.

I was given a dish garden of small succulents. There is a hole in the bottom of the dish. How do I water it?

Well, at least there is a hole. If there were none, the planting would have little survival potential. Water over the entire surface until water comes running out the bottom of the dish. Then allow the soil to become dry to just below the surface of the soil before rewatering. Young succulents often take quite a bit of water, and most dish gardens of this sort are made up of young, not miniature, plants.

I brought back a large and healthy cactus from Florida to Connecticut, and now it's growing spindly. What can I do?

Send it back to Florida or move it into a house with very bright sun.

Growing large cacti is a problem for indoor gardeners—even those with bright sun. If you can grow your cactus outdoors for much of the year—on a balcony or terrace, say—and keep it dormant the rest of the year by growing it cool indoors, you may be able to grow really fine large cacti.

In climates without frost, of course, cacti should be grown outdoors year round.

If cactus plants need only a little water, why do you talk about watering them well? Well?

Who said cacti need little water? They are adapted to do without water for periods of time. But when it rains in the desert, the cacti take the water up and very quickly.

No, cacti will take lots of water (in a well-drained soil), when in active growth. When not in active growth, *then* they need little water.

Do all cacti require full sun to flower? I just don't have it.

Mammillarias will flower in the moderate sun of a partially blocked east window—the flowers are small, but there are many of them.

Gymnocalyciums (called "chin cacti") flower very well in that same moderate sun (if given a winter dormancy), and they make the large flowers for which cacti are so justly famous.

Are there any cactus plants that do have leaves?

Pereskia is a vining genus of true cactus with leaves, but the leaves will drop if it doesn't get enough water.

Incidentally, unlike most cactus flowers, which are scentless, pereskia flowers have a strong lemon scent.

It is winter, but all my cacti are growing, not dormant. I thought they were supposed to be dormant.

Indoors, where temperatures tend to be constant, cacti must be *deliberately put* into dormancy.

Cacti and cactuslike succulents need a winter dormancy because the reduced sun is not enough to keep their growth compact. Also, many cacti will not flower for you without a winter dormancy period.

To put a cactus into dormancy, set it in a cool place (not freezing) in the brightest sun possible. Water only enough to keep the plants from shriveling—perhaps once a month between November and February.

I inherited a big Christmas cactus from my son when he went to school, and I love it very much. But it's not doing well; the leaves are wrinkling. I keep it in good sun and water it a couple of tablespoons at a time when it is dry. I would hate to lose it. Can you suggest something?

You're teasing the plant, and it won't survive if you don't stop. *Zygocactus truncatus* (Christmas cactus) is a jungle cactus, and when in active growth it wants lots of water. The leaves are wrinkling from lack of water. Once you begin watering well, the leaves should plump up. Water every time the surface of the soil goes dry, and water well—until water comes running out the bottom of the pot; then throw away the excess.

Around September or October, the plant may slow its growth, and then it can be allowed to go a bit drier between waterings—but no more than down to a depth of about ½ inch below the surface of the soil. Even then, water well and discard the excess.

The long nights and cool temperatures of fall stimulate bud formation in zygocactus.

How dry should I let an orchid cactus go between waterings?

While in active growth, not dry at all. *Epiphyllum ackermannii,* or any of the other cacti going under the "orchid cactus" moniker, is a jungle epiphyte and wants watering as soon as its soil goes surface dry. In the dim months, when it slows its growth, you can allow it to go a bit drier: say, to ¼ inch below the surface of the soil.

I'm about to transplant the darling of my collection—a tall cephalo-cereus. Do you have any suggestions?

Pot dry! Cactus roots are so easily damaged and then rotted. Allow the plant to dry for a full week before repotting, pot into soil that is virtually dry, and then don't water for a week or two. And think clean thoughts.

I bought a 4-foot-tall cereus cactus (I'm ashamed to tell you what I paid for it). I keep it in my brightest light (a clear east window), and water it when it is dry about 2 inches below the soil (it's in a 12-inch pot). But in the months I've had it, it hasn't grown at all. Why? What can I do?

You don't have enough sun.

You really can't expect a plant that has been raised in full outdoor sun for years (as yours had to be) to be grateful for your lousy east window. Be happy that it doesn't grow. If it did, its growth would likely be noticeably weaker, and thinner. A cactus of that size becomes difficult to maintain indoors.

Try four tubes of supplementary fluorescent light. That should help a bit. Keep the plant cooler and put it outside any day it's warm enough. It is hard to turn Pennsylvania into Arizona.

My cereus cactus is going dark and soft on top. When I touch it, my finger goes right in. What is it, and what can I do about it?

It sounds like some kind of rot. Perhaps the top was wounded and then some water got into the wound. It's impossible to know the cause for sure.

As for the cure, cut away the top until you see no more rot. Be cruel (to be kind) : cut far enough down or you'll lose the plant. And do use a sterile knife or you may just spread the fungus. Then dust the wound with a commercial fungicide or with flowers of sulfur. *And keep water off the wound.* Your cereus will likely make new growth just below the cut.

I recently inherited two large 3½-foot plants of rabbit-ear cactus in 12-inch pots. The soil seems about half sand. How do I water them? They sit in a south window.

While your *Opuntia microdasys* (rabbit-ears) are in active growth (from February or March to October), they should be allowed to go dry down to about 2 inches below the surface of the soil in pots that big. (In smaller pots, they would go dry down to an inch or so.)

They should have a dormant period in the late fall/early winter: cool temperatures (down to about 50° to 60°F.), during which they require less water. Water plants of this size about once a month during dormancy.

I have had a Christmas cactus for about three years and it has never bloomed. Would it bloom if I transplanted it into a larger pot?

No, Christmas cacti do better if a little potbound.

With *Zygocactus truncatus* (Christmas cactus), bud set is a matter of a balance between cool temperatures and long nights. If you keep yours where the temperature is constant, it is unlikely to bloom, and if it doesn't get 12 to 14 hours of darkness every night during the fall, it is *most* unlikely to flower.

Grown close to the window, your plant will get some temperature drop every night. But you must provide long nights of uninterrupted darkness. If your window is dark (without bright street lights) and the room doesn't have light at night, it will likely flower on its own. Otherwise, cover the plant at 6 in the evening and uncover it at 8 in the morning. Or, put it into a dark closet at night and take it out during the day.

During this time, the plant will demand less water. Buds should set after about 9 weeks of long nights.

The rest of the year, give it plenty of sun, and water, and some food.

I was told I was underwatering my Easter cactus. I watered it more—and now it's dead! Just rotted out. Did I get bad advice?

Perhaps this comes under the heading of "a little learning is a dangerous thing."

Your *Schlumbergera gaertneri* (Easter cactus) does drink a lot—certainly as compared to desert cacti. But you can't take a starving person and then feed that person a bunch of heavy meals. Similarly, you can't take a plant that has been starving for water and then drown it. Severe drying damages the roots; heavy watering then causes rot of those few remaining roots. That's how you lost your plant.

Your adviser was right to recommend increased watering, but you should have increased the watering a bit at a time—say, 10 percent or 20 percent a week until the plant was being watered appropriately for the season. Live and learn (if you're lucky).

What is the best time of year to repot cacti and succulents?

We like to repot most succulents only when they are in active growth: usually in early spring.

CASUARINACEAE   Casuarina Family

In Nassau, on Paradise Island, we saw a hundred-year-old planting of graceful and beautiful casuarina trees, reaching more than 80 feet tall and swaying in the wind. On Bermuda, we saw hedges of them, cut to 3 feet and dense and bushy. *That* is adaptability.

I have had absolutely no luck with Norfolk Island pine. Is there another indoor pine tree I might do better with? I do have bright sun.

Few growers have success with *Araucaria excelsa* (Norfolk Island pine). Even on Bermuda, where these tender conifers grow very tall, lots of them look poor, windblown, and leggy.

Perhaps you might have more success with another tender but more adaptable tree, also from the South Pacific: *Casuarina equisetifolia* (Australian pine). It has long needles and a very graceful look and is well adapted to adverse conditions (poor soil, wind, sea spray). It seems much more flexible (in both senses) than Norfolk Island pine.

Give your casuarina full sun, plenty of water, at least moderate humidity, and avoid excessive heat.

Casuarinas can be groomed to almost any shape and size, so, to keep yours compact, be an aggressive groomer. One warning: they are known as "trash" trees. They drop old needles (and cones when mature outdoors), but that is natural as new needles are made. If yours is kept cut back, that shouldn't be a problem.

COMMELINACEAE   Dayflower Family

For the most part, members of the Commelina family are sun-lovers, and if you don't succeed with them, try more sun. (*Rhoeo spathacea*—Moses-in-the-cradle—is an exception, being quite content with bright light and a minimum of direct sun.) Most have interesting foliage, variegated or fuzzy—or both. But their flowers are small and, true to the family, last only one day each—though usually a succession of blooms are produced.

In addition to the plants questioned in this section, you might want to try *Siderasis fuscata:* its leaves are covered with fuzzy brown hairs, and have a silver stripe down their centers. We have found it slow-growing and more upright than pendant.

My tradescantia is not hanging!! It just grows upright. It's almost a foot tall and it doesn't hang. Should I be happy that I have a rarity? Or am I doing something wrong? I thought I was getting a hanging plant.

Many plants sold in hanging baskets are of a *pendant* ("hang-down") habit, but your tradescantia is of a *creeping* habit in nature, and what it is actually doing is looking for a place to root at more places along its stem.

When young, the plant does tend to grow upright for a while. As it matures, as the stems grow longer and heavier, they will hang down—but they will always curl up at the tip. Be patient: it's only showing a family trait.

Why doesn't my purple heart flower?

Sun! *Setcreasea purpurea* (purple heart) is an easy flowerer (easier than most of its relatives in the Commelina family: zebrina, tradescantia, gibasis, etc.) if it is given even moderate sun. Low light will also make the stems weak-looking and leggy.

I bought a lovely Tahitian bridal veil plant in flower, but it has since stopped flowering. How do I make it flower in my north window?

You don't. *Gibasis geniculata* (formerly *Tripogandra multiflora*— Tahitian bridal veil) needs sun to do well. An unobstructed west window, or an east at least, is needed for flowering.

This member of the Commelina family is super lovely, but it is not for growers with poor light and/or low humidity.

My Moses-in-a-boat just doesn't grow. It has made a couple of offsets, but in the year I've had it, it hasn't grown past 8 or 9 inches tall. Should I change the soil?

Repot the plant only if the roots fill the pot.

We are forced to a conclusion: while most of the *Rhoeo spathacea* (oyster plant, Moses-in-the-cradle, etc.) grow to a maximum of about 18 inches, you are growing the dwarf form, which grows to only about 9 inches. So, what you have is not an unhealthy standard-size plant, but a healthy miniature.

My purple heart is turning green. Can it be getting too much sun? I keep it a few feet back from my window (east).

Setcreasea purpurea (purple heart) is a sun-lover—it is grown as an edging plant in Florida. Indoors, it must get as much sun as possible —and a few feet back from your east-facing window is impossible.

How do I root cuttings of *Purpurea purpurea?*

The plant is *Setcreasea purpurea* (known commonly as purple heart), and it is a member of the Dayflower family (commelinas).

It roots very readily. Take cuttings just below a node (that swelling in the stem where a leaf comes from—or came from). Root in any propagation medium, or water, or even just stick cuttings into the soil of the same pot.

How do I water my *Tradescantia navicularis?*

This unusual (and uncommon) member of the Commelina family is treated like a succulent. In a 4-inch to 6-inch pot, permit it to go dry down to about one knuckle depth before watering. Give it full sun.

Why am I having trouble with a *Cyanotis kewensis* plant? The stems don't hold up and the plant is pale and generally poor-looking.

Cyanotis kewensis, a member of the Commelina (Dayflower) family, takes a good deal of bright light and requires higher relative humidity than other commelinas. Allow it to go moderately dry between water-ings. Keep it well pinched back, to get a compact and bushy plant. But you can't have a bushy plant without bright light.

I have a wandering Jew with silver hairs—I mean I had it. It rotted and died. I did manage to save a piece, which I rooted in perlite, but how should I grow it? I don't want to lose it again.

It sounds like *Tradescantia sillamontana,* a plant that demands bright sun. But you probably killed it with overwatering. This tradescantia must go drier between waterings than most other members of the family.

COMPOSITAE   Daisy Family

This is a very large and varied family, with a great many possible, good, and excellent houseplants in it.

Have you tried some composite annuals in pots? Not just in the summer, but even in the wintertime—if you have enough sun: zinnia, ageratum, marigold. Ageratum comes in shades of blue, marigolds come in many shades of yellow and orange, and zinnia can be had in almost every color *but* true blue. Remember, sun and plenty of water (plus frequent showerings to get rid of bugs) are the secrets to success with annual Compositae in pots.

Cineraria (*Senecio cruentus*) is widely killed by growing it too warm. If you can keep it cool and bright it is a gorgeous plant. Rather than trying to carry it over after flowering, propagate it from tip cuttings, then grow on the cuttings raised in your own, rather than a greenhouse, environment.

French tarragon (*Artemisia dracunculus*) and wormwood (*A. absinthium*) are two herbs of this family possible in pots, but they take lots of sun and water.

Kleinia is an interesting succulent genus, easy to grow in a very well-drained soil and bright light, and the succulent forms of senecio are also interesting to try, though more difficult to manage, at least for us.

All in all, the Composite or Daisy family has a lot of challenges to offer.

My purple passion is growing like a vine, but the color is poor and the leaves seem a little weak. What does this plant prefer?

Good sun, and watering when the soil goes surface dry. There is a tendency to treat *Gynura aurantiaca* (purple passion) as a low-light and high-humidity exotic. It is actually a composite—in the same family as the garden daisy. When it flowers, gynura makes an orange daisylike flower (the species name means "golden").

If kept dim, it grows weak and long. With too little water, the leaves go limp. It propagates easily from tip cuttings.

We don't have enough sun to grow it well over the winter, so we take cuttings in the fall and pot them up in February to make a new plant.

How do I care for my leopard plant?

Ligularia tussilaginea aureo-maculata (leopard plant) wants constant moisture in a well-drained soil, moderate humidity (40 percent and higher), and bright light (it will tolerate some sun, but direct sun isn't needed). It will do better if you can keep it a bit cooler than the general run of your houseplants.

Its spotted leaves are quite attractive, but it is not the easiest of houseplants.

Can I grow sunflowers from sunflower seeds?

Certainly not from pumpkin seeds! And not from *roasted* sunflower seeds either. Roasting sterilizes seeds, but raw sunflower seeds from the health-food store or just sunflower seeds from a seed house will be fine.

Start them by pushing them just below the surface of a 3-inch pot full of damp long-fibered sphagnum moss.

But remember, you need sun to grow *Helianthus annuus* (common sunflower). In Greek, *helios* means sun, *anthus* means flower; so this is literally the sun's own flower, and it must be grown in full overhead sun, outdoors, on a sunny rooftop or terrace.

CORNACEAE　　　　　　　　　　　　　　　　　Dogwood Family

For some reason, *Aucuba japonica,* a shrub which will grow to 15 feet and which we have seen hardy as far north as Long Island, is often included in commercially made dish gardens or terrariums. That is a terrible fate for a shrub.

Actually, aucuba (gold-dust plant) makes an excellent potted shrub, more resistant to indoor conditions than many shrubs—provided it gets bright light.

But a dish garden?

My variegated aucuba is losing lower leaves. It is almost 4 feet tall, and I've had it indoors for years. The leaves are getting spotted yellow, then all yellow, then falling off. I'm treating it the same as always. Can you help me?

Aucuba japonica variegata (gold-dust plant) is a hardy shrub in the warmer half of the country, but still will make a good indoor plant. Though, truth to tell, we've seen it more successful in offices than in homes.

How long has it been since you've repotted it? It is, after all, a full-size, quite large-growing shrub, with a vigorous root system.

Water the plant and turn it out of the pot (get a friend to help if you must). Look at the root ball. If it fills the pot, then it's time for repotting. (However, we prefer *not* to repot in October, November, and December, when the days are getting shorter; we wait until January, when the days are getting longer.)

But you said something else: that you're treating the plant the same as you did when it was young. Plants change. Mature adult plants have different needs than young plants. Never make assumptions about your plants. Keep them under observation. Their reactions will tell you what they need: more water, less water, light, food, repotting, etc. That's why it is so rewarding to "play" in your garden every day—so that if your plant is sending you a message, you get it good and early.

CRASSULACEAE   Stonecrop Family

This is a big family, all succulent plants, with many houseplants in cultivation. The family is worldwide in distribution, but many of the plants originally came from the southern parts of Africa. Most members of this family will propagate from a single leaf.

For us, they do well on a kind of benign neglect. We put them in very bright windows, with as much direct sun as we can manage (it's not a lot), keep them somewhat potbound, repot seldom, feed seldom, make certain their soil mix drains quite well, and water them along with our other houseplants—or a little less often. Since many of them are small plants and pushed out where we sometimes have trouble seeing them, they get skipped in the watering from time to time. But they grow well for us.

Adromischus is an interesting genus, with short swollen leaves, sometimes with dark variegations on them.

Aeoniums grow in tight rosettes, and seem the most difficult of the family, often losing lower leaves and getting a sloppy leggy look.

Cotyledon is another genus in the Crassula family, and some of its species have thick hairy leaves—very attractive.

The genus crassula has many forms itself: *Crassula arborescens* (jade plant) is treelike, though much smaller, while *C. lycopodioides* is called toy cypress and has tiny leaves set overlapping and quite tight against each other.

Echeveria is a very handsome genus, from the New World (mostly Mexico), with a bluish waxy coat to the leaves of many of its species.

This is a real sun-lover. Don't handle the leaves because rubbing away that waxy covering will hurt the plant's chances of survival. They seem prone to rot if overwatered. Be certain your soil mix drains *very* well for echeverias, and reduce watering during the short days of winter and fall.

Sedum is another very popular genus in this family. Its name (in Latin) describes its habit, in nature, of "sitting" on (growing over) rocks. If you have even moderately bright light, *Sedum morganianum* (burro's-tail sedum) makes as handsome a houseplant as you can grow. Water it well and give it a quarter-turn weekly to keep it even.

Kalanchoe has been hybridized to make houseplants that flower brilliantly and over a long period of time, but the best flowerers (*Kalanchoe blossfeldiana* and its hybrids) need long nights (about 14 hours of uninterrupted darkness) to set bud. Other kalanchoes make great (and we mean great) foliage plants that are easy to grow. If you want delight from a plant, grow *K. daigremontiana,* which spontaneously forms plantlets along its leaf margins, or *K. tubiflora,* which does the same at its leaf tips.

The Crassula family is one to know and grow.

I bought a miniature jade a few weeks ago in a 2-inch pot. It's about 4 inches tall, and a root is coming out the bottom of the pot. Should I repot it?

We are loath to repot in November, when the days are at their shortest. Waiting just a few weeks more, until after the turn of the year, can give you a much better chance of success. Even waiting until just after the solstice will improve the odds, because there is a bit more light every day.

A root coming out of the bottom of a pot doesn't necessarily mean the plant needs repotting—it may just mean that the grower (as is the case with the vast majority of plants sold commercially) has failed to crock the bottom of the pot, and so there is nothing to contain the root. Many plants send roots right down to the bottom of the pot and out the hole if the bottom of the pot isn't crocked. It doesn't mean the plant wants repotting.

As with any plant, knock it out of its pot and take a look at the rootball. Only if it is full of roots do you repot.

How do you transplant a jade tree?

Carefully—very carefully. As with other succulents, allow the plant to go rather dry, then pot into fairly dry soil, without handling the roots any more than absolutely necessary, and, finally, don't water for a week or so.

I broke my jade right off a couple of inches above the soil. Is there anything I can do?

You can treat the top of your *Crassula arborescens* (jade plant) as if it were a large cutting. Cut the bottom of the stem straight across and allow the new cut to callus overnight, then stand it on sterile damp sand. You can hold it up with a stake if need be. Cut the part remaining in the pot straight across and dust the top with flowers of sulfur—it may sprout and you may end up with two plants.

Most cacti and other succulents will propagate in the same way.

I bought a crassula jade in a 3-inch pot, and the top looks quite crowded. Should I repot it?

You can't tell from the top growth whether or not it needs repotting; you have to look at the roots.

Just *before* the next time you would water the plant, turn your crassula out of its pot and look at the roots. If they fill the pot, then repot (repot with the soil fairly dry, into fairly dry soil, and don't water for two weeks) . If the roots don't fill the pot, wait. If the plant is top-heavy but the roots don't fill the pot, set the plant, pot and all, into a slightly larger clay pot. This will hold the plant upright without disturbing the roots.

Succulents, in general, should be repotted as little as possible. Their roots are subject to easy damage and rot.

I have had a jade plant for a long time, and now it is losing its leaves. I haven't changed its treatment. Is there something going around?

Not for jades.

How long has it been since you've repotted? Whenever anyone says he's had a plant for a long time and suddenly it's changed, we wonder about how long it's been since a repotting. Let the plant go dryish, then turn it out of its pot and see if the roots fill the pot—if they do, repot into fairly dry soil and don't water for a week or two.

If the plant doesn't need repotting, then you may have a root problem—and when a succulent gets root problems, it's always serious. If it's the roots, raise the humidity as high as you can until leaves stop dropping.

I have just bought a "life plant." How do I care for it?

There are several plants commonly (and more or less appropriately) called "life plant," and they all belong to the genus kalanchoe (bryophyllum section). They are so named because of their habit of producing plantlets along the margins or tips of their succulent leaves.

Kalanchoe daigremontiana is also known as "mother of thousands." If you grow this plant, you will have the tiny plantlets (they grow small roots right there on the leaf edge of the parent plant) falling and rooting all over your garden.

K. pinnata plants are also known as "floppers." This is the plant whose leaf you see advertised as "African Life Plant—pin a leaf to your curtain and see it grow." The leaf will form plantlets, but you have to put the plantlets in soil to have them grow. This plant will grow quite leggy, then flop over (hence, "floppers"), and the new plants will root from the old leaves.

K. tubiflora is the handsomest of the section (in our opinion). It is smaller, more compact, handsomely variegated, and the plantlets form only on the tips of the leaves.

K. crennata grows rather large for a pot plant, but it will go pink and flower in full sun. It, too, forms its plantlets (and rather *large* plantlets they are) at the tips of its leaves.

All these plants require full sun—or as much as you can give them. Allow them to go moderately dry between watering (but not bone dry).

Some will tend to grow very tall and leggy—cut these back to within a few inches of the soil, and they will often resprout. Cut off most of the stem (allow the cut to callus), and you can root the top, as well as the individual leaves.

CRUCIFERAE   Mustard Family

This is our favorite edible family: cabbage, cauliflower, broccoli, watercress, kale. And some of them can be grown in containers on sunny terraces or rooftops. If you have the space and like the challenge, try a broccoli in a 12-inch tub. After you cut the first set of flower buds, others will come. Broccoli is one of the best of the cut-and-come-again vegetables.

The Mustard family includes many beautifully decorative plants—mathiola (stocks), iberis (candytuft), lunaria (honesty), as well as the ornamental cabbages—but almost all are better suited to in-ground culture.

Can you recommend something low-growing to put around the base of a 12-inch pot of geraniums? The pot is on a south window and the geraniums are in marvelous flower, but they have lost quite a few of their lower leaves, and so I'd like to put in something compatible that will make it a little less naked-looking.

Lobularia (sweet alyssum) is a fine plant for your situation, though it would also do well in less sun than your south-facing window. It grows rapidly, is shallow-rooted, flowers very freely, and aside from watering needs little care. And those flowers are indeed *sweet*.

It may also be that adding the sweet alyssum to the pot will improve your geraniums. They are likely losing those lower leaves because of underwatering. In the long days of summer, they drink a lot of water.

CYCADACEAE   Sago Palm Family

These plants are often mistakenly called palms—but they aren't: they are considerably older in the world than palms are.

Cycads are slow-growing, and typified by a tuft of stiff palmlike foliage, growing in a rosette out of a thick trunk.

We enjoy them at botanical gardens because the gardens have space to grow and to display them and we do not. Being hangovers from the carboniferous age, they are not the best of houseplants, but they can be grown in a conservatory or large greenhouse, or outdoors year-round where there is no frost.

Why are the fronds of my zamia falling off? The plant is growing new fronds, but they seem thinner, with smaller leaves. Do these plants need a special plant food?

Zamias are cycads—among the very oldest of plants still alive on earth. They are not heavy feeders. They need full, strong sun, and from what you describe (the new fronds coming in leggy and etiolated), yours is simply not getting its sun.

What causes my zamia to turn yellow?

Probably overwatering. In pots, most cycads will want to go somewhat dry between waterings in a very well-drained soil rich in organic material.

My zamia has mealybug—and what a case of it! I dose with alcohol, I spray—and for a while it looks as if I've won, and then it's back. What can I do?

Your problem is twofold. First of all, you have to be certain that you get not only the white cottony masses and the whitish adults, but you also have to hunt down the small pink nymph stage. These creatures are much more active than the adults, and harder to get with the alcohol—but if you miss them, your mealies come back when these nymphs mature.

Second, do you see that fluffy area on your zamia where the new leaves grow from? That is mealybug heaven. They live and breed there, almost invisible unless you look for them. Take your alcohol-soaked cotton swab and dab every week and you'll likely beat them.

Have you used Ced-o-flora for mealybug? It is often quite effective.

My sago palm is making these strange things on top, and I think they are flowers—they look like a kind of droopy pine cone. Will I be able to pollinate the flowers and get seeds?

You are right, those are flowers, but you won't get seed. Those are male flowers. Sago palms (*Cycas revoluta*) are dioecious, which means male and female flowers are borne on separate plants (like holly), so unless you can introduce yours to a female in the neighborhood, no seed.

You can propagate your sago palm from offsets that form at its base.

CYPERACEAE   Sedge Family

This family includes the historically interesting papyrus plant (*Cyperus papyrus*). Members of this family make difficult houseplants, usually, because they are semiaquatic.

My dwarf umbrella plant is dying back from the tips, and I don't know what to do with it. I give it bright light and water it when the surface of the soil is dry. What am I doing wrong?

It sounds as if you are letting the plant go too dry. Your dwarf umbrella plant (*Cyperus diffusus*) and all the cyperuses should be kept evenly moist—in fact, most of them prefer to grow just *under* water.

Can I grow papyrus in my "water garden"? It's actually a galvanized iron tub on my terrace.

Cyperus papyrus, which is the famous papyrus plant of ancient Egypt, does very well in a water garden—outdoors, away from freezing temperatures, and where it can have room to grow 7 feet tall.

    Instead, try *Cyperus haspan viviparus,* the pygmy papyrus.

ERICACEAE   Heath Family

Heaths and heathers are the backbone of this family, and they are not truly suited to anything but in-ground culture, but many of the broad-leafed evergreens in this family are excellent for balcony growing. Plants such as hardy azalea, rhododendron, leucothoe, and especially pieris (andromeda) will do well on a balcony with even moderate sun, but you have to provide tubs at least 18 inches square. Do be certain to keep them well watered—especially during the summer months.

I got an azalea for Mother's Day. Can I keep it growing?

Yes, though azaleas are easily killed indoors in pots.

    Give them as much sun as they can take without the leaves burning (the leaves turn red with sunburn).

    Give them an acid soil or an acid food.

    Give them plenty of water. (They'll die if they dry.)

    Cut them back about halfway after flowering is finished.

    And, most important, keep the plants as cool as you can: they suffer from heat—especially in the winter.

    Hardy azaleas (ask the plant seller—he may know what he's been selling) can be planted outdoors in the north, and tender azaleas can be planted outdoors in the south. Hardy azaleas grow well in large tubs on balcony or terrace.

    A Rhododendron Society representative told us that most of the holiday azaleas sold are *tender.* We do wish that the plant wholesalers would label their azaleas as to variety, or at least as to hardiness.

EUPHORBIACEAE   Spurge Family

This is a large and varied family, and contains some super houseplants. The Euphorbiaceae are not related to cacti, but they evolved in the Old World in the same way that cacti evolved in our half of the world.

But as houseplants they are far superior to cacti.

Most make a white sap when cut, and this sap should be washed off your hands promptly if you touch it: it is a skin irritant for many people. When propagating from tip cuttings, allow the sap to dry before inserting a cutting into your rooting medium.

Euphorbia pulcherrima is poinsettia, the most widely sold plant in the United States. We no longer carry our poinsettias over from year to year—they are so readily available that we now buy new ones (and often new varieties) every year. Did you know that poinsettias can be had in color at any time of year? You could have them in the spring—but apparently there is consumer resistance to springtime poinsettias, and so they are as yet sold only in winter.

The most notable characteristic about the flowers of the Euphorbiaceae is that they are mostly not notable. The family makes tiny flowers, but they are often surrounded by colorful and persistent bracts (adapted leaves).

Most plants in this family love warmth and tolerate low humidity, which makes them excellent houseplants.

There are a few that are more difficult to grow, requiring higher humidity (jatropha, for example), or brighter sun (such as codiaeum —known as croton), but there are others that are so easy to flower (*Euphorbia millii*—crown of thorns—is one), or so colorful and carefree (*Synadenium grantii rubra*), or just plain fascinating (like *Euphorbia obesa*—the so-called golfball cactus—which has plants of different sexes and when young can be a perfectly spherical shape), that you could grow just members of this family and yet have a spectacular and fascinating plant collection.

My match-me-if-you-can is losing color: more and more of the leaves are just greenish. Should I repot it?

Move it into more sun. *Acalypha wilkesiana macrophylla* (match-me-if-you-can) is a sun-lover and loses color out of the sun. Now, if your letter had had a Florida postmark, we would have said the opposite: move it into less sun. Acalypha can bleach in full outdoor sun.

Can I grow *Euphorbia splendens,* the crown of thorns, under fluorescent lights? What I mean is, will it flower?

Yes, and quite well (though *Euphorbia millii* is a better name—an earlier name—than *Euphorbia splendens* for crown of thorns). The one problem is the tendency of *Euphorbia millii* to grow so upright.

We have found a multibranching and rather low-growing variety, *Euphorbia millii prostrata,* which not only stays fairly low and compact but is very floriferous, too. We've had one in constant flower, close under three cool-white tubes, for almost four years. *E. m. imperatae* is a handsomely compact variety that is quite floriferous.

Can I grow crown of thorns from seed?

We have done so—though not deliberately.

We grow *Euphorbia millii prostrata* (a compact crown of thorns) under bright fluorescent light (with plenty of water). In the same light tray we control insects with ladybug beetles. The ladybugs nose into everything, including our crown of thorns flowers, and pollinate them. We have had seed ripen and drop into nearby pots and sprout, making, eventually, nice small plants. We suppose the same thing could be done deliberately.

Why do the leaves of my crown of thorns turn yellow and fall off? It can't be overwatering—I water very little.

Why are you watering very little? If you water your *Euphorbia millii* (crown of thorns) very little, the leaves turn yellow and fall off. However, don't despair, more generous watering will cause new leaves to sprout from the old empty nodes.

My croton drops its beautiful leaves—what should I do?

Buy it a ticket to Bermuda, where it will have a fighting chance.

Codiaeum (croton) enjoys high humidity and constant moisture. And, as do other members of the Euphorbia family, it likes warm temperatures. Give it at least moderate sun (it will take plenty). Cut it back to encourage resprouting, and then shower it frequently to discourage spider mite. Watch out for scale and mealybug, too, while you're at it.

Is croton a low-light or full-sun plant?

In very bright light, codiaeum (croton) will do all right without direct sun, but it needs sun to really look its best. Sun brings out the colors. It will pine and decline in low light.

About the name: there is a true croton in this same Euphorbia family, but no one grows it as a houseplant. Your "croton" (*Codiaeum variegatum pictum*) has hundreds of cultivars, each one more beautiful in size, shape, and color than the next.

In tubs indoors (or outdoors in really warm climates) they make very striking plants.

My croton leaves are coming in plain green instead of red and green. I have it in low light and water once a week. What am I doing wrong?

Everything.

Codiaeum (croton) wants lots of water, frequent washing of the leaves, and bright sun. If it can't have bright sun, it will tolerate lower light, but only if you can keep it *cool*. High temperature plus low light equals green instead of variegated leaves.

Does croton flower?

Yes, codiaeum (croton) will flower, in bright sun. It is monoecious, which means that it makes flowers of two different sexes on the same plant (like begonias). The female flowers look like tiny dandelions. They are quite small and are borne many to a stem. The berries ripen dark. The plant can be grown from these seeds, but being hybrids, they won't come true from seed.

If yours summers outdoors (and winters indoors), you may see some flowers while it is outdoors, but then the plant will suffer leaf drop when brought inside.

My croton lost most of its leaves because I let it go dry. Can I prune it and start over again?

Yes. Prune it sharply, keep it warm and bright, and water moderately until new leaf growth begins.

You will get replacement leaf growth even if you don't prune, but then the bulk of the new leaves will come out at the top.

Pruning will give you a better-looking and healthier plant.

On Thanksgiving, I bought a plant that they told me is a euphorbia, and that the leaves would fall off, and that I should water it when it goes very dry. It looks like a cactus with flat leaves, and it's in a 3-inch pot and about 8 inches tall. Should I repot it?

Unless the plant is so potbound that it's a desperate case, wait to repot until the turn of the year. And then, don't repot unless the rootball pretty much fills the pot. If you do repot, move up only one size pot.

But that watering advice is for the birds (or for the true cacti). Euphorbias lose their leaves if allowed to go very dry between waterings. To keep the leaves and encourage flowering keep the plant well watered (not sopping wet).

Also, keep the plant out of drafts—they like warm temperatures.

Following your instructions, I reflowered my poinsettia (Thanks!), but it is quite a bit taller than I remember it from last year. Could my temperature (70° or a little lower) be to blame?

Could be. (And you're welcome!) Temperatures around 65°F. will keep your *Euphorbia pulcherrima* (poinsettia) more compact, as will frequent pinching out. But the most likely thing is that your plant has outgrown the effects of the dwarfing chemical used by the original grower. Poinsettias (and some mums and other flowering plants) are treated with chemicals to keep their growth compact (without affecting their flowering).

In the year you've had the plant (without further treatment), the chemical has (pretty much) been flushed from the plant's system and it is back into a more realistic growth pattern.

Why are my poinsettia leaves turning yellow and falling off?

Poinsettias belong to the family and genus euphorbia (*Euphorbia pulcherrima*), and with many of these plants, lack of water will cause yellowing and leaf drop. The resumption of moderate watering will then allow new leaves to form.

Euphorbias have great recovery powers, and given a chance they will readily resprout replacement leaves.

Can jatropha be grown as a houseplant?

Jatrophas are in the Euphorbia family, and most of that family will make successful houseplants. For your jatropha, provide a porous soil, ample watering, moderate humidity, and warm (normal house) temperatures.

Jatropha integerrima grows rather rangy, but *J. podagrica* will stay more compact and makes an interesting swollen stem.

I have recently bought a plant with pointed indented leaves and a thick trunk, though the plant isn't very tall. The label was rubbed out, but I think it said "Jat . . ." or something like that. Have you any idea of what it could be and what I might expect from it?

It sounds like it could be a jatropha, a member of the Euphorbia family—in which case you've got yourself an interesting plant.

It requires warm temperatures, good humidity, and ample water—and bright light with some sun. If you lived in Florida, you might expect it to grow into quite a tall shrub, but in a pot be content if it grows to 2 feet.

Don't allow it to dry out. If it gets leggy, cut it back to the thick stem and start over.

It will make a rather bizarre red flower head with small red flowers.

My devil's backbone cactus has lost all its leaves! The stem looks green and not dying, but all the colorful leaves are gone. Is this normal?

Pedilanthus tithymaloides (devil's backbone cactus) is no cactus, but it is in the Euphorbia family, and it is not unusual for members of this family to lose their leaves from lack of water. We've seen it with crown of thorns, with croton, and with many others. It is a protective mechanism to keep the plant alive in dry weather. Water your plant and keep it watered, and the leaves will return and stay.

GERANIACEAE   Geranium Family

This is a family that contains both hardy and tender plants, but they all prefer cool temperatures. Geraniums (pelargonium is their Latin name) will do better in the fall than in a hot summer.

And, generally, they will do best if allowed to grow potbound—don't be in any hurry to repot them.

There are a number of wild geraniums in this same family, but they are not suited for pot culture.

For our plant dollar, the easiest and most satisfactory of the pelargoniums for indoor culture are the miniature, or dwarf, geraniums and the scented-leaf geraniums. (The full-sized zonal geraniums do best for us outdoors, where they can get the full sun they crave.)

Dwarf geraniums give flowers about the same size as full-size plants, but produce many fewer of them to a flower head. Since they are less sun-demanding than their big brothers, we find them more apt to flower during winter or under fluorescent lights than the biggies.

Some people classify scented-leaf geraniums among the herbs, since they are so aromatic; when industry wants something rose-scented, they usually use rose geraniums, which smell much more of roses than roses do. We always keep plants of lemon-scented, nutmeg-scented, and peppermint-scented geraniums, just to touch as we move around. Even in locations too dim to flower them—after all, scented-leaf geraniums usually have quite forgettable flowers. And we save every leaf that falls or that we prune off, for our linens and clothes drawers.

Why are the lower leaves of my dwarf geranium turning yellow and falling off?

Too little sun perhaps? Dwarf geraniums need less sun than full-size plants, but they still need sun.

Or too little water? Geraniums are not at their best grown like cacti. In a well-drained soil they will take plenty of water.

Are miniature geraniums any harder to grow than the full-size plants?

Easier. They flower in less sun and will live in the same small pots for months and months.

We think the miniatures are terrific houseplants, while their full-size relations are really better suited to bedding outdoors, pots on the terrace, or windowbox plants. The full-size geraniums just don't get enough sun indoors to flower readily. The little ones are satisfied by bright light and will even flower under a bank of fluorescents.

Do I treat my miniature geraniums as I do my full-size geraniums for the winter? I mean, do I have to cut them back?

We don't. And we have only a blocked east exposure for them. But we grow them very cool, on the upper ledge of a cool window (the hot radiator is 3 feet below). Grown this cool and in this bright a window, and allowed to go rather dry between waterings, they even flower for us over the winter.

But if you have little sun over the winter and can't keep them cool, then by all means cut them back and allow them to resprout for new growth when the days get longer.

Of course, large geranium or miniature, you get only one flower head per branch, so do pinch them out to get branching.

I have been flowering geraniums all fall on my terrace. Do I have to throw them away now, or what?

Definitely "what."

Take 3- to 4-inch cuttings of your geraniums, cut away any flowers or buds, and remove all but a few top leaves. Allow the cut ends to callus for a few hours, and stick them into peat pellets (such as Jiffy-7's) or into damp sand—but do *not* cover them or set them into a plastic bag (because enclosed geraniums may rot). Keep them with your houseplants and water them regularly. When your cuttings are rooted, pot them up and give these young plants your best sun until you can put them outside. They'll flower when the sun is strong enough.

As for your original plants, keep them in their pots, in your sunniest, coolest indoor place, and reduce watering until they resprout with new growth.

You have to be very careful not to overwater a leafless plant. Gradually return to a normal watering schedule as the plant grows more leaves.

Top-dress in the spring with about an inch of rich potting soil.

My geranium leaves are spotting. Are they pollution-sensitive?

Not generally, but if there was something especially corrosive in the air, of course the leaves (and your lungs) would show it.

Remove damaged leaves, and cut the plant back if leaf loss is extensive.

If your spots are quite circular, you may have a fungus. Again, remove spotted leaves and keep water off the remaining leaves. If damage is severe, you may have to throw the plant away.

I bought a geranium from a man on a truck and it was in flower. But now, after two months, there are no more flowers and the stem looks long and thin and the lower leaves are yellowing and dropping off. I keep the plant in an east window and water it about once a week. Did he sell me a lemon?

We don't recommend getting plants from men on trucks because where are they when you get a problem? But your difficulty sounds like too little sun. Leggy plants often indicate poor light, and geraniums specifically drop their lower leaves in inadequate light. Move your plant into more sun and don't treat it like a cactus—water it whenever it is dry down to about one knuckle's depth below the soil surface.

My ivy geranium hanging basket just dried up and died. I do fine with other geraniums—what's the difference?

Ivy geraniums are poor houseplants (though they do well in greenhouses or on sun porches). They want cooler temperatures, higher humidity, and more water than the zonal geraniums. And they are mite prone. Treat them to a weekly prophylactic wash, under and over the leaves.

Will you recommend some easy-to-grow scented geraniums? I don't have a lot of sun; will they survive on my blocked east windowsill?

It depends on how blocked. They need some sun and a good deal of bright light to make strong growth, but the scented-leaf geraniums will thrive in conditions that cause a zonal geranium (ordinary garden geranium) to grow weak and floppy.

Most are easy. Exceptions include "Prince Rupert" (*Pelargonium crispum* 'Prince Rupert Variegatum'), a variegated lemon-scented with tightly curled leaves that is prone to rot with overwatering and demands bright sun and cool temperatures, and nutmeg-scented geranium (*P. x fragrans*), which may do poorly in normally warm indoor temperatures.

For a start, try rose-scented (*Pelargonium graveolens*), oak-leafed (*P. quercifolium*), and peppermint-scented (*P. tomentosum*). This last has delightfully furry leaves.

Allow them to go moderately dry between waterings, and pinch out to keep your plants bushy. Any lost leaves should go into a sachet or leaf bowl. The leaves dry to a crisp without any special treatment.

Do I have to cut back my scented geraniums for the winter as I do my zonals?

No, not as severely.

Zonals get cut back to within a couple of inches of the soil line. Your scented-leaf geraniums will grow quite well if cut back about 25 percent and kept in a very bright and cool window, and grown through the winter.

I bought a pot of a small-leafed plant, with rounded, kind of lobed leaves, looking and acting like a ground cover, and it has flowered for me, making these flowers that look a little like the flowers of my scented geraniums, but they are white, with purplish spots. Can you tell me what it is?

Our guess would be *Erodium pelargoniflorum,* a delightful small plant of the Geranium family. Give it cool evenings, bright light with some direct sun, and water when the soil is dry about $1/4$ inch below its surface. And don't be surprised if it grows more upright as it matures.

If you get seeds, plant them up.

GESNERIACEAE   African Violet Family

We will always have a soft feeling in our horticultural heart for the gesneriads, in part because of our own involvement with growing and hybridizing the plants of this family in an organized fashion with other members of the American Gloxinia and Gesneriad Society, but mostly because they are such attractive and easy plants (officers of other houseplant societies who want equal time will just have to write their own books) .

The trouble with most of the plants in the Gesneriad family is that they don't—aside from African violets (saintpaulia) and aeschynanthus (lipstick plant) —have cutesy common names. Who can be happy growing *Nematanthus perianthomega* when they could be growing "pink-polka-dot" plant? On the face of it, which would you buy: *Gesneria cuneifolia* or cobra plant? Not that pink-polka-dot plant (*Hypoestes sanguinolenta*) and cobra plant (calathea) aren't beautiful and terrific as houseplants—but it does put the gesneriads at a disadvantage.

Koellikeria erinoides and *Gesneria cuneifolia* both make excellent terrarium plants. The former makes scores of maroon and cream flowers held high over silver-spotted leaves; the latter may make orange or red flowers, depending on the variety.

Achimenes will make an excellent windowsill or balcony hanging basket for late summer bloom, provided your air is clean—pollution will blast its flower buds.

Episcias are terrestrial creepers with marvelously variegated foliage (mostly) , that make good hanging baskets in wide but shallow pots. Sun makes them flower but bleaches out leaf color. Moderately bright light brings out the leaf color but makes for scant bloom. They will have both bloom and good leaf color if under two or more tubes of fluorescent light.

Streptocarpus has become a more popular genus in recent years, and whereas before it was thought to be strictly a greenhouse plant, some are growing it as a summer bedding plant for part shade and many are growing it year round on windowsills or under lights. It wants bright light with some sun, but it does best if temperatures are kept on the cool side (below 70°F.) .

There are many many more gesneriads, enough to make a number of books on the subject. Go on. Try one. You'll like it.

There is a sticky light-colored dust on the leaves right under the blooms of my African violets. I wash it off, but it comes back. Do you have any idea of what it could be? It seems to be doing no harm.

It would be unusual, but it *could* be pollen from the flowers. If it washes away and does no harm, don't worry.

I have been waiting for *weeks* for my African violet leaf to make a new plant. The leaf looks healthy, it even has formed some roots, but no

new African violets. It is in vermiculite, in a high humidity, and on my north windowsill. Are there some African violets that just won't come from a leaf?

Not so far as we know—but some can be terribly slow. Not that a few weeks is so long to wait. It may take months before you have plantlets large enough to separate.

Perhaps too much petiole (leaf stem) was left on the leaf. Leave about 1 inch of petiole—more slows things down. If all else fails, remove the leaf and then reset it in another part of your prop box. The movement seems to stimulate sprouting (we don't know why). And be patient. As long as the leaf is plump and healthy-looking, you have the chance of plantlets sprouting.

Are African violets low-light or bright-light plants? I have read both.

African violets (saintpaulia hybrids) are very durable and flexible plants—that's what accounts for their long-term popularity.

They will flower in an unobstructed north window, and they will flower in a south window (as long as good air circulation keeps the temperatures down).

Under fluorescent lights, while they will flower somewhat at the ends of your fluorescent tubes, they will flower better in the middle and grown close to the tubes.

Generally, the more light, the more flowers.

Are miniature African violets demanding?

They are easy—easy, easy, easy. Keep them in 2½-inch pots, give them the same humidity and watering as full-size plants—and they will flower in even less light.

Why won't my African violet flower? I keep them in good sun and give them a good organic fish emulsion for food.

If your "good organic food" consists solely of fish emulsion, that's your answer. Fish emulsion is an excellent food and provides needed trace elements. But it is high in nitrogen. Flowering plants need phosphorus; too much nitrogen can inhibit flowering. Use fish emulsion only one feeding in four. The other times you are going to have to use a food with a lot of phosphorus (a high middle number). If you wish to continue organically, try incorporating some ground phosphate rock into your potting mix.

How should I feed my African violets?

Feed them every two weeks while they are in active growth and flowering, with 15–30–15 plant food or fish emulsion (three feedings of 15–30–15 to one of fish emulsion), at half the strength recommended on the label.

Slow down the feeding if your windows are dull in the winter.

If your African violets are in a soilless mix, however, you can feed constantly: that is, a solution at one-sixteenth strength with every feeding.

Why are random leaves of my African violets turning black?

Black? Dark brown, more likely. Sounds like botrytis, a fungus disease which can spread to other plants. Your best bet is to throw out all affected plants and to clean out the area with rubbing alcohol.

Next time, provide better air circulation and keep cool water off the leaves of your saintpaulias (African violets).

My African violets all lean out the window. How can I get them to grow flat and level with the ground?

Your African violets are just turning their leaves toward the light. If you give them a quarter-turn every few days, they will stay level.

Are African violets really from Africa?

Yes, the original plants from which our modern hybrids come *are* from Africa—mostly from Tanganyika. But they are definitely *not* violets, which are in the Viola family.

Are some African violets seasonal bloomers? Mine go out of flower in the winter but my friend's stay in bloom.

African violets (saintpaulias) are *not* seasonal. They are neither long-day plants nor long-night plants, but are what is known as day-neutral: as long as they have enough light they can, and will, flower at any time of year.

Windowsill growers have the problem of reduced natural light in the fall and winter. Your friend obviously has a brighter window.

If you want winter bloom, you'll have to move *your* plants to a brighter window. But then be patient: after they have enough light, your African violets will take five or six weeks to set bud.

I propagate my African violets from leaves, and they grow multiple crowns. I've looked for it in books, but I can't find out when and how to divide them.

What you seem to be doing is potting up everything that pops up from the leaf into one pot. Those are several plantlets, and that's why you have multiple crowns: because you begin with multiple plants.

The time to divide is when the new plantlets are about 1 inch to 1½ inches tall. Separate the plantlets from the parent leaf and (handling by a leaf, not by the roots) place them on a piece of light-colored paper. With a clean knife, separate the plantlets near the roots (you'll see where they join once you've shaken off a bit of the rooting medium). Each parent leaf should give you three or more plantlets.

Pot each plantlet into a separate pot with normal African violet soil.

Don't be frightened of this kind of handling. It is less traumatic to a young plant with a few short roots to be handled this way than it is for a mature plant to be separated from another mature plant.

And, with practice, it becomes a simple process.

Do I have to cut the deadheads off my African violets?

If you don't cut the deadheads off some plants, they form seeds and are shy to set more bloom.

African violets seldom self-seed. In fact, the hybrids we grow are difficult to pollinate, even by hand. So, flowering does not inhibit additional flowering.

However, if you don't remove spent flowers, their presence may promote fungus.

So, do cut them off. Remove the pedicle (the flower stalk) as close to the stem as you can, and then scrape away any remaining stem with your fingernail. If any stem remains at all, you may get a sucker instead of a new flower stalk.

Can I mist the leaves of my African violets with plain water?

Absolutely. In fact, you can take your African violets (saintpaulias) to the sink and wash them off under the tap or spray (with tepid water—never allow cold water to touch African violet leaves).

They can then go right back under fluorescent light, but if you are growing in sun, allow the leaves to dry before you put them out (a water drop can act like a lens, permitting the sun to burn the leaves).

If you use a fine-mist spray, however, you can put them out immediately after misting.

My miniature African violet isn't flowering, even though I feed it 20–20–20 plant food and give it good light. Are these plants hard to flower?

Not at all; often easier than the full-sized plants.

There are a number of possibilities: switch to a 15–30–15 plant food if your soil mix is high in nitrogen (the balanced food may not supply enough phosphorus); increase the light—even provide some direct sun if you can (or move the plant closer to your tubes if you are under fluorescents); finally, check your plant for suckers (miniature African violets have a tendency to sucker, and suckers inhibit flowering).

Another thought: how big a pot are you using? A miniature African violet should be in a pot from $2\frac{1}{4}$ to 3 inches in diameter. Larger than that may also delay flowering.

I started some African violet leaves in peat pots—can I grow the plantlets in them?

We prefer to peel away peat pots from the root ball—especially with houseplants. If any of the peat gets exposed above ground, it acts as a wick, drawing water from below out to the air. This means more watering and a greater chance of the plant suffering from lack of water. You could tear away just the upper half of the peat pot before you plant it. Peat pots also seem to be a locus for mold.

How big should the plantlets sprouting from the base of my African violet leaf be before I remove them and pot them up?

One to $1\frac{1}{2}$ inches.

Can I get more than one little African violet plant from a leaf I laid down?

You should get several. They are all growing close together, however, and you will need some patience and care to separate them when you remove them from the parent leaf.

By the way, if the parent leaf is still healthy-looking, set it in again, with the hope of getting still more plantlets.

The flowers on my miniature sinningia seem to drop off very quickly. How can I make them stay on longer?

Some of the mini sinningias do drop their flowers rather quickly (*Sinningia* 'Pink Flare' drops its flowers within a few days), but as a rule, for all flowering plants, the cooler you keep them, the longer your flowers last (not cold enough to hurt the plant, of course). And in terrarium growing conditions, new flowers come in as fast as the old ones fade. For their size and weight, miniature sinningias are the world's most floriferous plants. And easy. Easy in an apartment or house or office.

Under lights I have a mini gloxinia called *Sinningia* 'Rex' that isn't doing anything. It has some leaves, but it isn't growing or flowering—can you suggest anything?

Sinningia 'Rex' is one of Lyndon Lyon's new hybrids—basically a compact gloxinia. It should be given moderately high humidity, as strong light as a saintpaulia (African violet), constant moisture, and warm temperatures.

If your *Sinningia* 'Rex' is standing still, just upgrade the environment. Move it closer to the lights, raise the humidity, give it more water.

You can propagate the plant from a single leaf, inserted into damp vermiculite or perlite and kept in high humidity (as you would with an African violet leaf). This is a slow method of propagation, but the new plant you grow from this leaf may do better for you than the one you bought from a greenhouse. It will have grown up knowing only your conditions.

Why are my gloxinia buds blasting? I grow them quite close to my fluorescent tubes.

Bud blast—the shriveling and dying of a flower bud before it opens—can be caused by any (or all) of several conditions.

It could be too little water (they should stay quite moist while in bud). Or too much heat (if the buds are against warm tubes, watch it). But the most common cause of bud blast with *Sinningia speciosa* (gloxinia) is too low humidity, especially if combined with high heat.

How do I dry off a gloxinia to put it into dormancy?

Reduce watering and reduce light, and your *Sinningia speciosa* (gloxinia) will start to die back. When the leaves are dry, cut off the stem, about $1/4$ inch above the soil. Keep the pot dryish but not bone dry until new growth starts.

But unless you are going on vacation why bother? Grown under fluorescent lights, gloxes don't have to go dormant. That is our experience and the experience of many other growers.

After flowering, cut the stem back to within 1/4 inch of the soil. (Of course, you can propagate the leaves and the tip cutting.) Reduce your watering somewhat, so that you don't rot the now-leafless plant. Shortly, the plant should make new growth, and, if kept in the same bright light that flowered it in the first place, it should, within a couple of months, be in bud again.

We're glad you asked, because the old books all say you need a dormancy after each flowering period.

I am going to buy a gloxinia tuber: how do I start it?

It's easy.

Sinningia speciosa (gloxinia) tubers should be started right in their pots—4- to 6- inch azalea pots (squat pots), in rich, well-drained soil that is kept just a bit damp—not too wet, or you can rot the tuber. We like to keep ours under fluorescent light from the beginning. The warmth stimulates the tuber, and it has light the moment it sprouts.

If the tuber is slow to sprout, we put it *on top* of a fluorescent fixture (where it is really warm). However, we lose one tuber in ten if we put them over the ballast that way—the water balance is precarious.

What can I do about the buds on my achimenes blasting?

Move to a location with less air pollution. Air pollution is murder on achimenes and smithiantha flowers (and on the foliage of green peppers).

Too, achimenes require a lot of water. They'll even go dormant if you chronically underwater them.

I bought a *Columnea* 'Moonglow' recently. What can I do to make it bushier? It has only two stems, but these are growing nicely.

Take a cutting from each stem and root both in a closed propagation box. After a few weeks when the roots are about 1 inch long, plant them into the same pot with the original plant. The parent stems will have branched by then because of the cutting.

Don't forget to pinch out the cuttings as well, as soon as you put them in the prop box, to encourage them to branch too.

I have success with several columneas in my windows and on my sun porch, but my new *Columnea teuscheri* has begun to drop its leaves. Why?

We know the answer to this one only because of a conversation we had three years ago with a professional greenhouse grower who brought one into a plant show.

Aside from demanding more water and higher humidity than most other columneas, *Columnea teuscheri* must be kept at *warm temperatures*. If your sun porch or window went below 60°F., then the plant might well have dropped its leaves from the cold.

You can cut your plant back sharply and expect it to resprout.

Talk to professional gardeners every chance you get—they know a lot.

My *Columnea microphylla* doesn't flower.

Ours doesn't either. Hardly anyone's does, at least outside of a greenhouse. *Columnea microphylla* can be very attractive, but it can also be very unrewarding.

If it is the small leaf-size that attracted you to this plant, look for a different gesneriad, one in the genus *codonanthe:* the foliage will be similar (though not as pendant) , but it will flower for you.

My columnea dropped all its leaves after repotting.

You must have really manhandled the roots—most gesneriads take repotting rather well.

Repot your columneas wet, move them up only one pot size, and keep the humidity high.

Now that your leaves have dropped, cut the stems back to within a few inches of the soil, keep the humidity high, and water moderately until (and if) the plant resprouts.

What kind of soil do you recommend for episcias?

Episcias are jungle-floor plants and should do well in the kind of mix you use for your African violets. Our basic mix works fine.

Equally important when growing episcias is the size and shape of the pot. Episcias like to spread, and will do best grown in an azalea pot or bulb pan rather large for the size of the plant. (Azalea pots are slightly wider than they are deep: 4 inches across for every 3 inches deep. Bulb pans are even more shallow.) The wide pot allows rooting as the plant crawls, and helps to maintain the proper high humidity.

For years I have been growing *Rechsteineria cardinalis*. My tuber is almost 6 inches across and it flowers beautifully. Recently I came across it in a catalog and saw that they've changed the name to

Sinningia cardinalis. I have grown sinningias, many of them, and I don't know of any that look like my cardinalis, or have the same growth habit or flower shape. I think my plant has been the victim of a mad scientist.

Not really mad—just a little annoyed sometimes.

In a way, you are right. The other sinningias do look different; they have different leaves and flowers, and their tubers don't stick up above the soil the way the former *Rechsteineria cardinalis* does. And for years botanists classified just that way: how does it look?

But with modern scientific techniques, taxonomists and botanists are classifying plants according to how they cross with each other, and according to parts you can't even see without a microscope.

Now, this may sound like heresy, but if you want to go on calling your plant rechsteineria, go ahead—we won't squeal. But if you want to find another one in a reputable grower's catalog, be prepared to look under *Sinningia cardinalis.*

By the way, have you ever grown the symmetrical form of the plant? Its name is *Sinningia cardinalis* 'George Kalmbacher,' discovered by and named for the late taxonomist of the Brooklyn Botanic Garden. It is the same in culture, but the flowers are not hooded.

GINKGOACEAE   Ginkgo Family

Ginkgos have no really close relatives. In fact, they were thought to have disappeared from the earth long ago—until some were found in China.

The female bears edible nuts—but raw the nuts have an offensive cheesy smell that makes the female tree undesirable for use in the front yard.

Seedling ginkgos can be trained into bonsai shape.

I have gathered some seed from under a ginkgo tree, and would like to know if I can start the plants from these seeds and how.

Unlike many hardy trees whose seeds require a freezing period before they will germinate, ginkgo seeds can be started as soon as they are gathered.

Soak the seed overnight and remove the outer soft matter. Take a 3-inch plastic pot and stuff it moderately full with damp long-haired sphagnum moss. Push one or two seeds into the moss, cover the top with clear plastic held on with a rubber band, and set it in a bright but not sunny location.

You should get germination within a month. Keep only one seedling in a pot.

And, please, don't set your heart on growing your seedling in a pot into a 30-foot tree, or on keeping it for more than a season or two unless you are willing to do bonsai work on it. Still, while you have it, it is lovely.

GRAMINEAE   Grass Family

This is a very large family—but with very few houseplants. The genera bambusa and sasa contain most of the plants called bamboo, and a few of them will grow in pots—but under average indoor conditions are unlikely to keep.

There are many decorative grasses in this family, most of which have never been tried as houseplants. One of them is *Oplismenus hirtellus,* and it was this plant that, at the beginning of a long chain of events, led to the writing of this book.

I got a cutting of a pretty little green-white-striped thing called "ribbon grass." I've put it into vermiculite in my closed propagation box, but if I'm lucky and it roots, how do I take care of it? Can I grow it under fluorescent lights? Is it really a grass?

Yes, *Oplismenus hirtellus* (ribbon grass or basket grass) is a true grass.

Yes, you can grow it under fluorescent lights, but you'll need four tubes, and even then don't hesitate to grow it right up close to the tubes—and it may even make tiny grassy flowers for you. For all the small size of the leaves and its dainty appearance, it loves light.

As for being lucky, we've found this a very easy plant to propagate from tip cuttings, and a rampant grower both in a greenhouse and under lights. We got ours from a greenhouseman who considered it a weed.

Give it plenty of water and moderate humidity and some direct sun if you're going to grow it in natural light. If it gets enough sun, it will be not only green and white but tinged with red as well.

LABIATAE   Mint Family

This is a family for anyone who enjoys good smells: it contains scores of aromatic herbs. To list just a few of our favorites: ocimum (basil), mentha (mint), majorana (sweet marjoram), lavendula (lavender), rosmarinus (rosemary), melissa (lemon balm), salvia (sage), and thymus (thyme). Most of these herbs do marvelously well in pots if you have a sunny window, but don't let them dry out.

It also contains popular houseplants such as coleus and plectranthus (Swedish ivy).

The family is characterized by being easy to grow, being easy to propagate, and having square stems. There are no plants we know of that come more quickly from tip cuttings than do mint and coleus and basil. They are even rapid from seed, and for years we used basil seed to demonstrate sexual propagation because basil yielded quick results with a high percentage of ultimate plants.

We were taught how to make a delicious drink from mint. The Mennonite friends who showed us how called it "meadow tea."

Bring a quart of water to the boil and shut it off. Take four sprigs of spearmint about 4 inches long, put them into a teapot, and pour the just-boiled water over them. Steep for about 15 minutes, then serve hot with honey or plain. Or allow to cool and then set into the refrigerator to serve chilled. Very refreshing.

Why would the leaves of my Swedish ivy be turning brown starting at the tips? It is in a bright window and I water it every two weeks. Should I feed it?

Don't feed it! Don't ever feed a plant in trouble. Except for acid-loving plants suffering from iron-poor sap, you only hurt a plant by feeding it when something is wrong with it.

Yours is probably a water deficiency. Plectranthus (there are several varieties of plectranthus called Swedish ivy) may have thick leaves, but it's not really very succulent, so it wants to be watered (in a moderate-sized pot) when the top ½ to ¾ inch of soil is dry.

Cut back any branches that are severely damaged, mist the leaves frequently, and increase the watering a bit at a time. You don't want to drown a plant that has been dying of thirst.

I have a large basket of Swedish ivy which seemed to be doing well, but now, after three months in my northeast window, the leaves are turning soft and brown. Does that sound like anything?

Yes, it sounds like your leaves are turning soft and brown. Aside from that, it sounds like too little light and too much water.

How do I propagate my red-stemmed Swedish ivy?

Plectranthus australis (Swedish ivy) is in the Mint family, and most members of this family root quite readily. We propagate them mostly in high humidity (a closed clear-plastic box with a 1½ inch layer of damp vermiculite—or perlite, or vermiculite and perlite mixed—in the bottom), but we also use peat pellets, and friends of ours use a glass of water.

By the way, don't worry if the stems color your fingers red—that will wash off eventually.

My Swedish ivy is looking dull instead of shiny, and it worries me. Can you think of a reason? Should I use leaf shine?

Do *not* use leaf shine. We never use leaf shine, because it clogs the stoma (pores) of the plant. If your leaves are looking dull, your culture is lacking something.

Plectranthus (Swedish ivy) is only a moderate drinker, and it has no special need for high humidity, but it does need more sun than most people give it: bright light with some direct sun is fine.

Also, have you rinsed the dust off your leaves lately?

I have a large basket of Swedish ivy that has been growing a little weakly lately. I cut it way back, and I'm rooting the cuttings. I want to make the basket bushier. My question is this: Will I damage the roots already in the pot if I dig holes with a pencil to put the new rooted cuttings into the old pot?

Perhaps some—but it will be worth it.

But a plectranthus (Swedish ivy—popularized in Sweden but native to Australia) cut too far back may not resprout. If you have as many as a dozen cuttings, why not just put them all into a fresh pot and start a new hanging basket?

Can I propagate my coleus from a single leaf?

No. A student of ours tried it, even though we said it couldn't be done. He kept the leaf alive for months, but it never made a plant.

My coleus is yellowing and in general looking pale and weak. I water it well, but the plant isn't doing well. I keep it on my sunniest windowsill—have you any suggestions?

Sounds like it could be a soil problem; either too heavy a soil or too long in the same pot. Does the water drain right through or does it sit there? How does the soil smell? Fresh? Or musty? Get your nose in there and sniff.

Try repotting into a fresh well-drained soil (and into a new pot—but don't move up in pot size unless the roots fill the pot) .

Cut the plant back a bit, too (about 25 percent) .

Or is yours a heat problem? Even in winter, the temperature in a sunny window can easily go over 100°F. If it is heat, provide air circulation, and cut the plant back as recommended.

My coleus is making weak growth. I think there is not enough sun for it in my window. I can give it to my sister, who has more sun, but what else can I do?

Cut it back to within two or three nodes of the soil. The plant should resprout and in good sun make sturdy growth. But remember to pinch out the new growth.

How can I get my coleus to grow in a mound shape instead of a single stalk?

Pinch out the young plant, then pinch out the new branches, and then pinch out the new new branches when they are a few inches long. This will give your coleus a very bushy look.

Of course, to keep the look, you'll probably have to keep on pinching through the growing season. (Can we get T-shirts with that slogan on them?—"Keep on pinchin'!")

I have had coleus cuttings in a glass of water for two months, since mid-September, and they are not rooting. They still have their leaves.

That is certainly unusual, especially since a coleus cutting will often start shooting roots after two or three days in the spring.

As a guess, we would suggest that the water temperature is too cold. Try a temperature around 76°F. (They do root at lower temperatures, but yours sounds a desperate case.)

Do you have fertilizer in the water? Perhaps a strong fertilizer solution is burning the root tips.

Should we pinch the growing tips of our coleus?

Yes, and pinch and pinch and pinch . . .

Especially indoors, coleus must be pinched frequently to be kept bushy. This keeps them out of flower, too, which encourages best leaf growth.

My coleus is growing very tall and weak. Why?

Outdoors, coleus are fine in part shade, but indoors they require bright light. Cut yours back and give it more sun.

My pot of coleus is wilted in the morning, but perks up after I water it. What do you think it is?

We think you are not watering enough—what do you think?

Are you watering plenty when you do water? Or are you just tickling the soil? If you are watering well, then the plant needs repotting into a larger pot.

LEGUMINOSAE   Pea Family

The Pea family includes a lot of beautiful tropical and hardy trees, but very few durable houseplants.

Phaseolus coccineus is scarlet runner bean, and it will make a lot of foliage in a bright window—for one season.

Albizzia julibrissin is called powderpuff tree (it is also mistakenly called mimosa—which is acacia—often enough to drive us up the wall). It can be grown from seeds gathered in the fall, when the pods drop from the tree. They sprout readily in a pot of dampened long-haired sphagnum moss, and will last a year or two if kept watered.

Those pods are typical of the family, as are the lovely lipped flowers and compound leaves.

If you are a teacher and looking for a class project, grow beans from seed—you'll understand where the story of Jack and the Beanstalk comes from.

My "sensitive plant" seems to be less sensitive. I mean, the leaves don't close and open as readily as they used to. Do they get less sensitive with age?

Yes, and they don't like to be pestered, either.

Keep your *Mimosa pudica* (sensitive plant) well watered, in bright light (with some sun) —and warm (above 65°F.). Below 60°F. it may not react at all, although perfectly healthy otherwise.

Sensitive plant and other members of the Pea family have compound leaves. That is, each leaf is made up of several leaflets. So, while the leaves do fold down, most of the action you are watching is the leaflets folding toward one another along the midrib of the leaf.

LILIACEAE   Lily Family

The Lily family is the most varied family you will ever find. It includes genera that are bulbous, that are herbaceous, that are woody, and that are succulent. It includes hardy and tender plants, edible plants (onions, garlic, shallots), low-light and full-sun plants, and some of the sweetest-smelling plants in the world.

Lilies themselves are usually considered to be strictly outdoor plants, but we have had success with them in pots on a windowsill that is only moderately bright. We ordered them in the fall from Oregon Bulb Farm and potted them immediately; lilies may have their top growth die back, but they are never completely dormant. We got flowers in the spring, some more flowering in the fall, and then more flowering the *following* spring. We had our greatest success with *Lilium* 'Cinnabar.'

More than ten years earlier, we had had a marvelous time with a started bulb of a plant called Ushida lily (*Lilium speciosum rubrum*). It flowered beautifully, but we then failed to carry it over.

Ornithogalum caudatum (false sea-onion) is a fascinating plant with a persistent bulbous base that grows resting on the surface of the soil. Bright light and plenty of water should keep it for you.

Ledebouria socialis (formerly known as *Scilla violacea*) grows beautifully and durably under fluorescent light. It may, seasonally, make heads of flowers for you. But its spotted foliage is attractive year round.

Bowiea volubilis, the true sea-onion, makes lacy vining foliage but then goes dormant. Reduce watering during the dormant period.

If you are seeking a really honestly and truly low-light plant, try *Aspidistra elatior* (cast-iron plant). They had a few at one Brooklyn Botanic Garden spring sale (we were helping out), but no one seemed interested in them, even though many growers were looking for low-light plants. Well, they are "old-fashioned," belonging to a previous generation, and they are so slow-growing that they are expensive—but they *live.*

Why are the needles on my asparagus fern (Meyeri) turning yellow and falling off? I keep the soil damp and I keep it out of the bright light. I see no signs of bugs. Could it be nematodes?

To begin at the end, it is unlikely in the extreme that you have nematodes—very few houseplant growers get nematodes. Your problems are cultural.

Asparagus meyeri is not a fern, though it is confusingly called asparagus fern. And if you treat it like a fern, with too little sun, the needles (which are really small branches—the plant has no leaves) will yellow and fall.

Set the plant in full sun and allow the soil to go dry down to a depth of about one knuckle below the surface before rewatering.

Cut away, right down to the soil, any stems with few or no needles. This will give the new growth light and space.

My *Asparagus sprengeri* is outgrowing my terrarium. What should I do?

You should take it out of the terrarium.

Decorative asparagus grows best in pots, where it can go rather dry between waterings.

But since your particular plant has adapted so well to its strange high-humidity life, you will have to give it special treatment for a while after bringing it out—namely, very high humidity.

The plant's correct name is *Asparagus densiflorus cv. 'Sprengeri.'* The Meyers asparagus is also a cultivar of *A. densiflorus*. We are sorry that sellers drop parts of the name.

Does asparagus fern need high humidity?

No. Though during the winter heating season all plants should have some additional humidity.

We prefer to call these plants "ornamental asparagus"—they *are* relatives of your favorite vegetable and they are *not* ferns at all.

Asparagus does love sun—both the eating kind and the ornamental kind.

How do I groom my asparagus fern?

All the ornamental asparagus (they *are* asparagus, they are *not* ferns) should have any yellowing and brown fronds cut back to the soil line to give new growth a chance.

Cutting off half a frond does not cause branching, though you can reduce the size of an unruly plant that way.

My *Asparagus sprengeri* is making long skinny stems, even though I treat it just as you said: lots of sun, and I allow it to go dry down to about 3/4 inch below the soil surface before I water again. Floss, you misled me.

O ye of little faith!

Your *Asparagus sprengeri* is in nature a vining plant when mature —but, in cultivation, it often stays juvenile in form, with few or no vining stems. The appearance of the vining stems means you are doing fine with it. Give them something to vine around, or cut the vines off if they really bother you. (Are we friends again?)

Why are the leaves of my *Aloe vera* yellowing? I give it full sun.

Aloe vera (burn plant) will yellow in full sun, going greener in moderate sun.

We know it's hard, but not all succulent plants thrive on full sun.

My *Aloe eru* is several years old and it has grown quite tall—and a bit rangy. It has made a couple of offsets near the base of the plant. Now, my question is, if I cut off the top, will the offsets be encouraged to grow, or will it kill the plant?

Aloe eru is a very handsome member of the genus, larger-growing than many in cultivation. By all means, cut the plant back to *two nodes* above the soil and dust the wound with fungicide or flowers of sulfur. (Flowers of sulfur is powdered mineral sulfur, and you can get it at a drugstore.)

As for the top, allow it to callus for two or three days, then propagate it in an *open* propagation box.

How do you use *Aloe vera* for skin burns?

Break off an inch of leaf and squeeze the jelly onto the burn: you will get some immediate relief. Repeat in an hour or so. The burn will heal much faster than usual.

Many cosmetics companies, large and small, are using it as an ingredient in skin creams and tanning lotions. So don't think of it just as a "burn" plant: you are growing your own beauty.

I have had an aspidistra for years and years. It hasn't grown much, but at least it has stayed green where a lot of other plants have died on me. Now the tips of its leaves are turning brown. It has never had much sun, and I let it get dry between waterings. Can you make a suggestion?

We hate to talk about repotting really old plants—they just don't take it well—but that could be the problem. Especially if it's been more than two years since you repotted.

If you do repot, do it very carefully. Also, trim away the brown parts, just to make the plant look better. Let us hope that with fresh soil, new growth will start again. Then, if you can, give it a bit more light, and water to match.

They call *Aspidistra elatior* cast-iron plant—well, even iron eventually rusts.

How can I propagate my ponytail plant?

We suppose *Beaucarnea recurvata* are possible from seed—though we've never seen them in flower and are only guessing. But they are propagable from the small offsets that occasionally grow from the thick bulblike stem.

Break or cut them off, allow the base to callus for a few hours, and root in just-damp medium in a closed propagation box.

A friend gave me a spider plant in a 2-inch pot. I moved it into a 6-inch pot right away with a package of potting soil, but I guess it was too late, because now the leaves are turning brown and dying. And how often do I water it? The soil stays wet a long time.

Sounds like two problems. First, although chlorophytums (spider plants) have roots strong enough to skip one pot size, even *they* will suffer going from a 2-inch to a 6-inch pot. That keeps too much wet soil around the roots. Next time, go from a 2-inch pot to a 4-inch pot—with most other plants you'd go from a 2-inch to a 2½-inch or 3-inch pot.

Also, it sounds as if your soil might be too heavy and so too slow to drain. Virtually every packaged potting soil should be lightened with the addition of perlite—say, 1 part perlite to 3 parts packaged soil.

We suggest you unpot the plant and repot it into a 4-inch pot with a lightened soil mix. Allow the soil to go dry down to ½ inch below the surface of the soil before you rewater. Mist it as often as possible. Give it bright light.

Why do the leaves of my spider plant turn first yellow at the tips, then brown, and then die back? The plant is still making healthy-looking new growth at the center.

How about just a few of the major possibilities?

Though a vigorous grower, chlorophytum (spider plant) must have a humidity around 40 percent to thrive. Lower humidity and your tips will brown.

Chlorophytum is in the Lily family and grows roots like mad.

Allowed to go too potbound, the tips of leaves will brown and die back.

Chlorophytum is not a heavy feeder, and overfertilization will cause yellowing and browning at the tips.

If your water is fluoridated, fluorine buildup can cause brown tips.

There are a number of more minor reasons.

At what stage do I pot up my spider offsets?

Chlorophytum (spider plant) offsets should be potted up when the roots are between ½ inch and 1 inch long and a pale whitish color. If they are shorter, the offset is not really prepared to take nutrition on its own; if they are longer or brownish, their power to take nutrition is reduced. Many will still work for you, no matter when you pot them, but with ½ inch to 1 inch of roots they begin root growth rapidly without any transplant shock.

One time we wanted a great many plants, so we took some offsets that were too young, put them under transparent plastic for a couple of weeks, and let them root and grow there. It worked fine.

How often must I repot my spider plant?

When the roots *really* fill the pot. And that may be twice in a good season. In fact, crowding of the roots may cause the leaf tips to turn brown. But don't repot unless the roots do fill the pot: chlorophytums (spider plants) are shy to bloom if kept overpotted.

I grew a spider plant outside for the summer and it did marvelously well, but I brought it inside, and the leaves are looking awful: brown and yellow and dying. I have it in the best light I can, but I just don't have any sun. What can I do?

Move!

Any plant grown in outdoor sun, then brought in to dim light, is going to lose leaves; the wonder would be if it didn't.

If you have no sun, put it in your brightest location and provide some supplementary light for it. Not that this will be enough. Next time, keep your indoor plants indoors: they get used to it. They don't make that lush growth you get outside, but they don't go into shock from being brought in either.

Chlorophytums (spider plants) need some direct sun to grow well and make offsets.

Can I hurt the leaves of my spider plant by spraying them with plain water?

Not at all. In fact, chlorophytum (spider plant) needs more humidity than most growers give it—that's one reason the leaf tips turn brown.
Spray away!

I've heard there are separate sexes of spider plant.

You've heard wrong. All chlorophytum (spider plant) flowers are "perfect": that is, contain both male and female sex parts.
The rumor probably began because some people do and some people don't succeed in flowering them.

Why has my spider plant never made babies?

Because of too low light (they are bright-light plants); or because of being too immature; or because it is living in too large a pot.
Pick whichever answer appeals to you.

Why is my spider plant no longer having babies? It was very prolific. I cut off the babies, planted them, and gave them away to friends. But now no more babies. Why? I haven't moved it or changed my watering.

Assuming that it's not just a matter of the season (in fall and winter, chlorophytums usually don't get enough sun to flower), and that you haven't repotted it recently, perhaps the plant wants R & R (repotting and rejuvenation). It is difficult to get a plant to grow well if the soil is depleted and the roots are very crowded.
Try this: Instead of potting up to a larger size, divide the plant with a sharp sterile knife, like a pie cut into four equal wedges. Pot each piece into a pot about *half* the size of the original pot, in fresh, well-drained soil. Put the new plants into bright sun, and allow the roots some growing time, and we feel certain you'll soon be giving away chlorophytum offsets again.

What is proper care for a spider plant?

Chlorophytums (spider plants) want bright sun, moderate humidity (40 percent or better), and moderate watering (allow the soil to go dry down to about $1/2$ inch below the surface before rewatering) for best growth. Of course, they will get along on less than this optimal care.

My husband and I bought a three-stemmed marginata a few months ago, and it didn't drop dead on us, but it never did well either. It lost a leaf or so at a time, until, finally, all three stems were bare. You know, "not with a bang but a whimper." We dug the plant up to see if there was a bug in the soil, and there were hardly any roots! Now, did these rot away on us? Is there a bug that eats roots?

Your problem is simple but sad. Nothing ate the roots—they were never there.

In the tropics, where *Dracaena marginata* are propagated and grown for the United States market, they cut bare unrooted canes from a large mature plant and stick them (one, two, three, or four at a time) into pots of soil. Because of the nature of dracaenas, they sprout roots and leaves. But in the tropics, the roots and leaves develop at the same time, and because of the favorable environment, you can have a lot of leaves with very little rooting. The plants are shipped north, and, because they have never been well rooted, they start to die. Some have better root systems and so survive; some are coddled along into survival; and many die.

We don't recommend buying multistemmed pots of dracaenas in the first place—that's buying trouble from root competition. But if you do buy a dracaena, give its stem a very little wiggle before you pay your money. If the stem seems firm in the pot, then you likely have a good root system. If the stem wiggles readily, give it the go-by and look for another.

You talk a lot about air-layering dracaenas, but at my office the top broke off a corn plant and I took it home and it rooted in vermiculite.

We are not surprised. In Puerto Rico, where they propagate the bulk of the dracaenas, they do it by cutting the canes and sticking one to three canes into a pot, where they root and sprout.

Still, when you can, air-layering provides surer propagation in the home, and a stronger plant.

And, remember, nobody loves a wise-guy. But we'll forgive you this time.

What can I do to make my marginata branch lower down on the bare stem?

Bend it over.

If you can tie down your *Dracaena marginata* so that the growing tip is lower than the bend, it should be fooled into thinking that it has been pruned, and it may create a new "growing tip" and branch at the highest point.

Be careful not to break or even crimp the stem, as that creates new problems and can kill off the top.

The roots are showing at the bottom of the stem of my marginata. Does this indicate a need for repotting? Should I bury the roots?

No, on both counts. Mature dracaenas can show roots at their base without indicating anything wrong. It may just mean that you are watering with too heavy a stream of water—washing away some of the soil with the vigorous stream. If so, stop watering so hard.

But, now that your *Dracaena marginata* is showing its knees, don't cover them with soil.

Can you tell me why the edges of the leaves on my corn plant turn yellow?

The leaves of a *Dracaena massangeana* (corn plant) can yellow along the edges for a number of reasons.

Are you feeding too heavily? (By that, we mean, are you feeding according to label directions?)

Is your humidity too low?

Are you letting the plant go too dry between waterings? (The leaves shouldn't be allowed to droop.)

Do you live in a community with heavily fluoridated water? (The fluorine accumulates at the leaf edges.) If so, allow your water to stand in an open bucket overnight.

Finally, if this is a new plant, it may be suffering from shock. If so, put the entire plant into a plastic bag until the yellowing stops spreading (it won't "heal"), then punch a hole in the bag every morning, until it is in shreds. At that point the plant should be acclimated to your humidity.

My dracaenas are so thin! How can I get them to grow as thick as the ones I see in florists?

You can't. The thick canes are grown in the tropics (or subtropics), chopped into long pieces, rooted (we hope), and sent north to make you jealous.

If your canes are weak, stake them. Use a stake no higher than the plant, but make certain it is firm in the pot or it will provide no support.

Passing through Chinatown the other day, I noticed a store window in which there were some very odd things: there were these "sticks" of

various thicknesses, all less than a foot or so high, with wax on top, and stuck into large pots of soil. They all had prices on them, and I assume they had something to do with plants—but what?

Those were dracaena canes, hopefully rooting in those pots, and waiting to sprout. We have seen them too (or others) and feel the prices were too high.

The wax on top is to keep them from rotting.

Without the wax, that's just the way they do it in Florida and Puerto Rico, too. And once sprouted, they ship them north, whether they are well rooted or not.

Does *Dracaena marginata* go dormant?

No. Many houseplants will slow down in the winter, some dramatically, but few actually have a dormancy. If your *Dracaena marginata* has stopped growing, perhaps it is responding to the dull months. Or, perhaps it is responding to an "artificial winter"—that is, a poor indoor environment. Plant growth relates to the environment: if your plants are growing too slowly, perhaps you need more light, or more humidity, or a better soil, or more accurate watering. Take your pick.

My *Dracaena sanderiana* has a patch right across the leaf that's turning brown—right across the entire leaf! And there are brown patches on nearby leaves too. Why does it hate me?

Because you leave the plant in full sun. Or that's what it sounds like at any rate—sunburn.

Dracaenas sunburn easily in direct sun, but they do need bright light (they'll take some morning sun without burning).

Cut away the badly damaged leaf because it will not heal.

How do I care for my *Dracaena compacta?* It doesn't seem to be doing anything.

Dracaena deremensis 'Compacta' (that is its full name) is very slow-growing. It doesn't form the canes that other dracaenas do. The varietal name 'Compacta' tells the story. We've had one in a 5-inch azalea pot for two years, and it has grown perhaps 4 inches.

Of course, we've kept it in shade, not fed it, and watered it irregularly. With more light and better care, it might have grown 6 inches instead.

My *Dracaena* 'Tricolor' looks weak and pale. Why?

For our money, you can keep *Dracaena marginata* 'Tricolor'—it *always* looks weak and pale.

If you want to try it, give it a bit more sun than you would *Dracaena marginata,* and don't let it dry out between watering. If it is grown close to fluorescent tubes the heat will bleach it further.

Why do the lower leaves of my *Dracaena marginata* turn brown and fall off?

Most likely too little water. We can't imagine where the idea started that these plants want to go quite dry before waterings. Feel the soil. When it goes dry down to ½ inch below the surface of the soil (in a large pot), water well.

I bought a *Dracaena marginata* with three stems coming out of a 10-inch pot. It was fine for a while, but now the smallest stem has gone lousy. It looks rotten and has no leaves left. Is there anything I can do?

Yes, you can stop buying dracaenas with more than one stem to the pot. These are three separate plants, and the roots compete for the soil; if one plant is substantially weaker, it will get strangled out—as seems to have happened in your case. And your troubles may not be over yet. The remaining plants may go into competition with each other, or the roots of the dead plant may rot, causing damage to the roots of the healthy plants.

Pull on the stem of the dead plant. If it comes out readily, fine. Fill the hole with potting soil—and good luck.

If the stem doesn't come out readily, you may try to dig out the dead plant and separate the others, but be gentle. It's a case of being damned if you do separate them and taking the chance of rot if you don't.

My marginata is leggy, and I planted some striped wandering Jew in the soil around the stalk. Will that root so deeply as to compete with the marginata?

No, but there will be other problems. *Dracaena marginata* will often burn in direct sun, and it needs to go dry only to about ½ inch below the surface of the soil. Your *Zebrina pendula,* however, wants bright sun and to go dry down to about 1 inch below the surface of the soil. The principle is sound, but the plants are really incompatible. Try a cissus instead.

I've been growing the top of a dracaena in water for almost a year. (It broke off while we were moving.) It has filled the vase with roots, and I should like to pot it up into soil. What do you think?

We think you shouldn't do it. Plants that have been growing for a long time in water really have a tough time making the transition to soil. You see, roots grown in water form a kind of sheath which permits the roots to have some necessary air, though underwater. Soil-grown roots don't have or need that sheath—they take air directly from the air in the soil.

Your dracaena would have to make a whole new set of soil roots appropriate to taking water, air, and nutrition from damp soil instead of from water. And it may not be able to make it. You have something attractive now—why not keep it that way?

Change the water from time to time. It's not necessary to feed, but if you feel you must do something, put 1/32 of a teaspoon (a half pinch) of water-soluble plant food into the vase. But it isn't really necessary.

The top of one branch broke off my reflexis plant. Should I cut it back and paint it? Or what?

Let's assume you mean *Pleomele reflexa* (a relative of the dracaenas). If you've just lost the tip and have leaves left, you can paint the wound—or you can drip melted wax over it to protect it.

If you've lost most of or all of the leaves, cut off the stem to within an inch of the soil. Cut the leftover stem into 3-inch pieces and lay them in damp rooting medium, horizontally, half buried, and they may root.

You can expect your original stem to resprout from just below the cut.

Do haworthias want bright sun or moderate light?

Either, if they are the fenestral or "window"-type haworthias. These are truly fascinating plants. They have a translucency in their surface which permits light to strike the interior of the leaf. In moderate sun, the surface of the leaf is more translucent, permitting more of the sun in. In bright sun, less sun is allowed in. Just like the newest sunglasses—they are sun-sensitive.

Lithops (living stones) have a similar mechanism, but they are difficult for most growers.

Haworthias will tolerate erratic care, though they prefer to go only moderately dry between waterings. They will even flower in quite moderate sun. Reduce watering somewhat during the dim months, but they don't take a true dormancy.

How much sun should I give my snake plant? And how much should I water it?

Snake plants (*Sansevieria fasciata*) are well known for being plants that will survive in low light, but if you give yours *some* sun, a good-size pot, and ample water, it will thrive and may well flower for you.

In Bermuda, we saw them as bedding plants in almost full outdoor sun. In Nassau, we saw them growing near the beach. They were a bit pale—but they were growing.

What's the best way to propagate snake plants?

Sansevierias (snake plant, lucky plant, etc.) spread by thick under-ground rhizomes. The rhizome grows away from the main plant and then a new growth sprouts. The plant can be divided by cutting through the rhizome and roots. Propagation by division gives you a plant immediately.

Leaf cuttings give you more plants, but they are much slower (as the individual sections must first root and then sprout from the base) and require a special propagation medium such as sand or perlite.

Do snake plants flower?

Yes, given good conditions (bright light with some sun, and moderate watering) they will flower and fruit—and you can grow new plants from the seeds.

Why are my yucca leaves turning yellow and dying? I keep it out of direct sun and give it a cup of water once a week.

Yucca is a full-sun plant, and it takes as much water as, say, a dracaena. If you got those ideas from a book, burn it. If you got the advice from a plant store, picket it.

MALVACEAE   Mallow Family

The Mallow family includes several very decorative hardy and tender shrubs. Hibiscus, to us its most beautiful genus, deserves wider use as a houseplant. We have found it more durable than other more widely grown potted shrubs. Okra, the vegetable, is an edible annual form of hibiscus.

For you city or suburban gardeners looking for a handsome and reliable flowering shrub, try another hibiscus: *Hibiscus syriacus* (althea or rose of Sharon). This clean and sturdy plant is a marvelous summer flowerer, well suited to small plots or large-container culture.

We have seen advertisements lately for another member of this family: cotton (gossypium). Strange the things people will sell (and buy!).

I have a flowering maple plant that I bought a few weeks ago. I keep it outdoors in bright sun and don't water it until it's half-dry, but the buds are dropping and the leaves are turning yellow and falling off. Why?

Abutilon (flowering maple) is a dramatic and beautiful houseplant, but not easy to manage.

First of all, it is not an outdoor maple. That maple moniker is really misleading. It is not used to full outdoor sun, and you may be burning the leaves. On a windowsill, it will take all the sun you can give it, but that is much less than outdoor sun.

Second, it needs much more water than you're giving it. Water your abutilon well when the surface of the soil goes dry.

Also, keep track of the rootball; don't allow the plant to become potbound or your troubles will increase.

In these late spring months, humidity is no problem, but when you get to the heating months, you are going to have to provide supplementary humidity for the plant (as well as for yourself). A minimum of 35 or 40 percent relative humidity will be your goal.

What would be your recommendation for a flowering shrub on a windowsill that gets morning sun? I don't want something that needs special winter treatment—but I do want something with really nice flowers.

We are in love with our hibiscus (*Hibiscus rosa-sinensis*). It has flowered its second year. It spent its first winter just inside our brightest windowsill, close to the window. It flowers magnificently, late in the summer and early fall (with more sun, it would flower later and earlier). The flowers don't last long, but they are large and spectacular.

The only drawback (if you consider it that) is that the plant does require frequent watering. Allowed to go at all dry, it will drop buds and leaves. We went away for three weeks and our plant sitter was careless and allowed our gem to dry out. We came back to a bare stem; but rather than just cry, we watered the plant *lightly* and waited. Within about ten days there was sign of resprouting at the tips and at a few places along the stem. We cut the main stem back to above a live branch and a few sproutings (yes, we sacrificed the tip), and two weeks later, the plant was in bushy lush growth. Waiting to cut back allowed us, with this shrubby tropical plant, to see the best place to prune.

How far back can I prune my potted hibiscus? It looks very leggy and ratty.

In Bermuda, we saw in-ground hibiscus being cut back to within 6 inches of the soil, and the gardener-horticulturist who did it assured us they cut them back like that every year. If we were to do such heavy pruning on ours, we would wait until early spring, when the plant is likeliest to be in rapid growth.

If hibiscus is pruned sharply in early spring, and kept in sun, you should expect flowering in the summer.

MARANTACEAE   Arrowroot Family

There are lots of good low-light houseplants in this family, but they are often misunderstood: they want good humidity (near 40 percent), lots of water, and warm temperatures. Most failures with marantas (prayer plants) and their relatives can be traced to low temperature, low humidity, and/or low water.

One aquatic plant in the Arrowroot family, *Thalia dealbata* (water canna), is suited to a sunny rooftop or terrace water garden. It is supposed to be tender in the northern states, but we have seen it hardy as far north as Brooklyn, New York.

Other genera in this family that you may not know are ctenanthe (which can be quite colorful and seems able to hang on in dim and rather dry locations—though it wants constant moisture and moderate light to do well) and stromanthe (which looks a lot like ctenanthe). Of course, for color there is nothing to match calathea (often known as cobra plant).

You may think prayer plants (marantas) and these other close relatives don't flower: they do, but the flowers are small and may be hidden among the leaves.

Why do the tips of my prayer plant leaves turn brown and dry up?

Either low humidity or too little water. Marantas (prayer plants) do best in high humidity, with lots of water, and a very well-drained soil high in organic matter; but they need only moderate light. Pot them into wide shallow pots to give their spreading habit a chance.

By the way, they do not climb, so if you purchase one tied onto a totem, take off the ties and allow the plant to grow horizontally.

Can I grow cobra plants in a north window?

In the summer, yes, but in the winter they will have to be moved away from the glass. Calathea (cobra plant) and its relatives—maranta and ctenanthe—want *warm* temperatures, and a north window is too cool in winter.

MELASTOMACEAE Meadow-beauty Family

This family contains relatively few houseplants, but they all have interestingly exotic foliage or flowering habits.

Medinilla magnifica has leathery leaves with pale veins and bears panicles of flowers hanging downward. It prefers to be slightly pot-bound, but needs good humidity.

We had great success with *Sonerila margaritacea* (it has marvelous silver variegations on its leaves) in a *terrarium*.

Tibouchina semidecandra (glory bush) grows with a shrubby habit and is suited to a greenhouse, or a high-humidity window, where it can produce its hairy leaves and purple flowers.

I have bought a weird little plant with hairs and spots on the leaves, called "bartonia." But I can't find it in a book. Do you know what it needs? Does it flower?

If the plant is *Bertolonia maculata* (which it sounds like), it certainly does flower: small pink-purple star-shaped flowers, which are borne on a zigzag stem that continues to grow and flower in moderate light (say, under two tubes of fluorescent light). It also forms a thick hairy stem—a very unusual and handsome plant.

Keep it moist and in high humidity. For us it does best in a terrarium.

MORACEAE Mulberry Family

This is a family of great economic importance. Aside from mulberries themselves, we get rope, rubber, dyes, medicines, figs, and breadfruit from it.

In addition, it is of great economic importance to plant sellers, as most of the ficus plants sold soon die. This kind of built-in obsolescence, combined with their ability for rapid growth in the tropics, makes them very popular with plant wholesalers.

All this mortality among plants of *Ficus elastica* (rubber tree) and *Ficus benjamina* (weeping fig) and *Ficus lyrata* (fiddle-leaf fig) is unnecessary, too, because they really are durable and desirable as houseplants—if they are just given enough water, enough root room, and, most of all, enough bright light (with as much direct sun as the leaves can stand without burning).

We've grown another member of this family most successfully: *Dorstenia hildebrandtii*. This really odd little succulent plant has been in flower for us under lights, continuously, for *four years*.

Why are the leaves of my *Ficus benjamina* turning yellow and falling off?

Too low light, too little water, or cold temperatures will do it. But if *none* of these obtains, we have discovered something that seems to help: next time you water, use a mixture of 1 gallon of tepid water plus 1 tablespoon of chlorine bleach (mixed well).

Use this combination once every few months. We're not certain why this works: perhaps the problem is a mineral lack and the chlorine bleach amends it.

My weeping fig tree lost a lot of its leaves. Since I put it in better sun it's making new leaves—but mostly at the tips. What can I do to make it leaf out farther up?

That's simple—but not easy. The only way you're going to get those *Ficus benjamina* (weeping fig) leaves to grow closer to the trunk is to cut some of the branches back. Go over the plant and cut back about one branch in six—about halfway. When those branches are in leaf, cut back another one in six—and so on. It is a slow and scary process, but you can't cut back the whole plant without shocking it severely.

One good thing: this will give you many lovely 6-inch cuttings which will root (use a bit of rooting hormone and a box of damp sand) and provide you with many presents for friends.

I own a plant store, and I want to take exception to something you said on your radio program. You said *Ficus benjamina* likes lots of water. We sell *Ficus benjamina* in 12-inch metal tubs (as they are shipped up from Florida), and if watered heavily they will rot. You shouldn't make blanket statements.

The soil in those tubs is field soil, and *much* too heavy for house-plants—and galvanized iron (the most common metal) a poor pot material. Plants coming north in that kind of soil and that sort of pot should be repotted. Put into an appropriately light and well-drained soil, *Ficus benjamina* (weeping fig) and all the houseplant ficuses will take as much water as you give them (as long as you don't let them sit in that water).

No, we stick by what we said: give *Ficus benjamina* lots of water.

Despite food and water, my weeping fig tree has been dropping leaves. Perhaps the plant resents being moved into our new apartment. It had a bigger window at our old place.

No doubt it is the light. *Ficus benjamina* (weeping fig) needs bright sun to do best. It will adapt to somewhat reduced light, but it will lose a frightening number of leaves along the way.

I have a rubber tree I would like to encourage to branch. Is there anything I can do?

Not specifically. With most houseplants you can pinch out the growing tip and expect branching. When a young *Ficus elastica* (rubber tree) is pinched, most often it will just send out one side shoot and you no longer have a symmetrical plant. When mature, rubber trees often branch spontaneously.

So, give the plant excellent culture (bright light, ample water) and when it's 3 or 4 feet tall and growing vigorously it may branch on its own, or at least reward your pinch then with two branches.

My rubber plant has sat on the windowsill for months without growing. It has a new leaf coming on top, but that leaf just sits there. Otherwise the plant looks healthy. Should I feed it?

God, no! Feed only plants that are in active growth.

It is not uncommon for *Ficus elastica* (rubber plant) to slow down its growth radically in the dim months—or as a result of a shock. It's certainly a better reaction than dropping leaves.

If you can, place it in a sunnier location and increase the temperature a few degrees. That may stimulate it into growth.

Every time my rubber tree makes a new leaf it drops an old one. It seems healthy. What could it be?

It could be a need for repotting. Rubber trees are trees, after all.

Or, you could be watering too little. They want rewatering when the soil is dry down to only about 1/4 inch below the surface.

Or, perhaps you're giving yours too little light. They want sun.

This kind of action, an old leaf lost for every new one gained, indicates a plant in precarious balance. At such times, the plant holds on to the young growth and gives up the old. If the period of poor environmental conditions is extended, you can be left with a growing tip and no mature leaves at all. Improve your environment.

Why should the young leaves of my rubber tree be dying?

Root damage, most likely. Perhaps caused by improper watering in too heavy a soil. This is a serious condition. More serious than the loss of older leaves.

Put the whole plant under a transparent plastic tent or in a large plastic bag until it is definitely dead or shows signs of recovering.

My rubber tree is losing its growing tip—it is just peeling away. I don't know what to do.

If the outer skin of that "growing tip" has turned dark brown or black and is "peeling away" to show healthy green underneath, then don't worry: what's happening is that the new leaf (it grows pointing up) has finally decided to throw off its stipule (leaf covering) and open.

If, however, the growing lead is actually dying, then you may be in trouble—physical-damage trouble (your cat or child chewed on it) or root trouble (over- or underwatering, most likely). The plant should recover rapidly from mechanical damage and start a new lead. However, root damage is quite serious and, if that is the case, the plant may not recover. If root damage seems probable, reduce your watering somewhat, give the plant better light, and raise its humidity considerably—and don't feed at all.

You say that rubber plants need sun and lots of water; my grandmother's grows as if it were in the jungle, but she has no sun and lets it go dry.

Plants can't read gardening books, but they will adapt—sometimes—and it's certainly true that if you can get a *Ficus elastica* through its first year in poor conditions, it will survive almost anything. But the operative word is "if." Most rubber trees in poor conditions don't survive past their first year. Your grandmother is lucky.

I blush to admit it, but I've had three rubber trees of various sizes rot on me in the past year. I don't seem to be able to water correctly. If I

water well, the soil takes forever to dry out—if I water lightly, the soil gets hard and dry. Just how do you water rubber trees?

You're looking at it the wrong way. Your problem isn't inaccurate watering so much as too heavy a soil. Any plant in too heavy a soil should be repotted. Try this: make up a soil mix of equal parts peat/perlite/vermiculite/topsoil, and then add another equal part (by volume) of long-fibered sphagnum moss cut into pieces no more than ½ inch long. You can cut it with a scissors. This will give you a fantastically well-drained soil, one which will be very difficult to overwater.

By the way, all ficuses, including *Ficus elastica* (rubber tree), want a good deal of water (feel the soil; when it is dry on the surface, water well) while in active growth.

You say that rubber trees need sun, but I want to grow mine in a bright window without direct sun. What can I do?

You can provide some supplementary light for it: a 100-watt spotlight about 3 to 4 feet from the leaves.

To tell the truth, *Ficus elastica* (rubber tree) is a very adaptable plant. It will grow in somewhat reduced light (not in a dark corner), but it will throw some of its leaves and make leggy growth.

I bought a hanging basket of creeping fig for $20, and the leaves are green, but they feel very dry and papery.

That papery feel is the way the plant feels. *Ficus pumila* (creeping fig), also known as *Ficus repens,* is a lovely plant and strong-growing under the right conditions: bright light, lots of water, and high humidity. In a humid greenhouse (or a tropical country) it will grow up a rough wall. Propagate it from tip cuttings pinned to the rooting medium in a closed propagation box. (Hairpins or broken paper clips do the pinning.)

I bought a lovely tiny ivy I'd never seen before. The leaves feel like paper, and are shaped like little oak leaves (but without points). Do you know what it could be?

It could be *Ficus pumila quercifolia* (oakleaf creeping fig). A little gem of a vine. We saw a lovely one about 6 inches tall, but very bushy, growing under glass on a piece of cholla cactus skeleton. It makes a good ground cover in a terrarium. It does need high humidity and bright light—though it will do well with some direct sun. It is a big drinker, and if you let it go dry it dies.

I have a fiddle-leaf fig in a 12-inch pot and it needs repotting. Can I move to a 17-inch pot?

We wouldn't recommend it. Though there is more leeway in pot size with a large plant (you can often skip a size with a big plant), and even though *Ficus lyrata* (fiddle-leaf fig) and all the ficuses are vigorous growers, we suggest you move up only to a 14-inch pot or tub. It probably means annual repotting, but otherwise all that empty wet soil around the ficus's roots can lead to root damage.

How can I propagate my Indian laurel?

Ficus indica (Indian laurel) propagates readily from tip cuttings or by air-layering.

MUSACEAE   Banana Family

The Banana family is poorly suited to houseplant culture: the leaves are very large and there are relatively few of them. The plants really prefer tropical or subtropical conditions.

Though they are called trees, they are not woody plants at all. They are herbaceous.

Some growers have success with *Ravenala madagascariensis,* the traveler's tree. It is a most handsome plant, with bananalike foliage, but in a huge fan. It will grow in nature to dozens of feet. To succeed as a houseplant it must have a large pot, bright sun, and tropical humidity.

Can I get fruit starting with a dwarf banana bulb?

The ads say yes, but we've never known anyone to do it indoors. Bananas need high humidity, warm temperatures, and constant moisture, all this together with full sun.

It really burns us up to see advertisements making ridiculous claims for banana plants—or other plants, too. Where are the consumer advocates when this kind of deceptive advertising goes down? We know that phony plant ads are unlikely to affect your health or safety, but they do rip off a lot of growers.

I saw beautiful bird-of-paradise plants both in the ground and in large tubs growing outdoors in Bermuda. They are so beautiful. Can they be grown indoors as houseplants in the north?

Yes, if you are determined enough. *Strelitzia reginae* must be quite mature and quite crowded in its container before it will flower, and then only if it has had bright sun, plenty of water, and general good culture (which includes rather cool winters—evening temperatures around 60°F.) for years.

Does bird-of-paradise need sun?

Strelitzia reginae (bird-of-paradise) needs as much sun as you can give it—and more! And that goes for other members of the Ginger and Musa families (close relatives) too: musa (banana), heliconia (lobster claws), ornamental ginger, etc.

MYRSINACEAE　　　　　　　　　　　　Myrsine Family

This is a small family with few houseplants in it.

Myrsine africana (African boxwood) has small leaves and can be kept cut back to a compact houseplant. Give it bright light, and don't allow it to dry out.

Ardisia crispa (coralberry) is an easy and durable houseplant, thriving under those same conditions, but surviving erratic watering and lower light.

Can I grow ardisia from the seed in the red berries?

Yes; allow the seed to ripen. Then lay the seed on a bed of damp milled sphagnum moss (over some potting soil in a 4-inch plastic pot), mist, cover lightly with more damp moss, and cover the pot with a sheet of clear plastic. Set in a warm bright place without direct sun. The transparent plastic helps to keep the seed bed moist until your seed germinates.

MYRTACEAE　　　　　　　　　　　　　Myrtle Family

The Myrtaceae include a number of tropical fruit crops that are also growable as houseplants: *Eugenia uniflora* (Surinam cherry), psidium (guava), *Feijoa sellowiana* (pineapple guava). They will all start from seed and, given a large pot, plenty of light with good sun, ample water, and moderate humidity, will grow into really handsome specimen plants—though they are unlikely to flower and fruit for you indoors.

I bought a plant with a label in it that said "Myrtle." The myrtle I know has much larger leaves. These leaves are only about ½ inch long, and quite thin—like the cut-off tips of podocarpus leaves. They are shiny and dark green. Can you help me identify the plant?

You have indeed bought a myrtle: *Myrtus communis microphylla,* small-leafed myrtle.

We have one and we love it. Keep it well pinched to promote branching, don't let it dry out (that's how we lost our first one), give it bright light with direct sun, and a winter humidity no lower than 35 percent.

It propagates (though slowly) from tip cuttings in damp sand in a closed propagation box.

NYCTAGINACEAE   Four-o'clock Family

While mirabilis (four-o'clock), the afternoon-blooming vine for which the family is known, does not make an indoor vine, bougainvillaea, given ample water, sun, humidity, and root room, certainly does. Bougainvillaea is a tropical vine with stunning bracts that come in many rich and pastel colors.

I have a bougainvillaea shrub in a pot on an east window (partly blocked), but it doesn't flower. I've had it more than a year. How can I force it into flower?

Buy it a plane ticket for Puerto Rico!

Or give it lots more sun. By the way, bougainvillaea is a vine, not a shrub. It wants a large pot, too, and ample water. Be proud that you've kept it alive over a winter in a heated apartment.

How long should my bougainvillaea flowers last?

The colorful parts of a bougainvillaea are its bracts, large adapted leaves which cup the insignificant white flowers. The flowers last only a few days, but the bracts should persist for weeks.

Will bougainvillaea flower indoors?

Yes, both under fluorescent lights and on a sunny windowsill. Pinch the plant out when young because it has a rangy, vining habit.

NYMPHAEACEAE   Water Lily Family

This is a small family of aquatic perennials, most with large floating
leaves, not houseplants at all in the accepted sense of the word, but
quite suited to sunny rooftop or terrace culture. They *must* have sun,
but need little root room or feeding.

Nymphaea is the genus of the water lilies, and you can have them
from pygmies to giants with flowers almost a foot across.

Victoria (water platter), named after Queen Victoria, can have
leaves over 6 feet across.

Cabomba (water shield) is a desirable companion plant if you are
planning a container water garden.

Though there are hardy water lilies, none of these plants can live
outdoors year round in a shallow container.

**At Longwood Gardens, in Kennett Square, Pennsylvania, I saw a wa-
ter lily in a half-barrel, with some other tiny plants. Is this a practical
idea for a balcony?**

Yes, if you've got sun—in the shade it won't work.

Take a clean half-barrel and wash it very well. Lay some clean
potting soil a few inches deep in the bottom of the barrel and set in
your nymphaea (water lily) bulb. Cover the soil with an inch of
gravel. Gently run in water to within 2 inches of the rim of the barrel.
The gravel holds the soil in place.

Add some water fern, either azola or salvinia, and there you are.

We suggest a pygmy nymphaea, and one that is tender. You won't
be able to keep it over the winter unless you move to a frost-free part
of the country, but it makes good fast growth in late spring and early
summer.

At the end of the season you can scoop the water fern out and
overwinter it indoors.

Even hardy water lilies are difficult to store in balcony conditions
because they cannot stand a hard freeze.

OLEACEAE   Olive or Lilac Family

This is a family of shrubs and trees, often with fragrant flowers. Given
coolish nights (temperatures around 60°F.) in winter, some of them
can make lovely houseplants.

Osmanthus fragrans is sweet olive, a plant with delightfully fragrant flowers. We've seen it grow over 7 feet tall in a private greenhouse.

We have grown rooted branches of forsythia for a season, but they won't winter over for us in a pot.

I'm having difficulty flowering and growing jasmine. Do they have special needs?

They need bright light and good watering—and many of them need cool temperatures to do well. Try *Jasminum sambac*. It doesn't need coolness and often makes a successful houseplant.

I bought this shiny-leafed houseplant at a garden sale: *Ligustrum amurense*. Can you tell me how to care for it?

Your "houseplant" isn't a houseplant. It is Amur privet, a handsome hardy shrub used as a hedge. We don't think it will do well indoors over the winter without a dormancy period. Of course, you could try growing it in a 16-inch pot on a balcony, protected against the winter. But it's not a houseplant.

The wages of impulse buying is privet.

ONAGRACEAE Fuchsia or Evening Primrose Family

Fuchsia, the plant of greatest interest for us in this family, has been so vigorously hybridized that there are miniatures and giants and variously colored flowers and forms—if you are interested, that is.

While we admire fuchsia as a porch and balcony plant outside, it is too much of a problem indoors. Fuchsia is most attractive to whitefly and can serve as locus of infection for the rest of one's houseplant collection.

Godetia is an annual-growing member of the family, with handsome flowers. It is possible in a pot if you can keep the evening temperatures coolish, but likely to do poorly in midsummer heat. Keep in bright sun and well watered.

How do fuchsia do indoors?

Fair to poor.

We've seen them as fair plants, grown in quite cool temperatures and given plenty of water. But in a room warm enough for people to be comfortable, fuchsia growth indoors is weak; and it becomes very attractive to whitefly.

I transplanted my fuchsia, and now it is all wilted and losing its leaves. Why?

Transplant shock, probably. Which means that you handled the roots too roughly. Why handle them at all? Contact with the hand's warmth can hurt roots, so try not to touch them with your hand.

A plant in trauma must be given high humidity. Mist the leaves and cover the plant with a plastic bag. The leaves should revive. If you've lost a lot, you'll want to cut the plant back.

My mother gave me a present of a lovely fuchsia for our new apartment, but it seems to droop quite a bit and the soil is always dry. What can I do?

Lord love you, water it more!

Fuchsias will droop if allowed to dry.

The leaves of my fuchsia are going pale. I grow it in a south window. Could it be too much sun?

Pale leaves on a fuchsia are much more likely to be the result of too much heat—too much sun would *brown* the leaves.

Open the window a bit more or put a small fan in the window for circulation. That will lower the temperature.

ORCHIDACEAE   Orchid Family

This is a huge and fascinating family, with worldwide distribution, even to the Arctic.

When orchids were first brought into European cultivation it was thought that very special conditions, greenhouses, and expensive equipment were necessary to grow and flower them. And it's true that in the temperate zone the orchids that thrive in mountainous places (like the Andes) have to be provided with an artificially cooled or specially maintained environment. But there are so many orchids that are *easy* to grow: phalaenopsis, paphiopedilums, species cattleyas, intermediate miltonias, brassavolas, epidendrums—the list could go on and on.

Mostly what you need to grow orchids is a little money to buy the plants (they certainly cost more than geraniums), a willingness to try, and a willingness to allow a couple to die until you find which do best for you.

There are many ways to categorize orchids. For watering purposes, we like to think of them as either having or lacking pseudobulbs. (Pseudobulbs are swollen stems from which leaves grow. Many orchids can be propagated from a few of these pseudobulbs separated from the parent plant and set into an appropriate medium.)

Orchids with pseudobulbs have a water-storage mechanism, and so they should be allowed to dry out between waterings. In high humidity, the growing medium should be allowed to go quite dry; in moderate humidity, only somewhat dry.

Orchids without pseudobulbs have little water-retaining ability, and so should be kept more or less evenly moist.

Orchids are also traditionally classified into temperature ranges: "cool" orchids are often from cool mountainous regions, "warm" growers from jungle areas. We try to avoid the so-called cool orchids, and choose for our indoor plants from those listed as warm or intermediate. Our experience has been very positive, even with plants for which our growing conditions are supposed to be too hot. Orchids are tough, durable, adaptable plants, and if you can keep one alive as a foliage plant for years, you will often see it flower, even if the conditions are far from ideal.

Orchids must have air around their roots. Now, all plants require some air in their potting mix, but for orchids, most need a great deal of air around their roots. Especially epiphytic orchids. (Epiphytes are plants that grow on other plants.) In Florida, we saw vanda orchids being grown on a mesh fence, without any soil mix at all. Cattleya orchid roots grow out of their pots, and should be allowed to. Orchid growing media have been chosen to provide this air and a minimum of nutrition.

Tree-fern fiber holds water well but is mostly air. It stays intact a long time. When it is mixed with coarse perlite, many orchids thrive in it.

Fir-bark chips decompose after a while (which means more frequent repotting), and they take nitrogen from the soil as they do. Still, they make a good medium for orchids without pseudobulbs.

Osmunda fiber is difficult to find, and while it is recommended (almost exclusively) in early orchid books, it has fallen from favor with many growers.

Terrestrial orchids, such as ludisia (jewel orchid) —this is one of our favorite and easiest houseplants—and goodyera (rattlesnake orchid) will take a small amount of soil in their mix. Their roots need somewhat less aeration. But even these plants need a fluffy mix (say, small fir-bark chips, coarse perlite, lightened houseplant soil, and leaf mold in equal parts).

Orchids can be quite expensive, especially if you insist on buying them from local florists as flowering plants. Amateurs generally propagate their own orchids vegetatively, from divisions or offsets (they are extremely slow from seed). These amateurs will often sell their excess propagations to fellow members at meetings of local chapters of the American Orchid Society. Bought there, young plants can be quite inexpensive, and you get the bonus of being able to discuss the conditions in which the plant was grown *with the grower.* That is better than a book.

All in all, don't be frightened when you hear the word "orchid." Orchids can be quite simple to grow, and they are magnificently rewarding.

Are orchids really too delicate for a beginning grower? I don't have a greenhouse.

Orchids are not delicate; they are among the toughest and most durable of plants, tolerant of a broader range of treatment than almost anything you can name. In the wild they may well outlive people.

Flowering them is another matter, however, and that can require special conditions: temperature drops at night, special temperature ranges, special foods, high humidity, etc. This is what gives orchids their bad reputation. So, if you are willing to grow them as *foliage* plants, orchids are very simple. And there are even orchids which will flower easily under windowsill conditions: To name a few: *Epidendrum cochleatum, Laeliocattleya* 'Rojo,' *Phalaenopsis amabile* hybrids, *Paphiopaedilum maudiae.*

Can I grow a bletilla orchid as a houseplant?

Only if you are very, very determined.

Bletilla is a hardy terrestrial orchid, and it won't tolerate warm temperatures.

Give it moderate humidity, ample water, a woodsy growing medium, bright diffused light, cool winter and fall temperatures, and nightly prayers.

My cymbidium orchids all have black spots on the leaves now. Some of the leaves yellow and fall off, though the plants flower well. What's happening?

It seems cymbidium virus is happening.

Sterilize your tools after working with your cymbidiums, and keep insects under control. Plants can live for years with cymbidium virus, but the plants do eventually peter out. Whom did you buy the infected plants from? Don't shop there again.

There is no cure.

We wish *we* could flower cymbids, but they require a cool greenhouse in most of the world.

Is there really any such thing as a "windowsill orchid"?

Absolutely. For us the easiest is *Epidendrum cochleatum,* the Peruvian clamshell orchid. The flowers are small but fragrant and interestingly shell-shaped. We grow ours on our obstructed east windowsill and treat it like any other houseplant, providing no special humidity or watering. It does grow, however, in coarse fir-bark chips, not soil.

I have read conflicting things about phalaenopsis orchids (moth orchids). Are they a good beginner's orchid or a difficult one?

While there are some cool-growing phalaenopsis which require special care, most of the so-called moth orchids are super for beginners. They will require careful watering and high humidity in the winter, but they will flower in quite moderate light. Tree-fern fiber and perlite or just fir-bark chips are satisfactory media, but if the medium gets soggy, the roots can rot.

This was the first orchid we ever flowered.

My mother came back from Florida with a corsage orchid plant for me. (She knows how I feel about plants.) Can I reasonably expect it to grow in my window?

Generally, cattleya orchids (the type most often referred to as "corsage orchid") are bright-sun plants, which require evening temperatures around 60°F., and moderate humidity. Since these orchids have pseudobulbs (those swellings between the leaves and the soil), let yours go moderately dry between waterings.

Without bright sun, humidity over 40 percent, and a 15° temperature drop at night, you are unlikely to reflower it—though cattleyas do make interesting foliage plants.

Can I grow cattleya orchids under fluorescent lights?

Try the smaller-growing *species* cattleyas under lights (even two tubes—though four are better). Their flowers are smaller and less showy than most of the hybrids, but they flower more freely.

I bought a cattleya orchid from a greenhouse and it came with a dividend—a weed with pretty yellow flowers and small three-part leaves. Do I have to pull it out? Do you know what it could be?

Most likely some tender oxalis—they are common weeds in greenhouses. They need a lot of sun to keep flowering—but then your cattleya will probably need a lot of sun, too.

There's no need to pull out your dividend: it is shallow-rooted and not competitive. In fact, it can be a bird dog for your watering: when your orchid is in normal growth, it will need watering at just about the time the oxalis wilts!

I repotted my *Laeliocattleya* 'Muriel Turner' last year, but it seemed to "climb" out of its pot so quickly. How often should a plant like this be repotted?

Laeliocattleya 'Muriel Turner,' like many of the laeliocats, is quite a compact plant, and it would be quite happy in a 4-inch pot.

The current thinking among the orchid society members that we know is that this cattleya type of orchid should really be allowed to grow out of and over its pot: that it shouldn't be repotted until the roots are *very* out of the pot. So, unless the medium has rotted away, one should certainly go at least two years between repottings.

One of your problems may be that you set your plant in the middle of the pot last time you repotted. This type of orchid grows its rhizome in only one direction. So, next time, determine the direction of the new growth (it's easy enough to see where the growth buds are), and place the *back* of the plant against one edge of the pot. If your plant lives on a windowsill, let the front face out.

Orchids are often set back by repotting, so you want to repot yours as seldom as possible.

My *Vanda coerulea* orchid, mounted on tree fern, is shriveling up. What do vandas need?

Mostly full sun—which is difficult for them to get indoors, except in a greenhouse.

Also, tree-fern mountings are more appropriate for the tropics or for greenhouses than ordinary house culture; tree fern needs high humidity to make it most effective. Perhaps a medium such as fir bark in a pot would be simpler for you.

Also check the roots of your vanda to see that they are in good condition: white and plump. It sounds as if they might be in trouble.

Provide plenty of humidity along with full sun.

They are heavy feeders, too, but don't feed your plant until it looks healthier.

The roots of my bulbophyllum orchid have rotted completely. Have I lost the plant? The bulbs are still firm.

Your roots may rot if your potting mix is kept too moist, but you get a second chance with pseudobulbous orchids. Cut away the old root stubs; repot in fresh medium (holding the rootless pseudobulbs in place with a metal orchid clip) ; keep the humidity moderately high; and don't keep the medium wet.

Can I use miniature equitant oncidiums in a terrarium?

Equitant oncidiums are a group of tiny miniature orchids that grow in a fan shape. They are not really suited to a terrarium because they are epiphytes and need good air circulation. They grow very well mounted on a piece of rough cork bark. Keep the plant and its bark well misted and in bright light—even bright fluorescent light. These oncidiums can be started even without any roots. Just glue them to the bark with rubber cement. Eventually, a full set of roots will form and attach themselves to the bark.

For a good tiny terrarium orchid, try lockhartia (braid orchid) .

After flowering, the lower leaves of my jewel orchid turn pale and die. The new growth looks healthy.

Assuming you have the most available of the jewel orchids, *Ludisia discolor,* this plant flowers only on new growth. After flowering, you can encourage branching by pinching out the just-finished tips. The more branches, the more flower stalks.

The leaf loss is natural, but can be kept to a minimum by not overwatering after flowering.

I have lost a leaf from my ladyslipper orchid. It turned yellow, then shriveled—and the plant in general doesn't look as strong as it used to. I keep the fir bark damp and feed monthly. The leaves are clean. Does this sound like anything specific to you?

It sounds as if the plant were in root trouble. How long has it been since the fir bark was changed? Fir bark, a good mix for paphiopedi-lums (ladyslipper orchids) , does decay rather rapidly. You certainly can't expect it to last more than three years, especially if you keep it constantly moist. A better idea with paphs is to keep the humidity above 50 percent and to allow the medium to dry *very slightly* between waterings.

Turn your paph out of its pot, and examine the roots; if they are rotten, cut them away and dust the living ends with a fungicide. Then hold the plant in place over fresh damp potting medium with a metal clip.

If the roots are still healthy, just get rid of as much of the old medium as you can and pot into fresh. Have you considered tree-fern fiber mixed with coarse perlite as a medium? It is more durable.

Do orchids all need high humidity? Even with a humidifier I just can't get much above 40 percent in the winter.

New plants from greenhouses and very young plants need higher humidity than plants that have been in your conditions for a while. Buy in late spring. Summer humidity is always pretty high. By the time winter comes, they will have partially adjusted to your conditions—and you will have had time to save up for a better humidifier.

Do those brownish orchid roots still serve a function, or should I cut them off?

By all means cut them off—then dust the wounds with flowers of sulfur.

Healthy orchid roots are whitish, with a green growing tip. Actually, this white part is not a root at all, but a spongy material that absorbs water when it is provided, then slowly makes it available to the wiry root inside.

I have a small greenhouse in which I've been quite successful with many diverse plants. But I've always shied away from orchids because of this "warm," "medium", and "cool" business. My greenhouse, according to the orchid catalogs, would be classified as warm. Does this really mean I should not try to grow the others? Orchids are expensive, and I don't want to throw away my money.

Though you maintain a night temperature of about 65°F. through most of your greenhouse (which makes it a "warm" house), that doesn't mean that every corner of it is that temperature.

Buy yourself a minimum/maximum thermometer, and put it in various corners of the greenhouse (start with those farthest from the heat source or nearest the venting). You will likely find that there are places in your greenhouse ideal for intermediate or even cool growers.

The same holds true for windowsill gardeners. The microclimates that exist in the "cracks" of our growing areas can make a wider range of plants possible than we would have thought by just looking at the "average" temperature of the area.

OXALIDACEAE   Oxalis or Wood-sorrel Family

This is a family with many small plants, some of them good houseplants, some of them too sun-loving; some of them with persistent corms left in the soil, some without. They all tend to fold their compound leaves at night and open them during the day.

Biophytum sensitivum (life plant) will fold up if touched or chilled. Give it warm temperatures, bright light without direct sun (it will sunburn), plenty of water, and moderate humidity.

Oxalis lasiandra was a failure for us: very handsome variegated foliage sprouted from the corms, but we didn't have enough sun for the flowers.

Oxalis martiana aureo-reticulata is delightful in a terrarium, with its cloverlike foliage veined in yellow.

Oxalis deppei made handsome striped purple flowers for us in moderate sun.

Oxalis regnellii is very easy, even without sun.

Oxalis hedysaroides rubra (fire fern) has no persistent corms, but it does have the deepest red foliage of any plant we know, and is fairly durable if you grow it in a terrarium.

The leaves of my oxalis plant are drooping, and lately the soil never seems to dry. And the leaves close at night, too. I don't know the full Latin name, but it has three-petaled leaves and white flowers. Can you help me?

The leaves of most oxalis close and open as you describe, so that's not a problem.

Oxalis regnellii would fit—and if so, it may just be going dormant. This oxalis grows from a persistent storage bulb in the soil called a corm. It can go dormant: the leaves die back, but the corm persists and should sprout again.

If you have dug into the soil, found firm corms, and decided that the corms are going dormant, then reduce the watering for a while. The top growth will come, and watering can return to normal.

But *Oxalis regnellii* does not *have* to go dormant. It can stay in continuous growth and continuous flower year round. Therefore, there is something in your care or environment which put the plant into dormancy. Do you let the plant go dry between waterings? Don't. Do you let it get cold? Don't. Do you keep it in the dark? Don't.

PALMACEAE   Palm Family

Palms are not like trees. Trees are all dicots (their seeds have two food parts) ; palms are all monocots (their seeds have only one food part), which puts them closer to corn than to elms.

Palms have an interesting way of growing. Unlike trees which can grow wider and wider as they age and grow taller, palms grow in width and height until they reach their maximum width, and from then on grow only in height. If the growing tip of your palm is lost, the palm is lost.

Palms vary as to their cultural requirements, some preferring to go quite dry between waterings, others to stay somewhat moist; some demanding full sun, others burning in sun and thriving in reduced light.

Most often, those palms with spiny and leathery foliage are sun-tolerant; those with soft foliage are low-light-tolerant. It is important to know the variety of your palm, because you just can't generalize about palms.

Those varieties that make offsets at the base can be propagated by separation and potting of the offsets; otherwise, you are unlikely to propagate your palm. Under no circumstances try to air-layer your palm! The distribution of its meristematic tissue is wrong for air-layering or tip cuttings, and you will lose the plant.

The outside fronds of my miniature date palm are turning brown and dying. A friend said it might be sunburn, but it is in a northeast window and gets little sun. I keep it well watered. What should I do?

Get another friend—one who knows more about *Phoenix roebelenii* (miniature date palm). These durable palms want *bright sun* to thrive, and must go moderately dry between waterings.

I bought this lovely kentia palm and it seems pretty much to fill its 14-inch pot. Should I repot it?

Palms don't take repotting well, and they do quite well more pot-bound than most plants. With this combination, we repot our palms as seldom as possible, allowing them to really fill their pots.

If your *Howeia forsteriana* (kentia) is showing no sign of needing repotting (dying fronds, for example), we would *not recommend* repotting yet.

A few weeks ago, at the beginning of November, I bought a large palm tree—an areca. The plant store lady told me to spray twice a day and to water every fourteen days. But some of the outside leaves are dying. Now, I figured that it comes from a warm climate, so I put it in the boiler room, where there is a small window. What do you think?

We think you're killing the poor plant. The heat is too high and the humidity is too low.

Bring it into better light, normal home temperature, and moderate humidity (40 percent or better), cut away the browning fronds right down to the soil, increase your watering, and hope that the plant isn't so far damaged that it won't recover.

Chrysalidocarpus lutescens (areca palm) usually makes a tolerant houseplant—but not if you cook it.

I just bought a potted palm tree, and I don't know how to care for it. It had no name on it.

We hope you paid very little for it—otherwise, why buy a plant with no name from a seller who can't tell you how to care for it?

There are sun-loving palms and shade-loving palms and sun-tolerant palms and shade-tolerant palms. Look at the leaves of your palm. If they are spiny and leathery (or at least tough), then yours is probably a sun-lover or sun-tolerant. Give it bright sun and allow it to go dry down to about 1 inch below the surface of the soil in a 10-inch pot.

If, however, the leaves are smooth and soft (and bright green), then yours will probably be shade-tolerant. Grow these palms in bright light, but without much direct sun, and allow the soil to go dry down to about ½ inch below the surface before watering.

You realize, of course, that these are just "ballpark" suggestions and that you will have to keep an eye on your plant to see how it reacts, and be ready to change conditions if you see a negative reaction (leaf scorch means too much sun; leaf loss may mean too little sun or too little water).

It's been our observation that aside from the dwarf parlor palm, known in the trade as *Chamaedorea elegans* 'Bella' or *Neanthe bella*, most palms will take more sun than you supposed.

I recently bought a palm. I don't know its name, but it has large green leaves. I am growing it next to my phoenix palm, and that is doing

well, but this new palm is browning. Is it just shock? I mist it frequently.

It could be shock, but the best bet is that it is in too much sun. The phoenix is a bright-sun palm. If it is doing well, then you are likely giving it good sun and moderate water. If the palm next to it is browning, try putting it out of the direct sun and giving it more water.

But remember, the non-sun palms still prefer good bright light.

The trouble with palms that get any serious problem is that they often die.

We are about to transplant our miniature parlor palm. Do you have any hints for us?

Palms sometimes take repotting badly, so stack the cards in your own favor.

Transplant between January and August, when the roots are in most active growth. Make sure the plant is well watered before you transplant (unlike most plants), and water very well after transplanting.

Be prepared to provide high humidity for the transplantee, either by misting several times a day (ech!) or by covering your *Chamaedorea elegans* 'Bella' (parlor palm) with a plastic tent or large plastic bag.

However, after being in a bag for a couple of weeks, it will require another week or so of acclimatization before the plant is ready to live in the real world. Just poke a couple of holes in the bag (or lift the tent up a bit) every day. When the bag is in shreds, the palm should be ready to roll.

Is a red palm really red? Will it make a decent houseplant?

Its fruit is red and the new leaves come in with their centers red. But aside from that, red palm (*Dictyosperma album,* also known as *D. rubrum*) is as red as a white rhino is white.

But red or no, this is one fan palm that will make a good houseplant. Give it a large tub and it will acclimate itself to moderate light, moderate watering, and moderate humidity.

How blue is a blue palm? Reason I ask is I saw one in a catalog and the color as shown in the catalog would go well in my living room. But the other colors looked off—if you know what I mean.

We know what you mean. Some catalogs are more notable for their enthusiasm than their color accuracy.

A *Butia capitata* (blue palm) is less blue than a blue spruce—much less. (We were in Puerto Rico and asked a horticulturist at the Mayagüez Agricultural Research Station about how blue they grew, and he just laughed nervously—as if he were responsible for an inaccurate common name.)

Aside from not fitting your color scheme, butias are poor living-room palms. They have needlelike frond tips which can really hurt, and they require full sun. However, they will withstand relatively low humidity.

PANDANACEAE   Screw Pine Family

This is one of our favorite houseplants—and you know a houseplant has to be good for us to love it despite the scratches we get every time we move it or repot it. We have a plant of *Pandanus veitchii* (green leaves with lengthwise cream stripes) that we have loved for more than a decade. It now has 4-foot arching leaves that do for a room what every palm grower wishes a palm would do.

Pandanus is durable, resistant to everything but drowning, and will tolerate everything from bright sun to no sun and little light. The secret is in starting it young.

However, there is one leetle drawback with most pandanuses: spines—three rows of teeth (one row at each leaf margin and a third row on the underside of the midrib) ready to play "gotcha!" as you innocently wander by. If all those "teeth" are too much for you, try to find *Pandanus baptistii,* a spineless species.

Even in varieties without the spines you can distinguish pandanus from other look-alike plants by the prominent midrib running the length of the leaves.

Screw pine is so called because its leaves grow from the stem in a spiral (this is more noticeable in mature plants) .

Why are my screw pine leaves turning brown at the tips and dying back?

Pandanus (screw pine) is so durable that it takes a serious problem to damage it. Perhaps you have been fooled by the spines and are treating your plant as if it were a cactus. It isn't, and though it will stand erratic watering, the leaves will brown and die back if they are consistently underwatered.

My *Pandanus utilis* is several years old and about 5 feet tall. It is a lovely plant and has made half a dozen thick supporting aerial roots which have taken hold in the same pot. But now the central trunk seems to be rotting away. It is definitely coming apart (and so am I!). What can I do? I don't want to lose it.

The first thing is to take your finger off the panic button. *You have not necessarily lost the plant*—even if the stem does rot through. The stilt roots are capable of supporting the plant—certainly nutritionally, and perhaps physically, too.

We've seen the trunks of pandanuses rot out completely (in the tropics) and still go on. If the plant doesn't seem stable, use a sturdy stake or two to give it stability.

But why did the trunk rot in the first place? Overwatering, perhaps? An unnoticed (and untreated) injury? Too heavy a soil?

You will probably want to dust the living end of the trunk with flowers of sulfur. In fact, dusting with this fungicide now may stop or slow the rot.

My screw pine is making thick balancing roots out of its stem. Does this mean I should repot or something?

Pandanus veitchii (the plant most commonly called screw pine) and all pandanuses make these stilt roots when mature. It is a sign of nothing except that the plant is growing.

As for repotting, repot if the plant needs it: that is, if the rootball fills the pot. Pandanus, being large and prickly, is difficult to repot. However, it is a good idea to allow the stilt roots to find a home in soil.

How do I water a pandanus?

Don't keep it wet, but don't allow it to go bone dry. In a 10-inch pot, the soil can go dry down to about 1 inch below the surface before rewatering.

How can I root an offset from my pandanus?

We find the offsets of screw pine (pandanus) very easy to root. We just break one off and stick its bottom in damp vermiculite in a high-humidity propagation box. It will send out a thick taplike root and then minor roots. Pot it when that major root is about 1½ inches long.

PASSIFLORACEAE   Passionflower Family

The only genus in the Passionflower family important to us house-
planters is passiflora (the passionflower itself). The "passion" refers
not to Dorothy Lamour and Jon Hall, but to the Passion of Christ;
there is an entire symbology referring to the specific parts of the
flower.

As houseplants, the passifloras want lots of water and warm temperatures—they'll drop their leaves in protest, otherwise.

Passiflora trifasciata has done well for us trained around a wire
hoop.

For you outdoor gardeners, passifloras are not reliably hardy outside of the really subtropical parts of the States, but we have friends in
Lancaster County, Pennsylvania, who start passifloras indoors in mid-
winter, and by late summer this fast-growing vine covers a small
outdoor arbor.

Is *Passiflora trifasciata* easier or harder than *Passiflora caerulea*?

Easier to grow—harder to flower. We prefer *P. trifasciata* because of its
decorative leaves. Remember, don't let it get a chill and don't let it
dry out.

**I have no luck with passionflower vine. I've lost several. Is there a trick
to them?**

There are two things you must watch for with *Passiflora caerulea*.
First, that the plant you buy is well rooted, and second, that you never
allow it to go dry. It also wants bright sun and good humidity.

Passifloras do best if they are provided with a trellis on which to
climb. Even so, they are difficult to flower in a pot.

PIPERACEAE   Pepper Family

This is a small tropical family of vines and herbaceous plants, sometimes with very decorative leaves. The flowers are thin or thick spikes,
like erect rattails.

Yes, your peperomia is related to black pepper (*Piper nigrum*), but
not to various red peppers or green pepper or chile peppers, which are
all in the Solanum family.

Piper ornatum (variegated pepper) is even more closely related to black pepper, and it is a delightful vine, with dark-green leaves liberally laced with red. Not fast-growing, but handsome. Don't allow it to dry out, and give it a bright window.

Why do the leaves of my peperomia drop? They look perfectly healthy.

Peperomia leaves will drop at the least excuse:

    too little water;
    too much water;
    too low humidity;
    too low temperature.

They want a *very*, very well-drained soil, and to go somewhat dry between waterings. And remember, keep them warm and humid.

I have a *Peperomia orbicularis* in a terrarium, and it has begun to put out these small sticks. What are they and what should I do?

They are flowering spikes. The flowers are too small to see with your unaided eye. Do nothing.

How can I get rid of scale on my peperomia?

Swish the leaves and stems through warm soapy water, then rub gently at the scale with your fingers. It should come off readily.

Rinse in tepid clear water, and repeat the whole treatment at weekly intervals until you have the problem beaten.

This hand removal is very well suited to plants with succulent or leathery leaves, but it can be used on almost any plant once or twice.

My peperomia is top-heavy. It seems to be growing well, but even a stake won't keep some parts of it from hanging over. It is a large plant in a 7-inch pot. Can you suggest anything?

Cut it back some. Cut off some of the pendant parts and propagate them. And don't be afraid to use several stakes, each to hold up a single branch. But cut off the stakes just below the top of the plant; and hold the branches to the stakes with green twist-ties. After all, when you look at the plant, you want to see leaves and branches, not stakes and ties.

I bought a very interesting-looking peperomia with pale-green leaves, but now the new leaves are coming in dark green. What am I doing wrong?

You mean, what are you doing right! Peperomias get pale from too much sun. You are giving yours an appropriate amount of light, and so the leaves are coming in the proper color. There are many variegated peperomias, others in various shades of green, and one with a silvery green sheen (*Peperomia griseo-argentea*). But your question describes a plant going happy.

Why is my peperomia rotting?

Overwatering can cause rot in peperomias—especially in heavy soil. They are jungle-floor plants, adapted to living in a *most-well-drained* soil.

In good humidity and in the kind of soil described, allow your peperomias to go dry down to about ¾ inch (one knuckle's worth) below the surface of the soil (in a 4-inch pot) before rewatering thoroughly.

PITTOSPORACEAE   Pittosporum Family

Most of this family comes from way down south: Australia.

Pittosporum itself is a very handsome evergreen and can be grown into quite a large and decorative tub plant if you have a bright and cool place to winter it.

How far back can my leggy pittosporum be pruned?

Very far indeed.

But why did it go leggy? Make certain you give your pittosporum bright sun, and that it has moderately cool winter temperatures.

I have a large pittosporum on which the leaves droop and then perk up when I water them. What's the matter?

Let us put it as simply as we can—water more!

I have just bought a medium-size *Pittosporum tobira* for my terrace. Should I pinch it to make it branch?

No. Pittosporum branches freely without pinching.

Will my pittosporum flower?

Flower and fruit—if you give it enough sun. *Pittosporum tobira* flowers in the spring, a clump of small white flowers which are very fragrant. The fruit is not edible, but you can grow the plant from its seed.

Can pittosporum be grown as a houseplant?

We've seen it grown well as an office plant: a 2-foot shrub in a 10-inch pot, grown on top of a room divider, so that the top is within a few feet of the four 4-foot tubes of fluorescent light in the ceiling. The plant is watered when the soil is dry down to a depth of about ¾ inch below the surface.

My variegated pittosporum seems to be growing very slowly. I give it what you recommend (some sun and moderate watering). Is there anything else I can do?

You can be patient. It has been our observation that *Pittosporum tobira variegatum* (variegated pittosporum) *is* slower than all-green varieties. A feeding program (fish emulsion at half label dilution, once a month) when the plant is in active growth might help some.

The leaves of my pittosporum are reflexing back on themselves. I've looked for bugs and see none, and the soil smells all right and goes dry at a normal rate. Do you know why they would do this?

Before we answer your question, let us say that you are wise to sniff your soil—root problems often show themselves by a "sour" smell in the soil.

Supposing that by "reflexing," you mean curling under, then we have indeed seen the problem before, and it's hardly a problem.

Pittosporum tobira leaves in bright sun will curl under, while in low light they grow flat. And this just shows the adaptability of this marvelous shrub.

If you feel you must, by all means move your plant to lower light, but the curling does no harm, and in that much sun it may give you some flowers.

POLYGONACEAE   Buckwheat or Rhubarb Family

This is a family that shows great variety: important edibles (rhubarb and buckwheat) and the most undesirable of weeds (knotweed).

Rhubarb (*Rheum rhaponticum*) can be grown in a large tub on a sunny rooftop or terrace, but you are not likely to get much from it out of full sun.

Coccoloba uvifera (sea grape) makes a charming houseplant; its leaves have red veins when young, and it will grow to a good size (a couple of feet) in a single spring and summer, given sun and moisture.

For city gardeners with sun, there is no finer vine than *Polygonum aubertii* (silver-lace vine). Planted in the ground it will rapidly climb a fence and make masses of lacy summer flowers. On a sunny terrace, try it in 18-inch containers, but give it a latticework or some kind of mesh on which to climb. Beautiful.

In Bermuda I saw a magnificently beautiful tree: low, wide, with large and round leathery leaves (with red veins), and bunches of purple fruit like grapes. I brought in some of the seed. Can I grow the plant on my windowsill? And what is it?

The plant is *Coccoloba uvifera,* known in Bermuda as sea grape (because it grows well by the shore) and in Puerto Rico as cocoloba.

You can grow it from seed, and it is not difficult to manage if you can give it bright sun, moderate humidity, and constant moisture in a well-drained soil, as well as moderately cool evenings in the winter. If you can grow camellia, you can grow coccoloba. We are currently growing one started from Florida seed and it is behaving very well, but we are not likely to get it to yield the edible grapes that it bears in the tropics.

POLYPODIACEAE   Common Fern Family

Most of the ferns you will grow (barring tree ferns and some water ferns) belong to this family. It is a very ancient family: fossils of present ferns show that they existed 100 million years before flowering plants. We hope that impresses you.

If you have difficulty growing ferns, it may be an indication that you just don't have enough humidity, or that you aren't using a porous-enough soil mix.

Ferns are not big feeders and don't need a lot of soil, but they do need a lot of drainage. Long-haired sphagnum moss cut into small pieces, coarse perlite, tree-fern fiber, and even fine fir-bark chips have a place in their soil mix.

Ferns often make decorative hanging plants, but not if you are an erratic waterer. Hanging plants dry out faster than standing plants, and so you have to be even more conscientious about watering them. In a well-draining soil mix, ferns should be watered as soon as the surface of the soil is dry.

The fronds of the "Fluffy Ruffles" fern on my windowsill are drying up—turning brown and falling off. I have a Boston fern which is doing all right, but I really like the "Fluffy Ruffles." What do you think?

"Fluffy Ruffles" is really a mutation of that same Boston fern (*Nephrolepis exaltata*), but is much more demanding: it wants less sun, more water, and more humidity. When small, it can live in a terrarium.

I am growing a "Fluffy Ruffles" fern under lights, and the lower fronds are turning brown.

Either your fluorescent light setup is too warm or too dry, or both. "Fluffy Ruffles" wants high humidity and will not tolerate high heat.

Cut away all brown fronds right down to the ground to give the young and healthy fronds a chance. Then lower your temperature and raise your humidity.

What kind of humidity does a Boston fern need? Are they at all possible in an apartment? I mist and mist, but they won't do well for me.

If all that misting doesn't help, perhaps it's a light problem, not a humidity problem. *Nephrolepis exaltata* (Boston fern) needs a good deal of bright light, and with ample water and humidity, it will even thrive in a great deal of direct sun. So, try improving the light.

But to answer your question, if you can keep the humidity between 40 and 50 percent in its growing area, that should suffice.

My Boston fern is making these very skinny green roots out of its base. They look like thick hairy threads. What are they?

They are runners. *Nephrolepis exaltata* (Boston fern) and other members of this genus form runners and can be propagated by pinning one or more of them to the surface of a pot of damp soil. When a new plantlet begins to grow, cut the runner, and you'll have a new plant.

I have brought my Boston fern inside after a summer outdoors, and the fronds are turning brown at an alarming rate. Can you suggest something?

We suggest you don't put your plants outdoors for the summer because it is a tremendous shock to them when you bring them back inside.

Keep the humidity up on your *Nephrolepis exaltata* (Boston fern) and give it a very bright spot. These plants can take quite a bit of sun indoors.

What is the difference between a true fern and an asparagus fern?

Asparagus "ferns" are not ferns: they are asparagus; they flower and seed and fruit, whereas true ferns form spores.

On a cultural level, asparagus "ferns" (we wish people would call them "ornamental asparagus") prefer bright sun and moderate watering, and they do not particularly care about humidity: true ferns demand high humidity and constant moisture, and most are tolerant of moderate light.

My rabbit's-foot fern is losing its fronds. They are just falling off and no new ones are growing. I am getting panicky.

Hang loose.

Davallia fejeensis and many other "footed" ferns go dormant in the fall and lose their fronds. Keep the plant humid and warm, but reduce watering until the new fronds start to appear.

Over the last two months the new leaves on my bird's nest fern have turned brown, and now they have died. I misted it every other day because I thought ferns need humidity.

They do—and a lot more than one spraying every two days. The low humidity may have been a problem, but we don't think that's what bothered your *Asplenium nidus* (bird's nest fern). New growth dying is always a bad sign. We think you have root trouble. It might have been caused by underwatering—or by overwatering in too heavy a soil. The plant needs ample watering, but it must be in well-drained soil.

Root rot can be terminal. Put the whole plant into a plastic bag. This will raise the humidity to 100 percent, take demands off the roots, and give new roots a chance to form. Reduce watering somewhat, and consider repotting into very well-drained soil.

I tried to start fern spores on a bed of damp milled sphagnum moss as you suggested, but after a few months, all I got was a bed of green algae—can you suggest another method?

Are you certain you had algae? The first stage of fern-spore growth (prothallus) looks very much like algae. Try again on the damp milled sphagnum moss, and when you get that "algae," look at it under a magnifying glass. If the individuals look roughly heart-shaped, you do indeed have the prothallus stage. Then, spray the surface well with tepid water to permit fertilization (the males can get to the females only by swimming through water), and just wait for the young sporophytes to arise.

I have a "mother fern." What is it and why is it called that?

Probably what you have is *Asplenium viviparum* or *A. bulbiferum,* both of which are commonly called "mother fern" because of their habit of forming plantlets along the edges of their fronds. Pin a living frond down to damp growing medium in a high-humidity atmosphere and the plantlets will likely root. If they do, cut them away from the parent leaf when well rooted.

Asplenium viviparum is lacier and smaller than *A. bulbiferum.*

Is there any fern I can grow in an apartment?

The problem most of us have in growing ferns is humidity. And most ferns need a relative humidity above 50 percent to do really well. But there are some that will do all right in the 40 percent area (provided it goes *no lower* than that—40 percent is a bottom, not an average). You may think there is little difference between 40 and 50 percent—but ask your plants.

Pteris cretica (table fern) has a good reputation, and we've been surprised at the number of platyceriums (staghorn ferns) that are being grown in quite moderate humidity.

Finally, *Polypodium aureum* (golden bear's paw fern) is one that fern specialists recommend highly for apartment culture (it will take a bit more sun than most ferns).

My beautiful staghorn fern, mounted on long-hair sphagnum moss, rotted out on me! I'm desolate but would like to try again. Is there a better medium for platycerium?

Staghorn ferns make good houseplants if you're willing to take the extra trouble. (Visiting a friend's apartment recently, we parked in the garage and came up through the basement. There in the laundry room someone had hung a 24-inch platycerium over a washtub and was hosing it down!)

Long-fibered sphagnum is a good medium, but it holds water like mad. Allow several days drying between waterings (while keeping the humidity over 40 percent). Tree-fern fiber held between two rounded pieces of cork bark makes a most attractive hanging, and the watering is easier to manage.

PORTULACACEAE   Purslane Family

We had a lot of fun with the weed purslane (*Portulaca oleracea*— called pussley in some regions) on our television "Garden Spot." We cooked it, ate it, and then told how our viewers could do the same. The colonials brought it to this country from Europe as an edible potherb, long before all the multitude of hybrid vegetables came into our stores. If you want to try this succulent weed, just trim off the tough root, boil the leaves and stems in water for a few minutes, then chomp away. It smells and tastes like spinach, but without the acid bite.

Portulacaria afra tricolor is a handsome, small, colorful, upright succulent (nonedible, as far as we know), that does very well under fluorescent light.

Anacampseros rufescens is a delightful succulent, also small, but it will flower for you with little direct sun—uncharacteristic of the family.

I have a pot of portulaca growing (from seed) under fluorescent lights (two tubes), but I get very few flowers, and those I do get don't really open. Does portulaca need a special food?

No, but they do need sun, or, lacking that, stronger fluorescent light than you are providing.

But we really prefer to grow *Portulaca grandiflora* outside when possible, even if just in a pot on the outside of the windowsill.

PRIMULACEAE   Primrose Family

This is a family with a number of attractive plants in it, but mostly for greenhouse or outdoors because they require cool evening temperatures.

Can I regrow my cyclamen from the tuber?

You can, but it's unlikely to work out unless you have a cool greenhouse.

If you want to try, keep the dormant tuber (in its pot) in a cool place, almost dry, until it resprouts. A real watering at this time may rot the tuber. When new growth begins, bring your *Cyclamen persicum* (Persian cyclamen) into a cool bright place, and water it.

Commercial growers always start new plants from seed; it takes about eighteen months from seed to bloom time.

PUNICACEAE   Pomegranate Family

Pomegranates make handsome small plants, and they will fruit for you in home conditions. Give your seedling *Punica granatum* lots of water and as much sun as you can manage, good humidity, and frequent pinchings, and it will grow handsomely for you.

By the way, while dwarf pomegranate is the form mostly grown, even the full-size pomegranate (the kind whose fruit you will find for sale in your produce market) makes an excellent houseplant if pruned.

Since the beginning of December, many of my dwarf-pomegranate leaves have turned yellow and fallen off. I grow it in a bright window and keep it well watered. Why should the leaves fall off?

If that bright window is also a *cool* window, that may be your answer. Pomegranates are mostly evergreen, but in cool climates (where they are subjected to a cool winter—after all, they are not frost-hardy) they can drop all or some of their leaves in winter. They will then resprout in the warmer time. So, provide a little more warmth, and yours should resprout.

Can I grow a dwarf pomegranate from seed?

Yes, but only from the fruit of a dwarf pomegranate (*Punica granatum nana*). The pomegranate you buy in the greengrocer's (*Punica granatum*) will give you the standard-sized pomegranate shrub—which will also make a handsome pot plant.

Punica granatum would eventually grow to about 18 feet outdoors in a subtropical climate, whereas the dwarf form will reach only about 6 feet outdoors.

Whichever one you grow, you will want to prune it.

Are the fruit of my dwarf pomegranate edible?

Yes, when ripe. But, instead, we give the seeds to our friends, to grow new plants.

ROSACEAE   Rose Family

Aside from roses, there are many important garden and orchard plants
in the Rose family: raspberry, plum, peach, cherry, cotoneaster (a fine
shrub, the prostrate form, *Cotoneaster horizontalis,* is excellent for
planting at the base of street trees), pyrocantha, mountain ash, and
others.

You may not make a crop big enough to go into business, but
everblooming strawberries are quite appropriate for container culture
on a sunny terrace or balcony. Sorbus (mountain ash) will thrive
outdoors year round on your terrace, if you can give it enough sun and
a large enough container (a minimum of 2 feet square).

And for all of you who've never thought of it, while you are
planning your balcony garden—just picture roses in the sun.

If you can't picture roses on your balcony, try raphiolepis on your
windowsill. *Raphiolepis umbellata* (called coco plum in Bermuda) is
a delightful small shrub with dark leathery leaves and many handsome
though small white flowers. Give it a porous soil, bright light without
full sun, and plenty of water, and it should do beautifully for you.

**The leaves of my miniature rose are turning black and curling under.
Are they fungus-prone?**

No more so than full-size roses. But this doesn't sound like a fungus.
Check for spider mite. Cynthia Westcott ("the plant doctor") says
that mini roses have spider mites the way dogs have fleas.

What is the best pH for growing miniature roses?

Mini roses will grow very well in ordinary houseplant soil, with a pH
of around 6.5. Containered patio or terrace roses will also do well
there.

**I have a miniature rose in a pot on my windowsill. Do I prune it the
same way I prune my outdoor roses?**

Yes and no. Indoors, miniature roses have no dormant period and will
keep in growth year round, so no massive spring pruning is appropriate. But just as the larger roses need to be groomed, so must the
deadheads be trimmed off your mini, and the stem holding the spent
bloom cut back to a strong five-leaflet leaf. Better to cut a little too

much than too little. The cutting promotes branching and new flowers.

However, should your mini get ungainly and need sharper pruning, don't hesitate to cut it back as much as halfway.

Must I provide a cool winter climate for my miniature roses? I love them, but this is my first year growing them, so I would appreciate any help.

Most full-size roses must have a winter dormancy to do really well, but miniature roses, while just as hardy, are perfectly content to spend the entire year at normal house temperatures (65° to 75°F.), flowering as long as there is enough sun—or even under fluorescent lights.

I have black spot on one of my rose bushes (on my balcony). Do I have to spray?

Not necessarily, if you act fast. If you have other roses, separate them from the infected one. Cut away all affected leaves and burn them (don't compost). Then sterilize the tools. Keep water off the leaves, and water only early in the day, so no water is on the leaves as night comes (you can't help it if it rains—but that doesn't help). With this kind of care, you may not have to spray with a fungicide at all.

RUBIACEAE   Madder or Coffee Family

This is a family with some super houseplants in it.

Pentas (*Pentas lanceolata coccinea*—also known as Egyptian star flower) is grown widely as a garden plant, but we have had it under a four-tube fluorescent fixture for years, where it has been mostly in bloom, making its handsome heads of pink star-shaped flowers. It blooms only on new wood, but it branches freely (or you can pinch out the deadheads to encourage branching). Drying hurts it, so keep it evenly moist.

Ixora coccinea (flame of the woods) also has star-shaped flowers, but given sun and root room it will make a much larger plant. Pinch for branching and compactness, and feed every couple of months with an acid plant food.

Many members of this family are acid-lovers. If you want to learn about chlorosis, grow ixora or gardenia. Chlorosis is a deficiency disease caused by lack of iron and an insufficiently acid soil—the leaf yellows while the veins stay dark.

Hoffmannia is a genus of handsome plants, many variegated. Its square stems and quilted leaves are distinctive. But this is a genus to try only if you can maintain a minimum relative humidity of 40 percent. The leaves will turn brown at the edges and die in low winter humidity.

Serissa foetida variegata is a handsome little plant, flowering readily under fluorescent lights, but wanting constant moisture at its roots in a well-drained soil.

Coffea (coffee) makes a much better houseplant than you might think—though even if you get flowering, you won't get enough coffee berries to get more than a cup of coffee. It will do very well in bright light without any (or very little) direct sun, provided it has a fluffy, somewhat acid soil, and lots of water. Shower the plant weekly while it is of a handleable size—we have seen them 7 feet tall in an apartment.

We know we're fickle, but that's the way we are. And right now one of the plants we really adore is *Mitriostigma axillare*. Its leaves are dark and shiny, and it won't make a huge shrub, but it *flowers* and *stays in flower* for months, and even flowers in an unusual fashion: it makes bud clusters at its leaf axils (hence, "axillare"), and the flowers open one or two at a time from each axil. They are not quite as fragrant as gardenia, but they are fragrant. If you can find one—*buy it*.

Why are the leaves of my gardenia plant turning yellow and falling off? I see no bugs under my magnifying glass. The leaves just yellow and drop. I keep it in sun and water it about every ten days.

That's not nearly enough water for a gardenia. These plants will drop leaves if they go dry at all.

Feel the soil. If the *surface* is dry, water well.

Why can't I keep gardenias alive? I've had four, and they've all died on me.

Gardenias are difficult as houseplants—especially in the North.

They are mostly bought in early spring, when low humidity is a problem, but insufficient water is the main killer. They need good sun, high humidity, acid well-drained soil, and *lots of water*.

Mist frequently and well, use peat moss in the soil, feed with an acid food, cut back a bit after flowering, give it bright sun, and cool temperatures, watch out for spider mites, and yours *might* flower twice a year.

Also, the next time you bring one home, turn it out of its pot first thing: they are often sold very underpotted.

My friend and I bought nice little gardenias in 3-inch pots, but the leaves and buds started to drop almost at once on both plants. Could it be a disease?

Disease is always a possibility, but the likelihood is too little water and/or a need for repotting. These are related, really. Most of those gardenias in 3-inch pots are so potbound that they cannot readily take up enough water. And gardenias need *plenty* of water.

Repot your plants into 5-inch pots, in a well-drained acid soil, and your leaves should stop dropping.

How can I make the soil more acid for my gardenia?

Mix peat moss into the soil.
Cover the soil with a mulch of clean pine needles.
Feed at half strength with an acid plant food.
Choose any or all of the above.

I have an ixora plant in a 4-inch pot, in an east window, and I allow it to go about half-dry between waterings. But its leaves are turning yellow and drooping. Should I feed it or what?

The leaf loss is probably due to a too small pot, too little light, and too little water.

You didn't say how big your plant is. Ixora is a beautiful tropical or semitropical shrub which grows to about 6 feet. To keep it as a houseplant you must give it a fairly large pot, bright sun, at least moderate humidity, a porous soil, and *constant moisture,* at the roots. Two months after successfully repotting it into its new larger pot, feed monthly with 10–20–10 fertilizer at half strength, and you can expect it to flower.

Ixora coccinea (flame of the woods) doesn't have to be 6 feet tall, but it will take up room.

Is there any flowering shrub I can grow that will stay small?

We can suggest three: *Malpighia coccigera* (Malpighiaceae) (dwarf holly), *Lagerstroemia indica* 'Petite Pinkie' (Lythraceae) (crape myrtlette), and *Mitriostigma axillare.*

The malpighia is available widely and the myrtlette is available as seed from Geo. W. Park and Thompson & Morgan (see APPENDIX).

Our current pet is the mitriostigma, which has scented flowers and beautifully glossy foliage.

All should be kept quite well watered and in bright light. Keep the myrtlette and malpighia cut back and groomed to keep them compact.

And don't be in a hurry to repot.

RUTACEAE   Rue Family

The herb rue was an ingredient in a poison given to "erring maidens" in the Middle Ages.

On a more cheerful note, this is a family that contains *citrus plants* of all kinds—which must make it a favorite family with any house-plant grower. You don't grow any citrus at all? Plant a fresh seed from your morning grapefruit. It's as simple as that—as long as you can provide some sun.

Fortunella margarita (kumquat) is also easy from seed, and grows quite like citrus.

Why do the leaves of my orange tree turn yellow and fall off?

Citrus plants are acid-lovers. With too little acid in the soil, they will suffer from chlorosis (as will gardenias) : the leaves will turn yellow (the veins will stay dark) and fall. Use a pine-needle mulch or an acid plant food (at half strength) to supply acid.

My oranges and leaves are falling off! The leaves stay green, but they curl and seem dry. What's happening?

Sounds as if you're letting the plant go too dry between waterings. *Citrus mitis* (Calamondin orange) and other citruses want thorough rewatering when the surface is at all dry.

In the cold months, low humidity will cause this same kind of leaf and fruit drop. Mist the leaves frequently, and do what you can to keep the humidity above 30 percent.

Is there a flowering plant that can be a conversation piece all year round?

Citrus mitis (Calamondin orange) is a delight every minute of the year.

When in flower, the scent is glorious; the fruit stays on a long time, taking quite a while to ripen to orange. And the plant will often have ripe fruit and flowers *at the same time*. Given good care, the leaves are dark green and glossy.

Give it lots of water, year round. If you let it dry some, it will lose leaves; if you let it really dry, it will die.

Provide it with plenty of humidity, especially in the winter.

Cover the soil with clean pine needles (or give it a periodic dose with an acid plant food).

And give it full sun on your brightest windowsill. It will get by on less than full sun but not be as strong, and not as full of leaves.

My miniature citrus plants are not flowering. Are they long-night plants or something?

No, we've seen miniature oranges flower at any time of year.

Did you grow your plants from seed? We've read of them flowering from seed, but never known anyone to do it. Our citrus started from seed don't flower.

Are you feeding too much nitrogen? That inhibits flowering. Feed with a high-phosphorus (middle number) plant food.

Are the plants mature enough? Real youngsters won't flower.

Finally, are you giving them enough sun? They will flower in less sun than a geranium—but not a whole lot less.

Can I grow a plant from the seeds of my miniature orange? And how?

And how! If your miniature orange makes seeds, they should be fertile and should sprout readily. Just push the seed under damp soil in a pot and do not allow it to dry out.

The most important thing is that the seeds be planted promptly— immediately, really—before they have a chance to dry: the same is true of all citrus fruit and of most tropical fruit in general.

Once they are sprouted, give your citrus plants plenty of sun.

My orange tree suffered terribly from my four-week vacation. A friend was supposed to water it, but he was hospitalized. There seems to be some life, but it has lost lots of leaves.

You are in trouble, but perhaps not all is lost. Cut the plant back sharply—halfway at any rate—keep it in the sun, in a warm and humid location, and water only moderately until new growth (we hope) starts. Then water well.

The first of my Calamondin oranges tastes very sour. It is supposed to be edible. Am I doing something wrong?

"Edible" is the opposite of "poisonous." It doesn't mean "palatable."

Actually, the fruit of your *Citrus mitis* (Calamondin orange) can be used as if it were lemon in tea or in cooking. If you get a large crop, it can even make a good marmalade. We have a friend near Connecticut with a greenhouse who took *400 oranges* from one *Citrus mitis* at one time. It was an eight-year-old tree and required sharp cutting back that season.

I bought a lemon tree (Meyer lemon, it says on the stick), and it's supposed to have fruit all year. It did fine outdoors all summer. I mean it made great leaves, but no fruit. Why?

First of all, we don't feel responsible for the claims of plant sellers. Second, your lemon will bear when it is sufficiently mature, if it has enough sun and water, and if you give it an occasional feeding with a plant food with a high middle number (say, 15–30–15) and a big enough pot.

We have had citrus plants flower almost any month of the year that they feel like it, though most often in the winter. So you hang in there.

SALVINIACEAE   Salvinia Family

This is what you call a smallish family—two genera. Both are water ferns and very desirable as additions to container water gardens, or just in a dish on your windowsill. Do keep in mind that these are aquatic plants, and if you let their water evaporate, they will die.

I had a lovely dish of water fern (salvinia), but it just petered out. I was keeping it in my terrarium under fluorescent light and always had the dish full of water.

Salvinia and azola (another form of water fern) require bright light, including some sun. At the bottom of a terrarium it may be too shaded by other plants. We've had good success growing ours on a sunny windowsill.

When it does grow, divide it into separate dishes if it gets crowded.

SAXIFRAGACEAE   Saxifrage Family

This is a large and varied family with shrubs, trees, and herbaceous plants, edible and nonedible—almost everything except first-rate houseplants.

Saxifraga stolonifera is called hideously "strawberry begonia" and inaccurately "mother-of-thousands." We have found it at most mother of dozens—and pretty slow at that. It has never really done well for us—perhaps because it really prefers cool temperatures.

Astilbe grows well in shade on a balcony in a large pot—but don't let it dry out or you'll lose it.

And that most marvelous genus of shrubs—*hydrangea!*—is in this family, too. Give it a large tub and a protected corner, and it should do quite well outside year round on a part-shaded balcony.

I bought a beautiful hanging basket of piggyback plant, and within a few weeks the whole plant turned *grayish* and brown and just dried up! I went back to the plant store and got no satisfaction at all: he just said I probably overwatered it, but I didn't—I let it go dry between waterings, just as he told me. I'd like to try with piggyback again. What should I do?

First of all, buy your next plant at another store! The plant seller should be just as responsible for bad advice or an unhealthy plant as any other seller of poor merchandise.

Tolmiea menziesii (pickaback plant) is native to the northwest U.S. and southwest Canada, where it seldom freezes but is always cool and damp. Tolmiea is tolerant of almost any light but must have cool temperatures, high humidity, and lots of water.

For best results, grow them as new plants every year—propagating the new plant from the leaves of the old.

They are really not easy houseplants.

I bought some fish emulsion to use on a dracaena and used it on my piggyback. I spilled some on the leaves and it burned them. What can I do?

Almost anything will damage the leaves of *Tolmiea menziesii* (pickaback plant). Remove the damaged leaves and wash the plant off under the shower. But it sounds as if you may have been using the fish emulsion too strong. Use it (and any plant food) at *half* the strength recommended on the label—and, for most plants, half as often, too.

I have a pickaback plant. I have my choice to winter it in a south or a north window. Which would you suggest?

North. The cold (but not freezing) winter temperatures are very beneficial to tolmieas. In fact, your pickaback would probably be happy in that north window year round, provided it's bright.

SCROPHULARIACEAE   Snapdragon or Foxglove or Figwort Family

This is a large family, mostly of North American hardy perennials and annuals—generally cultivated outdoors or in greenhouses.

Calceolaria is the pocketbook plant, and easy enough to start from seed, but a cool-lover, and difficult to manage outside of a greenhouse. Buying one in flower can be most disappointing. They just collapse in the normally low humidity and high temperature of house conditions.

Cymbalaria muralis (Kenilworth ivy) is a delightful little plant, making tiny blue flowers even in part shade. Keep it moist.

Can I grow Mexican foxglove outside of a terrarium? I've lost one, but I'd like to try again.

Tetranema mexicanum (Mexican foxglove; it used to be *Allophyton mexicanum*) is a handsome small plant, about 8 inches at maturity, and freely flowering. It will grow outside of a terrarium if you keep it in moderate humidity and moderately bright light and, most important, keep it constantly moist. If you are an erratic waterer, then do keep it in a terrarium.

SELAGINELLACEAE   Selaginella Family

Again, a family with a single genus, though there are hundreds of varieties.

These are very old plants, survivors of the carboniferous age, and they will survive for you only if you treat them like invalids—keep them constantly moist and in high humidity.

If you have tried to transplant one and found it fulfilling a death wish, next time press the plant more firmly where you want it to root. We have a botanist friend who says selaginella must make good contact with its potting mix to root.

How much humidity does selaginella require?

In Puerto Rico they grow in the rain forest, but for most of us, selaginellas (spike mosses) are terrarium plants.

SOLANACEAE   Nightshade Family

This is a family of striking contradictions: edible fruit and poisonous leaves on the same plants (both tomatoes and potatoes have poisonous foliage). Other members of the family, such as tobacco, are narcotics; others, like petunia, just decorative.

Both tomato (*Lycopersicum esculentum*) and sweet peppers (*Capsicum annuum grossum*) can be grown in tubs on balconies or even on windowsills or under fluorescent lights. There are several decorative and miniature varieties of edible and ornamental peppers (they are all *Capsicum anuum*) which do beautifully indoors if they are provided with enough light and water.

Petunia has done well for us even in quite moderate light—though it threatened to take over an entire windowsill.

Cyphomandra betacea is widely advertised as the tree tomato, but we've never heard anyone brag of the crop he harvested, only of the whitefly that he had to get rid of. Its large leaves are decorative, but it is a bothersome plant.

Browallia is a beautiful little, blue-flowered hanger, and easy to grow.

My Jerusalem cherry made it through the summer and made flowers, but set no fruit. Why?

If the plant was inside, out of the breeze, perhaps the flowers were just not pollinated. We had the same problem. We bought one to show on our TV spot (on care of Christmas gift plants), then cut it back later in the winter. It branched and flowered in the spring, but set no fruit. As soon as the weather was warm enough to open the windows wide, we set it in the open window. There were no insect pollinators, but apparently the wind was enough, because we've got plenty of fruit now.

These plants are in the same family as tomatoes, and they can be pollinated indoors similarly: blowing into the open flowers; shaking the plant; poking the sex parts gently with a brush or cotton swab.

Do be warned that those lovely red fruits are poisonous, and very attractive to kiddies.

What does Jerusalem cherry need?

Moderate (to bright) sun and lots of water.

We have had a great time with our *Solanum pseudocapsicum*

(Jerusalem cherry). It has borne fruit and then germinated literally scores of new plants in the pots all around it. We do have to look out for mealybug and spider mite because these plants are bug-prone. We are looking in June at a 6-inch young darling with two of those yellow-centered white flowers already. We will pinch now for more branching, and the flowers of summer will become the red fruit that decorate our winter holidays.

Keep kids from the fruit, as it is poisonous.

Can you suggest a flowering hanging basket for a sunny window?

Try browallia—it's very lovely and readily produces blue flowers in a sunny window. Keep it pinched for bushy growth. Propagate from seed (it self-seeds readily) or from tip cuttings. Don't allow it to dry out.

THEACEAE   Tea Family

This is a handsome family of useful and ornamental trees and shrubs.

We don't grow *Thea sinensis* (Chinese tea), but we do grow, enjoy, and flower *Camellia japonica* (Japanese camellia). Camellias are quite shallow-rooted, which makes them well suited to pot culture, though they like to have coolish temperatures in the winter months. They do not need full windowsill sun to flower. One of our horticultural friends warns us not to turn our camellias once bud is set, or the buds will "break their necks."

My camellia made all these flower buds, but in spring when they opened, the flowers disappeared and I got only leaves. How could this happen? I didn't see any buds drop or anything.

You didn't have flower buds—you had *leaf* buds all along. Flower buds are fat; leaf buds are thin. Your camellia apparently did *not* set flower buds; perhaps you didn't give it even the modest amount of sun it needs to flower. Or perhaps your winter temperatures were too warm. We grow camellia right up against the glass, where it gets quite cool temperatures during the winter months.

TROPAEOLACEAE   Nasturtium Family

A one-genus family, but that is a delightful genus: tropaeolum (nasturtium).

Why do my nasturtium leaves turn yellow and dry up? I don't have a lot of light, but I understand they don't need much.

They don't need a lot of *sun,* but they will take all the bright light you can give them.

In addition, when was the last time you repotted? This is a fast grower and may have outrooted (so to speak) your pot.

Are you watering well? Nasturtiums take plenty of water, especially in the warm months of summer.

Finally, have you examined for bugs? Aphids are fond of nasturtiums, and a heavy infestation will kill the plant eventually. Take it to the sink and wash the undersides and tops of the leaves.

Aside from these, we can't imagine what the problem might be.

Is there any companion planting I can do on a windowsill? Or is that just for outdoor gardeners?

A lot of companion planting (planting two or more kinds of plants near one another to control insects) is largely for outdoor growers, because a great deal of the benefit of companion planting comes from root exudates: stuff the plant excretes from its roots which goes into the soil and keeps certain problems at bay.

However, one companion plant we've had success with is the common nasturtium. Pots of nasturtium placed among other windowsill plants will tend to attract aphids, but they do reduce the number of aphids on your more "desirable" plants. We put the "desirable" in quotes because for us, nasturtium is a very desirable summer and fall windowsill plant. Not only does it produce many flowers in moderate light and with little care, but the leaves and flowers are *edible.*

Nasturtium seeds are large (and also edible), they sprout quickly, and soon grow into flowering-size plants.

URTICACEAE   Nettle Family

This is a family you should know, especially if you are interested in terrarium plants.

Helxine (baby's-tears) is not a terrarium plant, but pilea and pellionia have varieties that are among the best foliage plants you can grow in a terrarium. Before we leave the wrong impression, pileas do flower readily, but their flowers are so tiny that they are not distinguishable as individual flowers without a magnifying glass.

My baby's-tears looks like hell—straggly and reaching for the light. I thought they were low-light plants.

Nope. *Helxine soleirolii* (baby's-tears) needs bright light, together with ample water and high humidity. It is not easy to keep outside a greenhouse.

My artillery fern is doing lousy in my terrarium. I thought this was a terrarium plant.

When we were in Puerto Rico, visiting the Botanical Gardens of the University of Puerto Rico, we saw *Pilea microphylla* (artillery fern), which is *not* a fern, growing in full sun as a border to a planting of vanda orchids. Now, the pilea was a little pale, indicating that this was a *bit* too much sun, but the leaves were not burning. Try giving your plant the constant moisture and high humidity of a terrarium, but give it much more light.

How much water does *Pilea involucrata* need? Mine seems always wilted. It can't be overwatering, because I let it go quite dry between waterings.

What are you so proud of? Pileas all take nearly constant moisture in a very well-drained soil.

What are those silvery marks on the aluminum plant?

Aluminum. No kidding. The plant (*Pilea cadierei*) can literally take the metal out of the soil and deposit it on its leaves.

VERBENACEAE   Verbena or Vervain Family

Clerodendrum is a very handsome vine in this family, with colorful and long-lasting bracts to its flowers. You can find it variegated or plain green, with white or with purple bracts. It needs moderate humidity and plenty of water to thrive.

Lantana is an excellent genus for houseplant growers, easy to maintain with lots of sun and water, not particularly choosy about humidity, and a year-round free bloomer. Don't hesitate to prune it somewhat for better shape.

Can I grow lantana as a houseplant? Or is it only good as a bedding plant?

Lantana camara is very adaptable—growing quite well in full sun, on a moderately bright windowsill, or under fluorescent lights.

Cut the deadheads off and the plant will branch and the branches will flower. Keep lantanas well washed: they are damnably attractive to whitefly.

Is hanging-basket lantana as easy to grow as the upright form?

Lantana montevidensis, which has a pendant habit, is more difficult to keep sightly and is less free-flowering than *Lantana camara,* the more common form. It will require more frequent and severe grooming and cutting back.

VITACEAE   Grape Family

This is a family of vines. Grapes (vitus) are probably the most important vines in the world. And the best vining foliage houseplants belong to this family too, in the cissus genus. At this moment we are growing six species and a mutation which may turn out to be something important. They are all low-care, attractive, and high-satisfaction plants.

Parthenocissus tricuspidata (Boston ivy) is of course a "grape," not an ivy. It is a deciduous climber, perfectly hardy in all but the very coldest parts of the United States, and perfectly suited to climbing up city walls and buildings.

Why do the leaves of my *Cissus discolor* turn brown and fall off?

Cissus discolor is a lovely vine, but it needs fairly high humidity, warm temperatures, and plenty of water to do well—as well as fairly bright light to bring out the color.

It is closely related to *Cissus rhombifolia* (grape ivy), but it is nowhere near as tolerant of marginal conditions.

Does kangaroo vine need sun?

Cissus antarctica (kangaroo vine) will do very well in bright light, without any direct sun at all. With a little direct sun, it really thrives. In dim light it will hang on by its fingernails—but it will live.

By the way, the more light you give it (or any plant), the more water it will need.

My grape ivy cuttings are slow to root. Why?

Try rooting your *Cissus rhombifolia* (grape ivy) cuttings at a slightly higher temperature and with more light than they now get.

Ours do beautifully in Jiffy-7's (perhaps because they are so easy to keep wet), but still it takes several weeks to get a well-rooted cutting.

Can I control mites on my grape ivy without spraying?

Fill a sink with tepid water and add a tablespoon or so of dishwashing liquid. Cover the soil with a piece of plastic (to hold the soil in), place your hand over the soil, invert, and swish the leaves and stems through the water several times. Wash off the soapy water with clear water.

Repeat at least once a week for a month. *Cissus rhombifolia* (grape ivy) is a tough plant: it can take it.

Why should my grape ivy be losing its leaves? It is in low light, but I keep it well watered.

You could also kick it occasionally. *Cissus rhombifolia* (grape ivy) will survive in low light, if allowed to go *moderately dry* between waterings.

Keeping it wet in low light will encourage root damage and leaf loss. Upgrade the environment. Give it more light *and* a little less water.

My Peruvian grape ivy is starting to grow long and leggy. I keep it in a sunny window (and it gets air circulation, too, so it can't be the temperature). Besides, I'm sure you won't be able to help me because that can't be the real name; it doesn't look like my grape ivy at all.

Appearances are deceiving you. The plant is *Cissus rotundifolia* (Peruvian grape ivy), and it is closely related to your *Cissus rhombifolia* (grape ivy), and it does come from Peru.

As for its current growth pattern, don't worry about it. When the plant gets mature, it starts doing what many of the cissus (and other members of the grape family) do when they get mature. They start to vine. You will no doubt soon see tendrils forming. For best results, give the plant something to vine upon.

Ours have been very tolerant of moderate light and erratic watering.

I would like to have two vines growing on the inside of my window—you know, one growing from each side. I tried scarlet runner bean, but it got too leggy and died out. I don't get much sun. Can you recommend something?

There are two cissuses that we have grown in this way. *Cissus adenopoda* has three-part leaves, a bit hairy, red underneath, and is a strong viner. The name *adenopoda* means "sticky foot," and if wounded it will exude a sticky sap.

Only slightly less vigorous is *Rhoicissus capensis* (oakleaf cissus), with downy leaves.

Provide strings (or even cup hooks), and these plants will make as good an indoor arbor as you can find. And they are both durable houseplants, though susceptible to mealybugs.

We did not provide strings, and both our cissus plants used the rest of our plant collection as climbing posts. That's O.K., until the day you want to move plants to wash the window.

Can you recommend an indoor vine for an east window?

We are very fond of *Cissus adenopoda*. This plant climbs by means of tendrils. It has three-leaflet leaves, olive-green above, reddish below. Very handsome. And very durable.

It will climb a dozen feet in a season.

Truth is, we are crazy about all the cissus plants. This genus of grape-related plants is varied, and full of interesting and desirable houseplants. It ranges from the commonest, such as *Cissus rhombifolia* (grape ivy), to a succulent cissus, *C. quadrangularis,* which looks like a stapelia or other segmented succulent, but also makes ivylike leaves at its nodes. Bizarre, but beautiful.

Will miniature grape ivy take the same care as my regular one?

Cissus striata (miniature grape ivy) is slower-growing and seems more susceptible to rotting out than *Cissus rhombifolia* (grape ivy), so give it more careful watering (allow it to go dry down to a depth of about ½ inch below the soil line). It also demands a higher humidity (about 40 percent) and slightly brighter light. Keep it well pinched, and *Cissus striata* should be quite satisfactory as a houseplant. It is rather slow to propagate from tip cuttings.

I bought a plant with light-green hairy leaves, sort of oak-shaped. I think it's a climber. Does it sound familiar?

Could be *Rhoicissus capensis* (oakleaf cissus), a close relative of the cissus plants (all of which are related to the true grape). This is a moderately strong climber, making a handsome houseplant in a moderately bright window. It is tolerant of erratic care, but susceptible to mealybug.

The tubbed grape vines on my terrace are not fruiting. Can you say why?

We can say several whys. Are they getting enough sun? (They need full sun.) Are they getting enough food? (They are gross feeders and would appreciate plenty of manure and rock phosphate.) Do you prune them back properly in the late winter/early spring? (See *The Pruning Manual,* by L. H. Bailey, for grape pruning.)

Part II ✿ ✿ ✿ ✿
Cultural Notes

Bugs: Friendly and Un-

Not all bugs are insects: insects are *segmented,* that is, their bodies are separated into more or less distinguishable sections. Some of the worst pests in your garden (aside from dogs, cats, and neighbors) are mites, which are not insects but spiders (arachnids).

We have what some of our friends think to be a strange attitude toward bugs. First of all, we don't panic when we see one, or a few. Second, we don't leap to the spray can. (For further discussion about poisons, see the next section: BUG JUICE.)

Whenever possible, we like to use mechanical controls on bugs—that is a fancy way of saying that we crush bugs with our fingers, or we take the afflicted plants to a sink or shower and wash the leaves with water.

But in recent years, our favorite means of bug control in our indoor garden is other bugs. We have found ladybugs to be an efficient, effective, and entertaining way of getting rid of aphids, scale, mealybug, and whitefly—the most common bug pests in the indoor garden. (See APPENDIX for mail-order ladybug sources.)

Don't scream and throw your hands up in the air when you find a bug among your plants. Bugs are not to panic over, they are to *control,* to reduce populations to a harmless level, but not to eradicate from the face of the earth.

My whole houseplant garden is infested with mites and mealybugs, and I'm tempted to throw the whole damned thing out. Before I do, do you have anything to suggest?

If all your houseplants are so bug-infested that everything seems lost, then perhaps the best thing to do *is* to start over again, with new clean plants. But you should know *why* your houseplants became so buggy. Were you careless about bringing in new plants? New plants should be carefully examined for insects and routinely isolated from your healthy houseplants. If you can't isolate them, put them into a plastic bag, until you are certain they are unbugged. Meanwhile, the plastic will keep any bugs from spreading.

Is your environment too warm? Bugs like it warmer than plants do.

Is it too dry? Mites seem to strike most severely in dry air situations.

Are your plants too crowded? Air circulation can be a help in a potentially buggy situation.

What has the general health of your plants been like? Bugs are attracted to sickly and weak plants. Apparently, weak plants give off a gas which attracts bugs. Is your situation too dark? Plants grown too dark make weak growth.

If your plants are growing poorly, you are likely to have bugs, too. Improve your growing conditions and be careful about what you bring into your garden, and even if you should get a bug, it will be easily controlled by washing or swishing through soapy water.

In the meanwhile, if you'd like to try to save your current collection, Pentac is a good control for severe infestations of mite, and Ced-o-flora will control mealybugs. Neither is particularly destructive to you or the environment.

My botanical garden tells me I have nematodes in my potting soil. I've thrown out most of my houseplants, but I have a few large foliage plants I'd like to save, if possible. The garden recommended a chemical, but I can't find it. Do you have a recommendation?

We can repeat to you a formula tested by a botanist and a commercial grower—they both say it works. Soak your plant for four hours (the water should be above the rim of the pot) in a solution of ½ teaspoon chlorine bleach and 1 quart of water.

Don't repeat this "drowning"; it's very hard on the roots.

We'd have the soil checked again after the soaking—to be certain. Prayer doesn't hurt.

I have a lot of little black fruit flies around my plants. What causes them?

What you have is probably fungus gnats. And it's not really much of a problem.

The insects don't eat your plants; rather they feed off decaying organic matter in the soil. The flies you see don't eat at all; it is the younger stage, the maggot stage, that eats—but not roots. (Don't be frightened by the word "maggot"—the maggot stage is a barely visible transparent worm, a fraction of an inch long.) The maggots can be killed by drowning them, using a mixture of 1 teaspoon of chlorine bleach to 1 quart of water. Sink the pot to over the rim in a pailful of this solution and allow it to soak for two or three hours.

But, though the fungus gnats are annoying when they land in your tea, they are not harming you. In fact, you would be amazed at the number of insects living in this world with you, without harming you.

I have found short transparent wireworms in my soil! Are they nematodes?

Our understanding is that there is only one species of nematode large enough to see easily—and that one won't hurt your plants. Harmful nematodes range in size from microscopic to one-tenth of an inch.

You may be looking at the maggots of fungus gnats. Fungus gnats can be eliminated by soaking the pot of soil for a few hours in a tepid solution of 1 teaspoon of chlorine bleach to 1 quart of water.

They aren't much of a problem.

Can I get rid of cyclamen mite without spraying? I have several African violets that are infested (according to the Botanical Garden), but I am sensitive to spray.

Cyclamen mites are sensitive, too. They are cool-lovers and are sensitive to heat. Immerse your entire plants in water at 110°F. for 15 minutes, and that may well do it for you. This hot water treatment won't work for spider mites (red spider).

Cyclamen mites are microscopic, persistent, and highly contagious, so it *might* be best to discard heavily infested plants.

I understand that spider mites are more likely to come if your plants live in a warm and dry atmosphere. Will raising my humidity get rid of them?

No, once established, red spider mites seem as happy in humid as dry conditions. But if you can lower your temperature, that will certainly slow them down. Their life cycle may be eight times as rapid at normal house temperatures like 75°F. as at 55°F.

I have spider mites on my pineapple sage. Is there anything I can do about it? Can I spray?

Before spraying—which would make your herb inedible—try the water torture. Fill a sink with cool soapy water and swish the plant through several times. Then rinse once in clear water. Repeat this every few days until the mites are defeated.

Growing your sage in a cooler place will slow the growth of the mite population.

I have white sticky stuff on my schefflera leaves. What is it and what can I do?

Sounds like mealybug. Remove with alcohol on a cotton swab, repeating every week for a month. In between, wash the plant in the shower (both above and below the leaves) frequently.

Can I spray my coleus with alcohol to get rid of mealybug?

God, no! Alcohol is a real desiccant. To treat the mealies with alcohol, put some on a cotton swab, and touch each white spot or area. And then wash the plant in tepid water afterward.

How can I get rid of mealybug on a gardenia? I tried the thing with alcohol on a Q-tip, but it didn't work.

If it didn't work, it's because you didn't keep after them long enough or often enough.

The alcohol should be applied (just dip the cotton swab into alcohol and touch the mealies) once a week for at least a month—or for as long as you find anything. And remember, young mealybugs are pink and active: it's the adults that are white and still.

Keep after them and you'll win.

Wash off the plant after each treatment.

How do I know if I have root mealybug—and how do I get rid of it?

Suspect root mealybug when growth is slow or distorted even though conditions are good. Unpot the suspected plant and look at its rootball. There will be actual patches of white on the outside of the ball.

The chemical controls are toxic, so we would recommend that you take cuttings and throw away the soil and plant. Check all plants near the affected one and keep them isolated.

Sorry.

Do whiteflies and spider mites lay eggs on furniture?

Not as far as we know—but mealybugs will breed in the cracks in pots, or in saucers—they are that dumb. But they've been around a long time, so how dumb can they be?

What would you recommend for scale on a Calamondin orange?

A thorough shower under warm (not hot) water, followed by massage. That is, gently rub the scaly places between thumb and forefinger. They will come off readily under the water. But you'll have to repeat the treatment every week until you see no more—and then keep an eye on the plant lest more should develop. Especially watch the stems; the brown of the scales matches the brown of the stems.

I have hard small brown bugs that don't move on my asparagus fern. What are they and what can I do about them? Under a magnifying glass they look like tiny turtle shells.

We wish all gardeners owned magnifying glasses as part of their basic equipment: it makes bug identification much easier.

You have scale—a piercing insect. For a bad case you may want to spray with Ced-o-flora. One spraying will often nail scale, but keep an eye out for a return infestation. If you've caught it early, you won't have to spray again. Fill a sink (or a tub, if it's a big plant) with warm water with some mild dishwashing liquid (don't use a laundry detergent) mixed in. Invert the pot and swish the foliage through the water several times. Keep your hand spread over the soil to hold that in.

After several swishes, reach in and gently rub at the scale with your fingers—they should come off.

Rinse with clear water. Repeat the washing a week later.

My orange tree has sticky stuff on the leaves. Is this natural?

It's natural for the scale insects causing it, but not for the orange. Swish it in warm soapy water (dishwashing detergent) and rub away the scale (they look like tiny turtle shells). If you must spray, Ced-o-flora is very effective against scale and not harmful to people.

What can I do about aphids on my African violets?

Saintpaulias (African violets) are not the preferred food for aphids, so we would strongly suggest you check your other plants for these bugs.

Take your African violets to the sink and wash them under a vigorous spray of tepid water. Be sure you cover the soil with some plastic, to keep the aphids from being washed back onto the soil.

This spraying should get rid of most of the adults. Repeat after a week—and every week until they are all gone.

If you are growing your African violets under fluorescent lights, you should seriously consider releasing ladybugs into your setup. They love to eat aphids.

I have bugs on my coleus. They look like aphids, but they are almost black. What should I do?

Aphids come in many colors. Just wash them off as you would their green cousins or let ladybugs eat them.

Can I use a systemic insecticide to get rid of a huge infestation of aphids?

We don't use systemics, and haven't used them. But we understand they take several weeks to work. Also, we have received complaints of plants slowing their growth after being treated with a systemic. Why not wash the plants at the sink? Aphids wash off readily. Or, if the plants are too big to bring to the sink or shower, hose them off in place. Or, if you are determined to use a spray, use Ced-o-flora which doesn't hurt anybody but bugs.

All the plants in one of my windows have this insect! When I water, these tiny pink bugs *jump into the air*—if you can believe it? What are they and how can I get rid of them?

Congratulations, you've got springtails, probably the most prevalent bug for indoor growers. But it is not an insect—it is a proto-insect, and insects may have evolved from them. They don't eat plants; they live on decaying organic matter in the soil. They spread easily through water that might come out the bottom of the pot when watering.

You can often get rid of them by soaking the pot in tepid water above the rim with some chlorine bleach in it (1 tablespoon to 1 gallon of water). Let the plant soak for a few hours.

Never do this to cacti and other succulents; and don't do it to any plant more than once every few months. After all, repeated overwatering can be more harmful to your plants than these rather harmless primitive creatures.

I have springtails in my windowbox planter. How can I get rid of them?

That is tough. Unless you want to poison them—and what's the point? They are not harming your plants. Try living with them for now, and next time you replant the box, use all new soil, and clean out the box with a solution of 9 parts hot water and 1 part chlorine bleach.

Or, if you can remove the windowbox from its brackets, prepare a solution of 1 tablespoon chlorine bleach to every gallon of tepid water in a bathtub, and set the box in so the soil is completely submerged. Allow the whole thing to soak for about six hours. But under no circumstances repeat the treatment, because this drastically overwaters your plants.

I have whitefly on my closed-in terrace. I can't spray because it opens onto my kitchen. Is there anything I can do?

If your terrace drains, by all means hose down the plants daily—especially under the leaves—with a strong fine mist spray. Whiteflies shed water, but the frequent hosing will reduce the numbers. Also, these serious pests are attracted to the color yellow. Put out yellow plastic pails coated with undiluted dormant oil. They will fly to the yellow, stick there, and die.

Ladybugs are a help: they will chomp on the eggs and young.

Use *either* the pail or the ladybugs, because the dormant oil will kill the ladybugs too.

I have these little white flying things on lantana and tomatoes on my balcony. Under a magnifying glass they look like tiny moths. There are also little transparent things (I think they are bugs, but they don't move). What can I do?

You've got one of the most serious problems a home gardener can have—whitefly (adult and nymph stages). And they love tomato and lantana (they also love basil and fuchsia).

If you choose to spray with a poison, there is a synthetic pyrethrum available which will get rid of whitefly in one application, but it is a real poison (unlike the real pyrethrums, which are not harmful to people). It is also quite expensive and not widely available.

Malathion or preparations containing pyrethrum and rotenone will kill the adults, but not the eggs, and so you will have to spray at least twice, five days apart (three times would be better). You see, one reason whiteflies are such a problem is that their life cycle is so fast: they can go from egg to mature adult in five days.

We have gotten rid of them on some plants by taking the plant to the sink (slowly, or they will just fly away) in the bathroom and washing it under cool water. Most of the adults fly to the light bulb, where they burn themselves to death (they *are* moths, you see) or to the bathroom mirror, where they are squished by hand. Frequent repetition will get rid of them.

Do this only on a cool and dull day (or time of day) —the whiteflies are relatively inactive then.

If all of these sound like too much to handle, throw the plants out. As we said, whiteflies are a very serious problem.

I have ants in my plants (ha!). My wife says get rid of them, but they don't really eat plants, do they?

You will be laughing from the other side of your compost heap when the scale, aphids, and mealybugs spread by the ants start to destroy your plants.

Ants are farmers; they plant these sucking insects and harvest the "honeydew" the plants secrete when pierced by the bugs. No, ants don't eat plants, but they are a real source of trouble.

We use round ant traps—we set them up on the ants' routes (they follow specific routes to and from places), and they seem to work without spraying.

I do believe I have some problems. The leaves of some of my plants are looking twisted and grayish, and I've seen these tiny black insects running around the leaves very fast. It's difficult to get a good look, but they are thin and shiny. Finally, there are some small black dots on the backs of my leaves—like a shiny scale. Can you help me?

First of all, you don't have several problems, you have only one—but that is enough: thrips.

They are not a common house pest, though they are common in greenhouses. The black spots are egg cases; the twisting and loss of color are caused by the adults.

You'll have to spray or discard the plants. When mature, thrips grow wings and will fly to your other plants.

Malathion, sprayed by label directions and repeated once, should get rid of them.

The next thing is to stop buying from the greenhouse that sold you the thrips.

I have roaches on my plants. Are they hurting the plants? How can I get rid of them?

Roaches don't do serious damage to your plants, but they will take nips out of growing tips, and this of course will lead to large holes later on.

We have had fair success with roach traps; and with boric acid left around a low saucer of water (the roaches track through the boric acid, then clean their limbs and poison themselves). We've also had plaster of paris recommended similarly.

Good sanitation (removal of dead leaves from the plant and soil) helps.

I never had roaches until I started a fluorescent-light garden; now what can I do?

Roaches *are* attracted to warm, wet places, such as light gardens tend to be, but if your sanitation is good (fallen leaves picked up, dying parts groomed away, soil removed from the surface of the trays), they don't seem much of a problem. At any rate, they are not breeding under your lights: find their nest and deal with them there. [See previous question.]

I'm having trouble with aphids and mealybugs in my fluorescent-light herb garden. I wash them off and alcohol the mealies, but they come back. I don't want to spray. Is there anything I can do?

Why don't you do what we did: use ladybugs. They really work under fluorescent lights. (See APPENDIX for sources.)

Conventional wisdom says ladybugs eat only aphids, but our experience is that they will eat any bug or bug egg they can stumble over.

Will ladybugs do a number on whitefly?

They will eliminate a small infestation, but nothing major. They cannot catch flying adults at all, but they will eat nymphs and eggs.

Ladybugs are dynamite against aphids and good with mealybugs.

Ladybugs have to stumble over something edible before they know it's food—and their eating of eggs and slow-moving nymphs can really keep a bug population down.

Can I use ladybugs to control bugs indoors?

Under lights, ladybugs are very effective. On a windowsill, much less so. They are attracted to the light and breezes and will fly out the open windows.

Are earthworms beneficial to houseplants?

Absolutely not! As helpful as they are in the outdoor garden, that is how destructive they can be in potted plants.

Earthworms tunnel through the garden soil, breaking it down and aerating it, and enriching it with their castings. In a pot, those same worms will create air pockets and make mud of the soil—both of which will damage your plant's roots.

We have spiders in our windowsill garden, and the webs tend to drive my husband berserk. He says they are eating the plants. I say they are eating the bugs that eat the plants.

You are right, so long as they are garden spiders, not tiny spider mites.

Garden spiders are flesh eaters—the flesh of insects, that is. But they do not eat a great deal. You would have to have *many* spiders for real pest control.

However, they do no harm; your husband is being unreasonable, and have you ever considered divorce?

I'm beside myself! I brought home several plants from a botanical garden plant sale and some extra soil. I mixed the soil with my own and potted into it. And now I see the soil has these round insect eggs in it! They are cream-colored, perfectly round, the biggest are about one-eighth inch across and the smallest about half that size. What can I do? I feel like suing the garden.

Don't sue—*that is fertilizer, not bugs.* The eggs of insect pests are not of that size or that roundness. What you have is a time-release fertilizer put in by the garden. Relax.

Bug Juice

We learned our gardening in an apartment, not an outside garden. Perhaps if our primary experience had been outdoors we'd have a different attitude toward poisons. After all, you can spray outdoors and then come indoors, and if the wind is right, the insecticides are not likely to contaminate you. In an apartment, where do you go to hide? The same is true for all indoor growing situations, not just apartments. If you spray indoors, the spray stays with you. If you spray outdoors and bring the plants inside, you bring the spray inside.

Early on in our gardening life, Stan sprayed with a nicotine spray (nicotine is a "natural" derivative from tobacco—but very poisonous). He was not careless: he did wear gloves and covered his face—though he failed to use a respirator. And he got sick from it.

Look, we can't say "never spray" to you. There may be times when it is a matter of spray or lose your collection. What we must say to you is that poison sprays should be your last line of defense against an unmanageable bug population—not your first choice. Shower your plants under water to wash off some bugs—especially mites and aphids. Go after bugs on the bottoms of leaves with your fingers—don't be too squeamish to squeeze. Use ladybug beetles (as we suggested in the previous section). Use flypaper strips—they may not be beautiful, but they can get a lot of fungus gnats and whiteflies. (There are other specific suggestions in this section.)

We grow plants, in part, to enrich our own immediate indoor environment. We feel we can damage that indoor environment only as a last resort.

I had aphids on my dracaena and sprayed it with an aerosol. Now it looks worse. Do aphids cause some other kind of disease? Should I spray one more time?

No—spray one *less* time.

First: *never* use an aerosol spray—the gas that propels the spray can really damage the plant close up.

Second: don't use an all-purpose spray—it treats a plant for problems it hasn't got and can *cause* problems.

Third: unless you absolutely must, don't use a premixed spray. Mix up the amount of spray you need for the problem you have, use it, and then throw away the leftovers.

And, last: why use a poison for aphids? They wash off with a stiff spray of water in the shower or at the sink.

In the meanwhile, reduce watering a little, pull it a *bit* out of the sun (if it has any sun), and mist the leaves frequently with tepid water.

What's the proper way to use a spray-can insecticide?

The proper way is to not use it at all.

Close enough to do good, the propellant can damage the plant. Far enough away not to do harm, you spray the whole world. Besides, spray cans are very suspect for what the propellants might be doing to you and to the environment.

Can I use Ced-o-flora as a dip?

No. It can harm your plant that way. In fact, you can't even spray too heavily. We did once, and the insecticide flowed down the leaves to the axils and *killed the plant*. Perhaps the oil base smothered the plant.

I sprayed with malathion according to the strength recommended on the label, but it seems to have damaged leaves on several of my plants. Why should that be?

Many insecticides can damage specific plants or genera. Read past the instructions and you'll see the warning about plants to stay away from.

Cut back the damaged parts. And do take note of which plants they are for next time.

Is it really dangerous to handle insecticide?

A study has shown that a wide range of insecticides persists on the hands of people who handle them for anywhere from a week to two years. So, just washing doesn't remove an insect poison from your hands.

Now, just how harmful that is to you, we can't say, but it certainly gives you pause to think.

I noticed a funny smell on my hands after planting my onion sets. Do they exude something?

The smell was probably fungicide (onion sets from nonorganic sources are usually treated with fungicide) .

Wash your hands well after handling onion sets—and don't eat the sets. Next time, work with disposable gloves or, at least, launderable work gloves.

Are rotenone and pyrethrum effective against spider mites?

Not really. Mites are not insects; they are arachnids. We use frequent washings for spider mite, or Pentac (a specific for mites, hence a miticide) in serious cases. Pyrethrum and rotenone, a good organic combination, are *insecticides* and will kill adult mites but not their eggs.

Many insecticides kill the *predators* of mites, and so can make your mite problem worse.

Composting—
Turning Garbage to Gold

One big problem in our modern industrial life is that we are a waste-producing society, both on a national and on a personal level. Composting makes you part of the solution.

Composting has always been thought of in terms of large piles of manure and leaves, and a person in bib overalls and a red bandanna pitchforking around. The picture may be valid, as far as it goes. Where it doesn't go is to the small compost bin that the indoor gardener can have on a balcony or fire escape (one of our NBC makeup men had his on a fire escape until he outgrew it and moved it up to the roof), and especially inside in a basement, on a closed porch, or in an apartment.

If you've read *The Apartment Gardener* and found no mention of composting (you would be amazed at how often we get that complaint over the telephones at WRVR-FM), that's because when we wrote *The Apartment Gardener,* we had that same parochial image of composting (and perhaps a little feeling that all composters were a little odd).

We have not bought a package of soil for four years now. We recycle all our vegetable wastes—we have the smallest garbage can in our building, and we feel that we are making a contribution.

Try composting—you'll like the soil it gives you and the feelings as well.

You've often mentioned living in an apartment, but in a magazine article you wrote that you had a compost heap. Do you have it on your balcony? My wife and I are apartment gardeners with a balcony, and the idea is intriguing.

We do live in an apartment and we do have a compost heap—but it's inside, not on our balcony. (Our "balcony" is 18 inches deep; an extended windowsill, really.)

But you can have a compost bin on your balcony. Provided your neighbors don't complain. (One friend of ours had hers in a large plastic garbage pail, and the neighbors complained that she was keeping garbage on her balcony. She had to remove it.)

The principles of composting are the same, however, indoors or out, so we'll describe our indoor compost bin (which we keep in a small spare room), and you can make your own adaptation.

We use a commercial compost bin made by Rotocrop. It is made of plastic and works quite well; but you can make your own out of ½-inch hardware cloth and 6-mil polyethylene (or its equivalent) plastic, winding up with a tubular bin about 24 inches across and 36 inches to 40 inches tall, with a "door" that swings out at the bottom. Indoors your bin needs no cover, but outdoors, if in a location that gets a lot of rain, you may want to figure on a cover as well.

Buy your materials: a piece of ½-inch hardware cloth 100 inches long (this will give you a 24-inch cylinder plus a 24-inch piece left over for the bottom) by 36 or 48 inches wide (depending on what you can find: if you are a person with short arms, you'll want the shorter height and may have to cut it down); and a piece of 6-mil plastic 6 feet long (it comes in 10-foot widths). You will also need cloth tape, cutting pliers, and rustproof wire.

Cut 2 feet off the hardware cloth and roll the remaining 76 inches into a cylinder (fasten it closed with some wire in two or three places). Cover the top and bottom edges with two thicknesses of the cloth tape (this is for safety—it has nothing to do with the compost), and set the cylinder aside. Cut off a 6-by-3-foot strip of plastic, fold it into a 3-foot square, and lay it on the floor, where your bin is to rest. This will keep water and damp compost off your wooden floor.

Set four bricks on edge on the plastic protector, within a 2-foot circle: these will serve to keep the bottom of your bin off the floor and permit some air circulation.

Cut a 2-foot hardware cloth bottom for your bin (this will not be attached) and place it on the bricks. Stand the cylinder and place it over the bottom (this does not have to be a very close fit). You're getting there.

Take the remaining plastic and cut out dozens of 2-inch holes (again, these will allow for air circulation). Line the inside of the bin with the holey plastic and cut away where it overlaps.

Now, with your cutters, cut a door into the side of the bin where it meets the bottom; it should extend about 10 inches above the bricks and be about 10 inches wide (cut it out completely, tape the edges for safety, cut a corresponding flap into the plastic, then wire the door back into place).

You have a plastic-lined metal cylinder, sitting on a doubled square of plastic, with a bottom and a door, and you are ready to compost.

There are really two important principles in composting: alternate the layers of materials and don't make any one layer too thick (a layer is "too thick" when it refuses to decompose rapidly).

Let's build a compost pile.

Start with a 2- or 3-inch-thick layer of vegetable wastes (lettuce or cabbage leaves, say, or lawn clippings). Cover this with a thin layer (¼ inch) of sawdust. Add an inch, say, of used potting soil, which you cover with a dusting of bone meal and a thin layer of dried cow manure. Now add a couple inches of ground-up leaves and twigs, and another layer of sawdust. Now a couple inches more of lettuce leaves or grass clippings or something else quick-rotting, and cover with sawdust. (Lettuce leaves are available in great quantities in front of supermarkets an hour before opening—waiting for the garbage collector; we have never had difficulty getting free sawdust from local carpentry shops.)

By now you get the point. Your heap is layered—and never a thick layer of any one thing. If you have lots of a single material, put it in several layers with soil or sawdust or manure or *something* in between.

Lettuce composts quickly, leaves compost slowly, solid twigs very slowly.

We always compost the hair from our brushes (Floss seems to have more of that than Stan does); coffee grounds or tea leaves, banana skins and corncobs are great.

Allow eggshells to dry very well and then crush them before adding them.

We use no meat at all in the heap because meat fats decompose slowly and they are attractive to creatures. Some fish leftovers will be a welcome addition, though, if you bury them in the heap and cover with sawdust.

By the way, unless you leave material rotting on the surface of your heap, your compost heap will have no smell at all, except the pleasant smell of the earth. Every time you put something on the heap, cover it with a little bit of sawdust or used soil, and you'll have no offensive smell.

Seaweed is a marvelous addition to the heap, when you can collect it (no need to wash it off).

Water your pile lightly after a week (you want to keep it damp, but not sopping wet), and then turn it (that is, mix it up so that the bottom material is closer to the top) with a trowel.

When you turn the heap, don't be surprised that it feels hot inside. This is an indication that the composting action (bacterial decay) is going on. If you feel no heat, then perhaps your heap is either too dry or too wet.

Your first compost should be ready to come out in about a month. Lift the door and the plastic flap, and trowel out your compost. You'll have to pasteurize your compost before using it indoors, because it will have weed seeds and bugs in it (see next question), but the rich growing material you have *made* is worth the small trouble.

Remember, every bit of "garbage" you compost instead of throwing away keeps the world just that much less polluted.

God loves the composter.

I want to sterilize my compost for use as a potting soil, but I'm afraid to use my oven because I've read that it smells so. Is there a chemical I can use?

Don't use chemicals for sterilization. You don't want sterile soil; soil should be alive—even for your houseplants. You want *pasteurized* soil: soil that has been raised to a temperature of 180° to 200°F. (no hotter) and held there for thirty minutes.

This relatively low temperature is high enough to destroy the tuberculosis bacillus, as was discovered by Louis Pasteur, and incidentally high enough to kill weed seed and most soil-borne pests.

The secret of keeping the smell at a minimum is to keep the temperature low and to take a long time to raise the soil temperature to 180°. It can take as long as an hour to get the soil to 180° this way, but it has very little smell.

We pasteurize our soil in a lasagna pan (a deep and large roasting pan). We heap the soil as high as we can safely, mound it in the center like a meatloaf, and stick a meat thermometer into the middle.

Why should I have to pasteurize compost?

Even compost made indoors (as ours is) contains insects, insect eggs, and weed seed (not to mention green pepper seeds, cantaloupe seeds, etc.). These may be irrelevant in the outdoor garden, but they can destroy your houseplants.

Can I use my compost directly from pasteurization, or must I lighten it?

Fill a pot with your compost, then water it. If the water drains through rapidly, then it is light enough. If the water sits on the surface and soaks through slowly, you should add a lightener. We make our potting mix of 2 parts pasteurized compost to 1 part coarse perlite.

Does compost need nutritional additives?

That depends on what you put into it. A well-balanced compost needs no additives (except perhaps for a lightener), but indoors it's tough to have a well-balanced compost.

If you don't use eggshells (and/or bone meal) for calcium on your heap, and wood ashes for potash, we would suggest you add those to your potting mix directly, though composting such mineral sources first makes the minerals more quickly available to your plants.

I have gotten flies on my compost heap. What can I do? Do you ever get flies?

Flies are attracted to the rotting vegetable material. They probably mean that you have not adequately covered the top layer of stuff with soil or sawdust or some other nonvegetable material. The only time we attracted flies was when we forgot to sprinkle sawdust over some rotten tomatoes we'd added to the heap.

Hang a flypaper strip over the bin, and that will do wonders. Also, they've got this terrific new thing for killing flies without poisons and without electricity and without any use of fuel: it's called a fly swatter.

I am planning to start an indoor compost heap, and what I seem to have mostly is clothes that no longer fit me and a lot of newspapers. Can I get rid of them by composting?

Small amounts of cloth and paper can be added to your compost bin, especially if they are shredded into thin strips and not allowed to form layers. The problem is that both cloth and paper are very slow to decompose, and, if allowed to form a layer, won't decompose at all and will hinder free passage of water in the heap.

If you want to recycle, give the clothes to Goodwill and the papers to a recycling plant. You stick to more rapidly decomposing stuff like food wastes and grass clippings.

Can I put my compost bin on the roof? Will I run into any special problems up there?

Do you mean aside from an irate landlord?

Yes, you can compost quite easily on a rooftop. It's just like composting on ground level. The only problem you are likely to encounter is water balance. Outdoors, your heap will be rained upon. If you cover it (recommended) you keep the rain out. Too much rain can cause the bacteria to stop working. But if you keep the rain out you must make arrangements for watering the heap, and this may be a problem on a rooftop. We know several growers who compost successfully on rooftops, both in a compost bin and in a compost heap without a real bin.

Come winter, you will find the heap doesn't really freeze (if it is big enough); its interior heat keeps it thawed. But it does work more slowly.

☞   ☞   ☞   ☞

Feeding, Overfeeding, and Food Elements

Since we have been potting into our homemade compost, we feed less than we used to. And even when we fed more, we always fed less than the manufacturers recommended on their package instructions. Most plant foods must have had their recommended dosages standardized on heavy feeders like African violets (saintpaulias), because they are just too much for the majority of the houseplants we grow.

Or, perhaps, those recommended rates were for plants growing in greenhouses. Plants in more vigorous growth can take more food. Plants growing in most of the indoor environments we've seen want a minimum of plant food.

Of course, there is the question of why feed at all, especially if you are growing in a mix with soil in it. Doesn't the soil provide all the nutrients a plant needs? Yes and no.

If your soil mix is well made, when you pot the plant into it, it will contain all the nutrients that a plant needs—especially if you have used a number of ingredients, all of which provide different food elements. As soon as you water, however, the nutrients are dissolved in the water (which is how the plant uses them) and much of it is washed out the bottom hole. Outdoors, these nutrients come back through percolation, but indoors they are leached out, never to return, leaving the plant, eventually, in want of a nutrient or nutrients.

Feeding helps to replace these washed-out nutrients.

Outdoors, we use only organic elements in our soil, because we are concerned with the effect of chemical fertilizers running off into local rivers and streams. Indoors, it is difficult to maintain a food balance organically by feeding. Many of the organic food additives are slow to break down and become available to the plant (it may be last year's bone meal feeding the plant this year). The problem could be solved, in a way, by frequent repotting into your organically enriched potting soil, but potting plants before they need it can make for more problems than it might solve.

All this is by way of leading up to the fact that we use water-soluble chemical plant foods indoors. In pots, there is little (if any) effect on the environment, and the plants get their needed supplements.

Growers who use soilless mixes for their plants scorn the idea of organic soil amendments at all. They are trying to avoid the organic, and must feed their plants with every watering (at a much reduced rate).

Plants need very little food. In a university study, it was found that in the course of a year, a *tree* used only *two ounces* of actual nutrients. We feed more than two ounces in the course of a year because most of our food is dribbled out the bottom of the pot.

As to the time-release fertilizers, we seldom use them, but we know a number of excellent growers who swear by them.

If you are interested in them, why not try a bit on one or two plants (not your favorites), and see how that works.

Which is good advice for any plant food you are considering. Don't rush into a wholesale program of feeding because it looks good on paper (or on television). Try it: you may not like it.

My wax begonias are rotting at the soil line.

Two possibilities leap to mind. A soil-line injury allows a fungus to enter; the area is wet down every time you water, and the fungus rots right through the stem.

Or, perhaps fertilizer salts at the soil line are cutting through your stem. This is especially likely if your *Begonia semperflorens* has been in the same soil a long time.

Take cuttings from what remains of the plant, and start over with new plants. Wax begonias come rapidly from tip cuttings.

My gloxinia leaves have drooped and are dying. There is a hard white mold on the soil, and it looks as if something has taken a bite out of the stem at the soil line. What can I use against the mold? And what kind of bug takes a chunk out of a stem?

No kind of insect. And that isn't mold, either. You have a buildup of mineral salts, which have eaten through the stem.

Remove the gloxinia (*Sinningia speciosa* hybrid) tuber from the soil and repot into fresh soil and a clean pot.

Sometimes these salts build up from the soil, sometimes from your fertilizer. Are you using a time-release fertilizer? Are you watering from the bottom? Are you overfeeding? Are you too long in the same soil?

Change some of your ways, or your problem will repeat itself.

I love to use clay pots with my African violets, but when the leaves touch the pot rim they yellow, then die. Is there anything I can do? I hate the look of plastic.

The leaf loss is caused by mineral salts which soak right into the clay pot and damage the leaf. We've solved the problem by waxing the rim of clay pots before we put African violets (saintpaulias) into them. Melt some candle wax in a metal dish and brush the wax over the rim in a generous layer with a cheap paintbrush (it's then ruined for anything else).

I have a white mold on the side of several of my clay flower pots—should I use a fungicide?

Lord, no. That's not a fungus, that is an accumulation of fertilizer salts. It's quite normal, especially when plants have been in their pots a long time, and it is generally not harmful.

Are you feeding a lot? Slow down. Some of that salty crust will wash or scrape away.

There is a hard white fungus on the surface of my soil and on my pots. What can I use to get rid of it?

A teaspoon.

That doesn't sound like a fungus but like a deposit of mineral salts. These salts are present in the soil (and any fertilizer you may use) and are released by the water. Scrape it away with that teaspoon. It will return eventually, but you can scrape again. Do get rid of it. Those salts can cut right through a soft plant stem at the neckline.

A number of my houseplants are showing a yellow edge. What could be causing that?

Fluorine—if your water is fluoridated. Allow your water to stand overnight in an open bucket before watering; this will allow some of the gases to evaporate off. Boiling water (*and allowing it to cool well*) before watering evaporates even more.

How do you feel about using slow-release fertilizers?

We know a few good growers who use them successfully by including the fertilizer in their basic soil mixes, so they obviously work for some.

But there can be problems: the pellets come with a dusting of the plant food on the outside, and this can give the plant a quick "jolt" at the beginning that can be harmful; with the food in the soil, you have extra fertilizer salts released with every watering, which means you cannot leach your soil with clear water, because the food is always present; if it is in the form of plastic-covered pellets, the plastic stays in the soil; and, finally, there are times of year when we don't want to feed our plants—if the food lasts for six months, it takes a great deal of forethought to *not* renew the food for several months before the plant requires the lighter diet.

Is whale emulsion as good a food as fish emulsion?

We don't use whale food at all—or any other whale products. These majestic creatures are endangered, and we won't contribute to their persecution.

How and what do I feed my bromeliads? I have two aechmeas, two cryptanthuses, and a neoregelia. The cryptanthuses have no vases, so where do I put the food?

Do not feed your bromeliads in their vases: you can severely damage your plants that way. However, do feel free to use feed on the potting mix. One feeding a month at half label strength would do well. Current thinking among bromel growers is that an occasional feeding is beneficial.

What should I feed my Cavendish banana? I want to encourage it to flower.

We don't know if it will flower for you at all, but the Bermudians swear by rain-washed seaweed as the best food for dwarf bananas (*Musa nana,* also known as *Musa cavendishii*) . *You* might try seaweed emulsion instead.

What should I feed my palms?

Dilute fish emulsion—they are light feeders.

I'm certain the numbers on plant foods have a meaning, but what? Or don't I need to know?

You need to know. And you need to know that a good plant food has *two* sets of numbers, one on the back and one on the front.

The front numbers (shown as three numbers joined by dashes, such as 15–30–15) represent the percentages (absolute, not relative) of nitrogen, phosphorus, and potassium the food contains. In the example, the numbers add up to 60 percent, which means that the product you've bought is 60 percent food (and 40 percent nonfood and trace elements—which we're now coming to).

On the back of the box, shown in decimal figures or percentages, is a list of minerals ("iron .027%" etc). These represent the *trace elements* in the food, and usually add up to less than 1 percent of the total—but trace elements are important.

A 15–30–15 plant food is a good formulation for flowering plants—and so are all formulas with the same proportions (5–10–5, 1–2–1, 14–28–14). A high-nitrogen food like fish emulsion has a formula (5–1–1, 5–2–2) which is good for foliage plants.

Orchid plants growing in fir bark want a food in the proportions of 20–10–10, 30–10–10.

We are distressed nowadays to see high-priced premixed plant foods. They promise that you won't suffer from fertilizer burn if you use them. And you sure won't. They are so dilute that they are about 97 percent water. What you really are paying for is water and a lot of packaging.

I read about N–P–K in houseplant books. What does N–P–K mean?

    N stands for Nitrogen
    P stands for Phosphorus
    K stands for Potassium

These are the three major elements of plant nutrition, and the bulk of the available food in any plant fertilizer.

If I have included bone meal in my cactus soil mix, should I still add some as a plant food?

Bone meal tends to wash out somewhat with watering. Also, it takes months to dissolve enough to be available to the plant as food. Finally, bone meal is about the only thing you can feed a plant without any fear of burning it.

So, yes, by all means scratch a teaspoonful into the surface of your 6-inch pot every six months or so. Bone meal is the best food for your cacti.

You've said you needn't feed newly potted plants. But what's the soonest I can feed?

Plants cannot take up nutrition from their roots until about two weeks after repotting. But we don't feed for the first two or three months after a potting, because the fresh soil has plenty of food.

Can I provide iron for my plants by letting an iron nail rust in the soil?

Very little of the iron in iron oxide (rust) is available to plants. Get a plant food containing "chelated iron" if your plants need iron.

I think I overfed my kentia palm. Several of the fronds are getting a streaky yellow.

That sounds like overfeeding, all right. Set the plant up where it can drain readily into a tub or something and water it slowly about five times the usual amount of tepid water, even after the water comes pouring out the bottom. Allow the plant to drain well and keep the leaves well misted.

Repeat this leaching for the next several waterings. Cut off the damaged leaves; they won't heal.

Really, what's the big deal about pH? After all, there is very little difference between a pH of 6.5 and one of 6.7 or even 7, isn't there?

We love questions like that because they show how smart we are.

On the pH scale, the differences progress logarithmically. A pH of 6 indicates a soil *ten times* as acid as one at pH 7. So, yes, there is a big difference between pH 6.5 and 6.7. Ask your plants.

Can we use seaweed we gather from the shore on our houseplants?

Seaweed is probably the most complete food material you can feed to plants, and a number of prepared seaweed emulsions are on the market.

Seaweed is a dynamite addition to your compost heap—for indoor *or* outdoor growing.

And you can get some benefit from it by just cutting it up and mixing it into houseplant soil or even laying it on top of the soil as a mulch. Better yet, try grinding it in the blender with some water, and then stirring the liquid thoroughly into some potting soil.

If you have access to a lot of seaweed, perhaps that can serve as an excuse to start an indoor or outdoor compost heap. By the way, seaweed you harvest from the ocean is richer than what you gather from the shoreline. Exposure to sun and drying reduces its nutritive value somewhat. (But it's still great.)

Humidity–
It May Not Be the Heat

Humidity, the moisture in the air, is little understood as a factor in plant well-being and seldom recognized as a factor in plant problems. Why are people fully able to accept that a plant is in trouble from a bug or disease, but unwilling to allow that their problem is humidity—something that is quite within their reach to improve?

During the warm months, humidity is usually high enough—except in continually arid regions. In fact, if the days are dull and the air very moist, fungus problems can arise from too high humidity. A little sun usually remedies that.

But during the heating months, the humidity nose-dives. The outdoor air is somewhat drier in winter. Taking that air and heating it—as we must for our own comfort—makes it even drier: too dry for plants and people. (A few people have humidification systems attached to their heating units, so air is moistened while being warmed; they are the smart ones.)

The surface of a leaf is like a little humidifier. The leaf gives off water vapor into the air just around itself, working to create a balance on both sides of the leaf membrane. If the humidity is high, the leaf works at a casual pace and little water is drawn up from the roots. If humidity is low, it draws more and more water from the roots. But a leaf is not a pump. The water rises only so fast. When water transpires at a faster rate than it can be replaced, the leaf burns and eventually that leaf is lost. (Usually, the leaf parts farthest from the circulatory system show such damage first: the tips or the margins.)

This shouldn't sound unfamiliar: your own mucous membranes keep your tissues moist similarly—your throat and nasal passages especially. Do you wake up of a winter morning with your nose hurting and your throat sore? You've lost a leaf—or at least been slightly damaged in the struggle to keep your membranes moist.

There are plants that are resistant to low humidity: cacti, because they have so little leaf surface; bromeliads; pandanus; sansevierias, aspidistra; euphorbias. But most other plants are damaged by low humidity. The damage may be a brown leaf tip (as in the case of dracaena), brown edges (as in the case of spathiphyllum), or the death of the whole plant (as with rex begonias).

If you don't give a damn about yourself or your shrinking wood furniture or wood floors (wood is damaged by low humidity, too), and you can't humidify your growing area, grow plants resistant to low humidity or grow your plants in a terrarium—there the humidity is maintained in that small space and the plants thrive.

But if you can, do raise your humidity. And don't just kid yourself that you have no problem. If your heat goes on, your humidity goes down.

Don't just take our word: buy a simple hygrometer to measure your humidity. You'll be shocked into investing in a humidifier or having pebble trays made to fit your radiators and windowsills (old refrigerator trays work just fine with a thick layer of gravel or perlite in the bottom).

As a final word, yes, misting is better than nothing.

Is it really necessary to have higher humidity in the winter?

Higher than you had last winter? You bet—unless you don't care about your plants, your nasal membranes, your wood furniture, and your floors.

The winter humidity in a cold climate can be as low as 6 percent for long stretches. Even cacti have trouble at that relative humidity.

Can I cover my light garden with plastic to raise the humidity?

Yes—and that is one solution to the low-humidity problem in a light garden. But there are two dangers.

An unvented plastic cover will hold in *heat* as well as humidity. And without air circulation, you may find yourself getting fungus problems.

Vent the plastic by punching holes high up, near the tubes, and use a very small whisper fan right in the light tray. This will achieve a compromise: the plastic will raise the humidity, but the vents and fan will provide air circulation and reduce the temperature.

What kind of humidifier should I get?

Check consumer publications for a recommended brand. But type and features are more important than brand.

Our preferred type operates by means of a pad which rotates through water; then a fan blows through the damp pad, dispersing the moistened air.

It should have a reservoir of 8 to 10 gallons—so you can go away for the weekend.

Automatic shut-off at a certain humidity level is desirable, as is automatic shut-off when empty.

It should be easy to fill.

Most of all, it should be easily disassembled for cleaning—and you will want to clean the pad and reservoir every week, during use. If you don't, a fungus can develop and spread into the atmosphere. Regular cleaning is better than adding chemicals to the water (which chemicals you then have to breathe) .

I use perlite in the "pebble" trays on my radiators, as you recommend, but they get algae. Can I use an algaecide to get rid of it?

Don't. There is no place for the algaecide to go, so it will stay there in your radiator trays. Also, if the algaecide comes into contact with any mosses you are trying to grow, it may kill them too.

We get some algae, but it doesn't do any harm—just sits there—as long as it doesn't touch the pots and get on them. Perlite is cheap, so when it becomes too unsightly we dump the trayful on our compost heap and refill the tray with fresh perlite. Perlite does not decompose and makes an excellent lightener for the compost.

Light–
Sun and Electric

How some of us can live in the dark holes we call apartments is beyond reason. People *need* light. That plants need light is easily seen: plants soon lose leaves if left in the dark, their foliage takes on a pale look, and stem growth is weak. People keep their symptoms inside, but they suffer just as much from lack of light. Our life changed for much the better when we painted our walls white instead of gray. We became more cheerful people, and our plants thrived.

Our living room got not a ray of light until we installed two banks of fluorescent lights and made this room into a growing gem—and raised ourselves from the slough of despond (an eternal winter) at the same time. There should be more research done on the effect of light on people.

So much can be done with artificial light! Under-cabinet areas in kitchens can be turned into herb gardens; bedrooms can be turned into orchidariums; terrariums can be grown in windowless bathrooms.

And not just inside the home, either. Many office buildings and public places are lit 24 hours a day with fluorescent light; why not turn them into light gardens? The power is being used—let it be used to good effect. Can you imagine New York's or Boston's subways growing plants! Think how the greenery will soothe commuters, and provide oxygen. It's a kind of green communism—in the future, we could all enjoy our communal subway plantings the same way we communally enjoy our street-tree plantings.

If you feel guilty about the electricity use involved in fluorescent-light gardening, cut out some other appliances: brush your teeth by hand; cut your roast by hand; eat untoasted bread!

If you can't afford fluorescent light and you live in a dungeon, perhaps you work in a bright office. Why not grow ten houseplants in the bright light there, and take home each plant for a week at a time? One week of dungeon life won't bother a plant that has nine weeks of bright sun.

If you've been flipping through these remarks to find something on *incandescent* lighting, here it comes: It is hot, it is expensive, and it is inefficient.

How many watts of incandescent light do I need with two 4-inch 40-watt fluorescent tubes?

None—if you use the combination of cool-white and warm-white tubes (50/50) recommended by the Indoor Light Gardening Society of America.

It was once thought that the red spectrum of incandescent bulbs was needed for flowering hard-to-flower plants like geraniums. But even these flower rapidly under cool-white and warm-white tubes, *if you provide* enough tubes (four for geraniums, as many as eight for some orchids) . *Intensity* of light seems more important than spectrum.

Are the special plant fluorescent lights really any better than ordinary tubes? They are certainly more expensive.

We, and most of the light-gardeners we know, grow successfully under a half-and-half combination of cool-white and warm-white fluorescents. Some of the special-spectrum tubes are quite good—others seem to affect the apparent color of the blooms more than the growth of the plant. Even orchid growers are using the cool-white/warm-white combination. It has yet to be shown to us that any of the special plant tubes are worth the extra money (or the extra trouble of getting them) .

However, some very respected garden writers do recommend them.

Can literally any plant be grown under fluorescents?

Literally anything can be grown under fluorescent lights—by someone. Various growers have various successes with various plants. At the extreme, we even know someone who is successfully flowering sun-loving cacti under fluorescents. We have a friend with an eight-tube setup on a variable-day-length timer who can flower vanda orchids.

But if you are looking for instant success, stay with plants requiring the middle range to low range of lights: gesneriads, begonias, peperomias, pileas, etc. These (and many, many others, of course) thrive under fluorescent lights without complex setups.

I have a damp basement and have this dream about turning it into a jungle with fluorescent lights. Can such a thing be done?

We have a friend who has ceilinged an entire large first-floor room in 4-foot fluorescent tubes. And we mean the whole ceiling. Perhaps you don't want to go that far—or perhaps you do. If you do, remember that buying parts is a lot cheaper than buying ready-made fixtures. Put up your lights so that the tubes are about 6 inches from center to center, and close up end to end.

Our friend uses warm-white tubes or warm-white deluxe. Apparently, when you provide that much light intensity, the spectrum doesn't matter.

Paint the walls flat white for even reflectance.

Be prepared to deal with air circulation (an exhaust fan) and heat. You will probably want to put your ballasts (the transformers built into each fluorescent fixture) in a cool place. Our friend has his set in the ceiling of an unheated garage, near the room.

And, finally, be prepared for the expense. Even though fluorescent light is cheaper than incandescent, the sheer number of tubes you use will run up a large electric bill.

Can I turn a wooden bookcase into a light garden?

Yes, light units of appropriate length can be screwed into the undersides of the shelves.

But bookcases don't make terrific light gardens. The shelves are usually too shallow and too close together, and since they are closed on all but one side, they provide poor air circulation. Small whisper fans can solve that problem.

Paint the insides white for good reflection and more efficient use of the light.

My fluorescent tubes seem to be dimming. When should I think of changing them?

Tubes start to die back from the ends the first day they go on. Most experts recommend changing after a year's use, but if you are as close with a buck as we are, you can go a year and a half.

By the way, don't change all your tubes at once. You can actually "burn" your plants.

Is one 15-watt fluorescent tube enough to grow plants?

Almost nothing will do well for you under that little light. You can start seedlings under one 15-watt tube, if you grow them almost touching the tube.

It breaks our hearts that there are firms marketing kits with just such a single tube, making outrageous claims. We think it is a rip-off.

Can I flower orchids under fluorescent lights?

Absolutely; the simple basic combination of warm white and cool white works well (50/50), though some growers like a combination of Gro-Lux Wide Spectrum and cool white.

Paphiopedilums and phalaenopsis will flower under two tubes; many lealiocattleya hybrids will flower under four tubes. For the sun-lovers you will need as many as eight tubes. With some orchids, day length is very important. We suggest you attend meetings of the American Orchid Society chapter near you, or read their journal; the *A.O.S. Bulletin* is a highly professional journal with many beautiful color photos. You get the journal (twelve issues a year) by joining the national society. Send $15 for annual membership to A.O.S., Botanical Museum of Harvard University, Cambridge, Massachusetts 02138.

What is your opinion of incandescent "plant lights"?

Low. Very low.

They are uneconomical and give off too much heat for the amount of light they produce.

When you say that a supplementary spotlight should be kept about 4 feet from a plant, do you mean from the pot or the leaves?

From the leaves; the pot doesn't get much benefit from supplementary light.

Place your bulb so that it is not directly over the plant, but at an angle. You don't want the bulb closer than about 4 feet, but you don't want only a few leaves that close and the rest too far away to get any benefit.

Will any plants at all grow for me under plain bulbs?

In a moderately bright room, you can grow several plants not too near a couple of 100-watt incandescent bulbs: nephthytis, syngonium, heartleaf philodendron, epipremnum (formerly called scindapsis or pothos), aspidistra, even spathiphyllum.

What is the one single biggest problem for the indoor grower?

Light, heat, and humidity.

Depending on your growing conditions, pick one or more—It's funny, but almost everyone who tells us how great she or he is with plants turns out to have a bright apartment.

Will ultraviolet lamps stimulate growth in my plants?

No, concentrated ultraviolet rays are harmful to plants. Most of the sun's ultraviolet is filtered out by the atmosphere.

My rooms are dark, and I have difficulty growing anything that needs sun. Must I go to the expense of putting in lights? I hate their glare and don't really have the money. Even if you don't have any suggestion, thanks for listening.

Well, you're welcome, but we do have a few suggestions.

Keep your windows washed. The dust can cut down on light dramatically.

Shower your plants to get rid of dust on leaves—that cuts out light, too.

Finally, paint your rooms white. A white wall reflects light beautifully, making the most of the little light you have. Also, friend, you will find a light-colored room much more cheering.

You might also consider growing plants with low light requirements.

I recently moved from a bright apartment to one with no sun at all. Is there anything I can grow? My windows face a narrow courtyard, so I get only indirect light.

That isn't indirect light, that's closet light. But, yes, there are some plants you can grow. (We were asked that same question by a writer at WNBC-TV and wise-guyed, "Have you tried plastic plants?" She replied, "Yes. They got little plastic bugs and died.")

Sansevieria (snake plant) will grow, if slowly, in a minimum of light—and several very handsome varieties are available.

Aglaonema (Chinese evergreen) will tolerate almost as low light—though you have to be prepared for it to go a bit leggy.

Spathiphyllum will probably grow well for you (though it probably won't flower), but you have to give it plenty of water.

If you can find an aspidistra, it will probably do well for you.

If you work in a bright office, our best solution is to buy all four plants and grow them in your office, *rotating one plant a week at home.* This way, each plant will have three weeks of bright office light, then one week in the Black Hole of Calcutta. They can all thrive on that kind of rotation.

Will any plants flower for me on my north-facing windowsill? I get bright light, but no direct sun.

You bet! Not geraniums or cacti, but still . . .

Spathiphyllums will love your exposure, as will aglaonemas (Chinese evergreen) and syngoniums.

If your exposure is a brilliant north or gets good reflection from across the street, try semperflorens begonias, or even African violets (saintpaulias), especially miniature African violets.

And, if you are adventurous and willing to maintain a terrarium, get yourself a few miniature sinningias (tiny relatives of African violets).

What will grow in a dark room?

If it's humid, mushrooms.

If dry and dark, nothing will grow—though some plants will *survive* for quite a while: sansevieria (snake plant) and aspidistra (cast-iron plant) for example.

Can you recommend a couple of dainty long-lasting shrubs for a bright living room?

This sounds suspiciously like a decorating question. Remember, plants are not furniture: they require care.

There are many handsome shrubs that will last a long while—with proper care. *Polyscias fruticosa* (Ming aralia) is extremely graceful, but it may take a while to get adjusted to you.

Ficus benjamina exotica (a more pendant form of weeping fig) has a shape that is positively willowish. And, if you can give it properly high humidity, *Dizygotheca elegantissima* (false aralia) is a real charmer.

What plants would you recommend for my south window?

Geraniums, miniature roses, and cacti all do well in south sun—but you'll have to keep the air circulating or the heat will get even the cacti. If you've a taste for the exotic, try a zamia. If you want a palm, try *Phoenix roebelinii* (dwarf date palm). Such bromeliads as *Aechmea fasciata* or pineapple (the kind you start yourself) should thrive in sun, as should *Hoya carnosa variegata* (variegated wax plant). And if you can manage the humidity and nighttime temperature drop, try cattleya or vanda orchids.

Other Environmental Conditions—If You Can't Find It Elsewhere, Look Here

Most plant problems are environmental problems: inaccurate watering, inappropriate light, over- or underfeeding, low humidity, poor soil mix, and dozens of other specific environmental conditions make your plants healthy or sick.

When you buy a plant, you take it from one environment (usually a tropical climate or a greenhouse) to another, usually much less favorable. Indoor plants seldom get any overhead sun or enough humidity in the winter. A soil well suited to a greenhouse may be much too heavy for your conditions. Constant watering and feeding may have pushed a plant along to grow to a large size quickly; when it comes into your garden, you treat it "normally" and it collapses.

We suggest you buy *small* plants and grow them on to specimen size—if you're lucky. And if you're unlucky, you haven't lost a large investment of either time or money. Besides, small plants are the most adaptable. They live closer to their soil, and so get the humidity that evaporates off the soil. They are not yet adapted to high living in a greenhouse. That's an important word for plant growers: *adapt*. Animals react to an unfavorable environment by leaving town; plants adapt (or die).

Given a chance, a plant will adapt to conditions that it should not ever be able to live in. Full-sun plants will adapt to low light;

epiphytes will adapt to growing in soil—*especially if you start them young.*

When we were new in the plant-advice biz, you might sometimes have found us saying that you couldn't raise a rubber tree in a dim room—until we had met any number of people who had done it. Plants can often be grown in a situation with one poor condition (such as too little light), but then you have to manage the other conditions (watering, etc.) *very carefully.*

We even got one call from a woman who had grown her jade plant (*Crassula arborescens*) in the same pot with no hole for ten years. Unbelievable! We insist on having holes in all our pots. She had managed by watering very critically. The plant had not grown, but it had lived—until one overwatering killed it.

That's not to say you can give any plant any treatment and expect it to grow gratefully and beautifully for you. Stick to what is *optimum* culture for your plants and you will most often come up with the best plants.

Plants, of course, adapt more readily to *improvements* in the environment than impoverishments. Occasionally a listener asks about moving to a darker apartment. We say sell or give away all of your current plants and start from scratch. The plants you are growing now, full-sized and beautiful as they are, are unlikely to adapt to the transition. Very few of our regular listeners and viewers have this problem, though, because after a year or so with us, they all move only to *sunnier* apartments and houses!

On January 1, I'm moving to a new residence about ten minutes by car from my apartment. What should I do to move my plants?

You have to watch out for three things: shock, cold, and whiplash.

Water your plants well just before you move them (except cacti and other succulents: they should be moved dry).

Wrap them well in paper for the trip to the car. The car doesn't have to be hot, but it should be warm.

Tall plants are a special problem because they especially suffer from being moved. Put tall plants into tall boxes, so that they don't move around. Cardboard egg crates stood on end are good for this—and for a quite tall plant you can tape two together.

In your new place, try to put your plants in similar exposures or brighter exposures. And, finally, coddle them for a few days (or more) with extra humidity.

Moving in the warm months is simpler: humidity is generally high and cold is not a problem. But when you move plants in late spring and summer, *heat* becomes a danger. Plants left in a closed car in a sunny parking lot while you have lunch will be cooked greens by the time you return. Keep a good deal of air circulating, or take the plants inside to lunch with you.

My daughter says I shouldn't have plants in my bedroom because they use up the oxygen. Is that true?

No. That is a dumb and destructive idea because it makes people fear plants.

Plants do use up some oxygen at night (it's part of a process called catabolism). But they make much more oxygen than that during the daylight (or lamplight) hours (by a process called photosynthesis).

Have plants in your bedroom, and tell your daughter to go wax her floor tile.

I am growing a number of vegetables in containers on my terrace, and, the other day, the leaves on all my peppers and eggplants were dissolved and spotted. I could see no bugs. Can you help me?

We can tell you what it is, but we can't help you. It is air pollution—to which peppers and eggplants are especially sensitive.

Cut away the worst leaves to give room to the healthy new growth—or move to a healthier climate.

The leaves of my avocado are turning pale, and they seem to have some sticky stuff on them. There is no scale I can see—or other bugs. We water it when the soil is a little dry, it is in an east-facing window (our brightest), and since it is in our kitchen it gets good humidity. What do you think it could be?

It could be a few things. But how about an off-the-wall question from us: Do you fry a lot? In a kitchen, this can be a real problem. The fat molecules will land on the leaves and leave a deposit which can gradually choke off the leaves and impair their ability to photosynthesize.

If this fits, wash off the leaves in a solution of dishwashing detergent, then in clear water, and take the plant out of the kitchen. If this is it and the damage hasn't gone too far, you can expect good recovery.

Is soot harmful to plant leaves?

Yes, and in two or three ways.

Soot is oily, and the oil in itself is slightly corrosive.

Soot deposits on leaves block the sun from the leaves.

And soot on your *windows* keeps sunlight off even your clean plants.

Water alone won't clean soot off leaves; you need some Ivory soap or dishwashing liquid (not laundry detergent) as an emulsifier—to de-oil the oil. You can fill a tub with soapy water, or fill a sink for small plants, and swish the leaves through until clean. Or you can spray the leaves with this same detergent mixture.

Either way, finish by rinsing the plant off with clear water.

What's the best way to handle watering of our plants when we go on our three weeks of vacation?

A reliable plantsitter, if you have access to one. A good babysitter usually has enough smarts. And don't feel ashamed to leave a detailed list of special watering problems. We do, and no one is insulted.

I'm going away for two weeks vacation and I'd like to do without a plantsitter for my light garden. What can I do besides putting the plants in plastic bags?

Reduce the number of hours of light. Set your timer for as little as eight hours of light out of the twenty-four. With less light, the plants will be less active and less demanding. This constitutes a subsistence diet for the plant. Then water the plants well, and drape a clear-plastic dropcloth over them. That should do it.

I'm going away for two weeks. Can I just tent in my window garden with plastic instead of bagging individual plants?

You can tent with plastic, but not in your window—the heat would dry out the plants. Just pull the plants back a bit, set up your tent, and water quite well—and you can go away with a good degree of confidence. Unless your plants normally need daily watering. *Very* heavy drinkers don't do well unless individually bagged.

I'm going away for a week. Can I put my plants (begonias, coleus, philo, etc.) in plastic bags?

Yes, certainly for a week. Water well, then allow each plant to drain. Put into the bag, inflate, and seal with a twist-tie. It is important that the leaves don't touch the bag, or the touching leaf may rot.

My job takes me out of town for a week at a time. What can I grow that will survive on that kind of watering schedule?

Bromeliads, orchids, cacti, and some other succulents will usually be fine.

But the best thing to grow if you're away for long periods is a terrarium. In a protected environment you can grow the most delicate exotics—and they will require little care.

I went away for two weeks and put my wax begonia inside a plastic bag. It was watered and the bag was inflated, so it didn't touch the leaves, but when I came back, there was a white fungus on the leaves! What can I do?

It sounds as if you left too much water in the bag. But fungus is relatively easy to deal with on *Begonia semperflorens* (wax begonia).

Cut off the affected leaves, improve the air circulation, put it into direct sun, and keep water off the leaves. Remember to allow the soil to go rather dry between waterings.

Also, after handling the fungusy leaves, be sure you clean your hands well. *You* can be the cause of spreading the fungus among other plants if you are not careful.

I have a white fuzzy fungus on my soil.

Mold, which is what it sounds like, is a sign that your soil may be too heavy. Scrape it off with a spoon and discard it.

Many molds, fungi, and other tiny things are harmless in themselves, but may be symptomatic. Does your soil stay too wet too long? They love the wet. Try a better-drained soil mix.

My African violets look like they have a gray powder on the center leaves, and they look crumpled.

Throw them out! It sounds as if you have botrytis—a fungus disease. Then, after you've thrown them out, wipe down your growing area with Lysol.

My English ivy has a powdery fungus on it. Can I cure it?

Plant pathologists we've known say you can't really cure fungus, just prevent it or prevent its spread.

However, improve your air circulation and keep water off the leaves. If desperate, you can spray with Benomyl 50 percent. (It is called Benomyl 50 percent; you then dilute it according to the instructions on the label.) We, however, prefer to discard a fungus-laden plant rather than spraying our own environment.

My angel-wing begonia has large brown papery spots on the leaves nearest the window. Do you know what that is?

Could be sunburn. Take the plant out of the window and then bring it back into the window a bit at a time over several days, to acclimate it to the sun

In springtime especially, even plants that want sun can get sunburn. Acclimation is the answer.

My massangeana has got sunburned. Is there anything I can do?

If the sunburn is across the entire leaf, cut off the leaf—sunburn doesn't heal. If it is across a small portion, you can trim it away or ignore it.

And, please, call it dracaena, if you want to, or *Dracaena massangeana,* but not just by the species name. That can lead to confusion.

The soil of my angel-wing begonia smells sour and doesn't dry, and the leaves are looking pale and droopy. What causes this?

It smells as if you have root rot. Take tip cuttings of whatever decent tops you have, and root them in an open or half-open propagation box.

Unpot the plant and begin breaking away the soil. You should find rotten roots. Keep breaking away until you find healthy roots. Then, with a sterile knife, make clean cuts so that only healthy roots are left—however few. Dust the living ends with flowers of sulfur or some other fungicide. Cut the stems back to within 6 inches of the soil, and repot into pasteurized soil and a clean (and smaller) pot. And the plant may survive.

Root rot is the most serious thing that can happen to a plant.

I bought a lovely coleus in a hanging basket (the plastic kind with a saucer attached). It is going brown—not just at the bottom but all over—and looks poor. I keep it in a bright east window and water it plenty (though it doesn't seem to dry out) and lately have even been misting it. But it keeps browning. What can I do?

You've got problems, and it sounds mostly like root damage. Those hanging baskets can be dangerous. If you don't tip the basket after watering, the saucer will hold a lot of water for a long time, giving the soil no chance to dry out at all. This constant moisture, combined with heavy greenhouse soil, helps create root rot.

You'll have to turn the plant out of its pot and look and sniff around for rotten roots: they look shriveled or mushy and dark instead of firm and light; they smell rotten. Cut away any rotten stuff back to live root. Dust the live ends with flowers of sulfur. And do cut back the top growth somewhat to compensate for the root loss. Now, using a regular-shaped flower pot, of a smaller size, to suit the new rootball, repot damp into a very well-drained soil mix. Keep out of direct sun for a week; keep the humidity high and the temperature warm; and with luck and God's help, your plant will be beautiful again.

Pinching, Pruning, and Grooming

Here is where plants are most *un*like animals. Take off the older, weaker, less efficient portions of a plant, and you encourage it to make better, younger, stronger growth.

Beauty in plants is not size: it is proportion, shape, good health, color—all of which are affected by grooming and pruning.

For many of us indoor gardeners, an ideal plant would be one that reaches a size that fits our growing area, and then stays that size. Well, with judicious pruning and root pruning, you can have just such a plant.

I often hear you speak of "pinching out." Could you say just how much of the plant you remove and why?

Removing the growing tip of a plant encourages branching—sometimes at the place pinched, sometimes lower down. One way to remove the growing tip is to take a tip cutting for propagation. Sometimes, with young plants, this is inappropriate, so, instead, we pinch out the growing tip and discard it.

To pinch out, you reach right into the growing tip of your plant with thumb and forefinger (or thumb and middle finger) and actually clip out (with your nails) the very tip of the stem, including the youngest leaf or leaves. Just removing the leaves won't do it: you must take out a bit of the stem tip.

In some plants, auxins (hormones) which inhibit branching gather in the tip, and removing those inhibiting auxins gives the side growths a real push.

How soon should I start pinching out a begonia cutting?

Pinch out the growing tip of your begonia cutting for the first time *when you put it into the propagating medium*. This ensures branching while the plant is still quite short.

Give it a second pinching-out the day you pot up your successfully rooted plantlet.

These two pinches—the day you put it into the propagation box and the day you take it out of the prop box—will give it a shapely healthy start in life.

What is "stopping" a plant?

That's British for pinching out. You've been reading English gardening books, haven't you? We hope you don't have trouble with the translation.

Do you have any particular opinion about root pruning? I mean, should you do it and when?

We are believers in root pruning under certain circumstances.

When you cut a plant's top growth back sharply, you should root-prune a similar amount (one-fourth off the top, one-fourth off the roots) —except, of course, when you cut back all the way. If you've ever top-pruned a plant sharply, had it resprout, and then just peter out, it was probably because the root system was too large for the top growth. Roots and branches must be in some kind of balance.

If you have plants that are in containers as large as you can manage but they need potting up, you may decide to root-prune them and return them to the same containers. In such cases, you top-prune a proportional amount. This is a technique especially useful with balcony and terrace plants in large containers.

Root pruning is least traumatic when done in the spring, when roots are in active growth. If you root-prune potted plants in the shortening days of autumn or in early winter, you have less chance of success.

Root-prune with sterilized and very sharp instruments, and treat the plants like invalids afterward, with extra-high humidity (a plastic emergency tent comes in handy here) and only moderate watering. Also, if you can manage it, provide bright light without direct sun.

Don't root-prune cacti or cactuslike succulents.

By pruning roots you are, in a sense, dwarfing your shrub or tree or plant. The maestros of root pruning are the practitioners of bonsai.

Can you settle some questions about staking houseplants? When is the best time to put in the stakes? How tall should the stakes be in relationship to the plant? What is the best material to use for stakes— wood, plastic, or what?

Staking is a part of growing healthy plants.

WHEN: Certainly you do the plant least harm if you put in the stakes as you transplant. This way no root damage is incurred and you can more easily change your mind about the location of a stake. But often the idea to stake comes long after potting. In general, we stake when a plant needs it. A floppy plant, insecure in its pot, does not grow vigorously. When plants show signs of flopping or of falling over (and they don't need repotting) , stake.

HOW TALL: There is no set rule about the height of stakes, but we prefer stakes that are no taller than their plants. We don't believe in "leaving room to grow." If the plant grows to need a taller stake, we restake. There is no cultural reason for this, but we consider those bare stakes unsightly: they detract from the good looks of the plant.

WHAT: Our preferred stakes are metal hyacinth stakes: thin, painted green, and almost invisible once in place. But these are inappropriate for tall plants or for plants needing heavy support. Bamboo stakes come in a variety of lengths and thicknesses, and are also painted green for invisibility. But we once staked a dieffenbachia with a mop handle because of the height and support it needed. Plastic doesn't make good staking material; it seldom has the rigidity for good support. And those small plastic trellises are ugly ugly ugly!

Should I tie a plant to a stake with soft wool or a Twist'em?

Either will do—anything that doesn't cut into the stem. But don't tie the plant directly to the stake. Twist the twist-tie around the stake completely and give it a turn so that it holds firmly (or tie the wool firmly to the stake) , and then make a more gentle loop around the stem of the plant.

Also, you'll want to tie in more than one place: two at least for good support. If you are not careful with your ties, you can snap off or strangle your plants instead of supporting them.

I shouldn't really be asking, since I've been doing it for two years, but something you said on the radio about grooming made me think about it. I crumble up my dead geranium or begonia leaves and put them on the surface of the soil. Before I did this the soil seemed to pull away from the sides of the pots, and it no longer does. But I don't seem to be able to get rid of some mites lately, and it has started me wondering if these leaves could be the reason.

We have always been amazed at how often people know the answers to their own questions.

It is generally good to put a mulch on the surface of your house-plants' soil. Even some excellent growers miss this chance to conserve houseplant moisture. Obviously, your plants needed a mulch if the soil was pulling away from the sides of their pots.

But what leaves are you using? If you groom off aging leaves and use them, or leaves that have died because of lack of water, fine. But if you are using leaves killed by bugs, then not so fine. The bugs (or their eggs) could well be alive even though the leaves are dead.

You can use the leaves you groom off as a mulch—but not if they have bugs on them.

Why should I groom the dead leaves off my houseplants? They fall off, don't they? Isn't it really better to let things look natural?

If you don't groom away the dying parts of a plant, they sap its strength and often inhibit the formation of new leaves. They are a drain on the plant, without contributing to either its appearance or its photosynthesis.

Yes, we like things to be natural, too, but we don't think that a plant that looks like the victim of an early autumn is any more natural than one with only healthy leaves and an attractive symmetry.

When do I cut back my avocado?

When it has lost all its leaves and would otherwise just die.

This is that old stuff about lopping off the young avocado stem to make it branch—and it is so much *stuff*. Avocados are pruned and pinched and groomed like any other tropical tree: to make them branch and improve their shape (and to get rid of dead or dying leaves). You cannot get a better plant by decapitating it—though if for some reason it becomes defoliated, cutting it back to within a few inches of the seed is likely to give you compact new growth.

✐ ✐ ✐ ✐

Pots and Potting—
Getting Potted

We've been through a lot, us old-timers. We've been through the time when plastic pots were new and needed explaining. And through the time of a real plastic shortage and a great increase in price. And then a time when a real variety of plastic pots was available, both in materials and in design. And now we seem to be having a boom in hanging baskets.

We have used and find all kinds of pots useful. Clay pots are especially good for large-growing plants; not only does their weight anchor the plant, but the clay allows the large rootball to dry out faster and reduces the chance of rot. This drying out also makes clay excellent for plants (such as orchids) that need air around their roots.

Plastic is marvelous where weight would be a problem (as it would be if you were crowding many plants onto a fragile shelf). Plastic is very desirable for plants that want to stay evenly moist—as do many gesneriads, including African violets (saintpaulias), and many begonias.

We love all kinds of hanging plants—and we hang all kinds of plants. If you have a real hanging plant, it may well prefer a moss-lined wire basket to a solid plastic hanging basket (many plants that do hang in their natural habitats need the great drainage you get from a moss-lined basket). Of course, the plastic basket keeps water from dripping onto your floors when you water, but are you growing floors or plants?

What does the potting future hold? Perhaps a growth of the awareness that there is a relationship between a plant and its pot, and that the two must be matched, both aesthetically and horticulturally.

How do I sterilize old flowerpots for reuse?

Use a solution of 9 parts hot water plus 1 part chlorine bleach. If the pots are obviously dirty add 1 or 2 tablespoons of detergent powder. Soak at least overnight, then rinse repeatedly in steaming hot water (to get rid of the chlorine).

Fertilizer salts will probably have to be scraped off with a knife.

You get crusty deposits of fertilizer salts on your pots and perhaps on your soil, even if you don't fertilize. The elements that naturally form the salts are there in the soil.

Can I drill holes into glazed pots without drainage holes?

We have a friend who says she does it with a high-speed drill, held at an angle (not drilled perpendicularly).

Can I reuse pots and soil from plants that have died?

It depends. If they've died from neglect—such as lack of water—yes, you can reuse the pots; and you can mix the soil into some fresh.

Soil from bug-infested plants should be thrown away. Composting and then pasteurizing the soil can get rid of the bug eggs, but otherwise it's too dangerous (it's no saving if you kill your plants to save a buck on soil).

All used pots should be soaked in a solution of 1 part of chlorine bleach to 9 parts hot water, and have all old soil washed out thoroughly. (For clay pots, then soak them again in clear hot water to disperse some of the chlorine.)

Used soil should be mixed with a bit of fresh soil and some lightener (sand, perlite, or vermiculite)—if it is reused at all. At best, it's a tolerable, not a recommended, practice. And if the soil is from buggy plants, then it is a disaster.

Should I tear the net off my Jiffy-7 peat pellet when I pot it up?

Yes, a bit, and carefully, so as not to disturb the young roots. Or use Jiffy-10 peat pellets, which don't leave a persistent plastic net in the soil.

Is crock in the bottom of a pot important?

What is important is keeping the soil in and the roots in, but permitting the water easy egress.

Some shallow-rooted plants do better if the amount of soil in a deep pot is reduced by adding crockery to the bottom of the pot. But shallow-rooted plants are best grown in shallow azalea pots or bulb pans. For these shallow pots, and for all small pots, we are now using plastic or aluminum screening in the bottom, instead of the usual broken clay pots and pieces of brick.

Why is it such a bad idea to repot in November and December? Is it because the days are so short? They are just as short in January, but you say it's all right to repot in January. What's the difference?

It's not just that the days are short in November and December. It is that *they are getting shorter* (up to December 21, when the year turns). In some way, plants detect and respond to this shortening day by slowing their growth. (Even under fluorescent lights, some plants will slow.) In January, though the days are short, they are *lengthening*. This lengthening is also detected by the plants, and many of them will show new growth in January, in response.

Roots follow the same pattern as top growth: they are active in the lengthening or long days, and almost inactive as the days shorten sharply in November and December.

Houseplants should be repotted when their roots will grow rapidly into the new soil. If not, rot may occur. So, we disrecommend repotting until the roots (and the top) are in active growth.

There are plants that are in active growth all year. You can tell that their roots are growing because they sprout new leaves at a goodly pace. These plants can be repotted as needed, any time of the year.

What is "turning a plant out"?

"Turning out" is removing a plant from its pot. With the palm of your hand spread over the soil, and with the stem between your two middle fingers, turn the plant upside down, tap the rim of the pot against a firm surface, then lift the pot off.

Is there any reason why I can't grow a hybrid "Patio" tomato in a hanging basket?

They do it at Longwood Gardens (Kennett Square, Pennsylvania). They put several plants in a 12-inch wire basket lined with long-haired sphagnum moss.

They plug the bottom hole of a small clay flowerpot and set it into the center of the moss, in the midst of the plants. The little pot is then kept full of water. The water seeps through the clay, providing constant moisture for the basket, hanging in full sun.

This pot-in-pot method should work for any plant that would benefit from constant moisture.

Can I grow coleus in a hanging basket?

Quite successfully! But keep your coleus in a basket well pinched. Yes, even more pinching than coleus in a standing pot: you don't want to call your coleus Rapunzel.

Is there any plant you wouldn't hang?

No. Every plant *could* hang. We have a friend with very narrow windowsills who hangs virtually everything. Only *weight* makes a houseplant ineligible for hanging. Of course, a plant whose habit is pendulous, trailing, vining, or prostrate looks more natural hanging than one that is stiffly upright. But we don't let that stop us.

I think you two are prejudiced! Against cachepots, that is. Stan especially never has a good word to say for them. What's the matter with an attractive outer pot to hide an ugly inner pot?

We choose not to take umbrage (besides, all our umbrage was taken last week).

We will tell you exactly what is wrong with cachepots. If they are of wicker or straw or a similar openwork material, nothing at all is wrong with them. They allow free passage of air and don't hold excess water.

But if they are solid and you are growing anything but aquatic plants, water can stay in their bottoms and promote root rot and at the very least encourage the roots to grow through the bottom of the pot—which makes repotting difficult. To grow plants in this kind of cachepot, you must go around and empty out the excess water half an hour after watering.

To tell the truth, Stan is a closet cachepot-queen. He has cachepots all over the place—and a few of them even have plants in them. But only plants that demand lots of water, and even then he goes around after watering and pours out the excess water.

Propagation– Making Little Ones from Big Ones

Propagation is probably the most intriguing aspect of horticulture, so exciting and diverse that one could study it for a lifetime.

Plants propagate in so many ways: in kalanchoes, plantlets complete with roots form along the edges of their leaves; sansevierias form underground runners which sprout at a distance from the parent plant; episcias form above-ground runners called stolons, which sprout into plantlets at their ends; many succulents will form new plants from a single leaf that falls to the ground. You are probably familiar with ordinary seed formation, but did you know that ferns have three-part sex lives, including the male swimming to the female gamete through a film of water? These are just teasers, hints of the variety of plant propagation.

And the best part is that so much of propagation is possible to the interested home grower. Propagation equipment is inexpensive and readily available, and home propagation often the only way to get an exotic or rare plant. We have often admired a plant, only to have someone offer us not the plant but a *piece* of the plant, which we took home and propagated. And there we were, with a lovely new plant at virtually no cost.

Commercial growers often grow what is easy to propagate, what comes quickly and grows quickly. You don't have to be affected by commercial considerations—you can propagate almost anything for pennies, once you know how.

Do propagate: there is no more fascinating or satisfying aspect to growing.

Can spider plants be grown from seed?

Yes, and the seeds are easy to come by: simply poke a clean brush or cotton swab into each flower—and that should be enough for pollination.

When the seed capsules open, tap the seeds out over a seeding medium, and they should germinate quite readily in a moist, warm environment.

I planted some date seeds, but nothing has happened for more than a month. I used nonpasteurized dates from the health-food store as you suggested.

Checking our notes on our last batch of date seeds, the first came up after two months, the third after *four* months. So, hang in there and keep the soil moist (and the faith).

We have heard that date seeds can take as long as a year and a half to sprout. We don't know if even we have that much patience.

I want to try growing ferns from spores, but how do I collect spores from my ferns?

You can wait until the sori (the spore cases) on the backs of the fronds open and drop the dustlike spores all over the place.

Or, after the spore cases have matured but haven't yet opened, cut a piece of frond off and stick it into an envelope. The sori will open and allow the spores to drop out.

If the sori are open, hold a legal-size envelope under the frond and tap it with a finger. The spores will drop into the envelope.

Can bromeliads be grown from seed?

Yes, on a sterile medium that does not hold too much water. But mostly it takes patience: your seedlings will be months old before they will be big enough to transplant.

Can bird-of-paradise be grown from seed?

Certainly. Score the seed with a nail file, soak it overnight in tepid water, and then thrust the seed into a 3-inch pot full of long-haired sphagnum moss. Cover the pot with transparent plastic; you must keep the moss constantly moist until the seed germinates.

You've talked us into it; we want to start our next spring's seeds indoors under fluorescent lights. How many tubes do we need, and of what kind?

Always glad to make a convert.

If you can grow your seedlings almost up against the tube, one single tube is enough. If you've two tubes, the seedling tops should be no closer than, say, 4 inches from the tubes. In the beginning, keep an eye on your seedlings. If they begin to bleach out, move them away.

Cool-white tubes are best for thrifty seedling growth.

Can I propagate columneas from the seed I take out of the berry?

Yes. In fact, we've seen the seed sprouting inside the berry.

The berry is ripe when the calyx curves way back. Lay the berry on blotting paper or a paper towel and spread it with a dull knife as you would a pat of butter. Separate as much of the berry from the seeds as you can, and plant the seeds on a bed of damp milled sphagnum moss over potting soil. Do not cover with more moss (because the seeds are so small), but cover the pot with a piece of clear plastic held on with a rubber band.

If the berry was quite ripe, the seed will sprout within weeks.

Remember, columneas are slow to bloom from seed, and of course hybrids don't come true from seed.

I plant seed and get good germination, but in a few days the seedlings droop over. Am I watering too much?

Your problem is a fungus disease called popularly (or *un*popularly) damping off. A ¼-inch layer of damp milled sphagnum moss over potting soil will keep the fungus at bay until the roots reach into the soil (where the fungus still lives). But by then the seedling will be old enough to be resistant.

Your alternative is to plant your seeds in 100 percent milled sphagnum moss. But, after seedlings have sprouted in the moss, they must be fed regularly and/or transplanted when very young.

You often speak of a "closed propagation box," and I'm afraid I don't get the picture.

Any clear plastic box of almost any size, with a layer of damp perlite or vermiculite in the bottom, can serve as a closed prop box. The only requirements are that it is transparent and that the cover fits securely. We want to create the kind of saturated atmosphere the greenhouse-man creates with misting.

The box holds in virtually all the moisture, cutting down the leaves' need to pull moisture from the roots (for the time being, the cutting has no roots).

Also, the clear box allows in light (it should not be kept in direct sun), which permits the leaves to function in a more or less normal way all the while.

Are clear plastic bags as good as clear plastic boxes for propagation?

No, they're not. Bags, being thinner and less rigid, permit the passage of air (and some water vapor), which the more rigid boxes do not. Cuttings in plastic bags dry out more quickly than those in plastic prop boxes. But some cuttings are just too big for a prop box and must be put into a sealed bag. Keep a more careful eye on your bagged cuttings.

In your book *The Apartment Gardener*, you recommend coarse vermiculite for a propagation box. I can get only fine vermiculite. Can I use that or should I switch to perlite?

You can use fine vermiculite, but it's not as good as the coarse. The fine holds more water and less air. Air is important for best root formation. Propagation is a bit slower in the fine. We have had satisfactory results mixing the fine vermiculite with coarse perlite.

We once dropped a prop box of fine vermiculite, because when wet it was so much heavier than we expected—we were too used to the light weight of the coarse vermiculite. That shows how much less water the coarse holds.

If fine vermiculite is all you can find, use it, but underwater it just a bit.

Sometimes you say to use rooting hormone and sometimes you say not to. I wish you'd make up your minds.

We have made up our minds: sometimes you do and sometimes you don't. With woody cuttings or with plants that take a long time to strike roots, by all means use a rooting hormone—one of the more powerful preparations in fact. But these hormones can be irritating if inhaled. Also, while they can hasten the formation of first roots, they can hinder the development of later roots. So we say don't use them on the vast majority of your soft quick-rooting cuttings.

For a school fund-raiser in two months, April, what plants will propagate very quickly from tip cuttings?

At this time of year, basil, our favorite herb, and coleus, which has so many leaf colors and forms. Both show roots within a few days and can be potted up in about ten days. And there is always a market for them.

   With more time and less money you could grow both from seed, which is how the professionals produce their coleus plants in the greenhouse.

I saw you demonstrate air-layering on your Garden Spot, and it seemed like a lot of trouble. How is it better than just taking a tip cutting?

First of all, not everything is suited to air-layering. We don't air-layer any cacti or other succulents. We don't air-layer plants with stems less than $\frac{1}{4}$ inch in diameter. We don't air-layer a plant unless it has a tough fibrous stem—such as ficus plants and dracaenas have.

   Air-layering enables you to propagate without the loss of a single leaf. The root system develops on the stem, and then is transplanted only when it is large enough to support the plant. Tip cuttings usually lose a leaf or so during propagation, and they are planted up when they have a minimum of root.

   Since air-layering is done in the open air of your room, air-layered plants don't need a period of adjustment (unless the roots are damaged when they are potted), as do all plants propagated in a high-humidity propagation box.

   And, air-layering enables us to propagate pieces much larger than could be accommodated in any of our closed propagation boxes.

   Yes, air-layering is some trouble, but it is also one of the safest means we know to propagate a big plant.

   We like questions like that.

How do I air-layer my rubber tree?

Air-layering is the same for all plants you air-layer.

   Take a sterile razor or very sharp knife (you can use alcohol to sterilize).

Plan to make your cut about 3 inches below the lowest leaf. Look at the spot and try to visualize the cut. (This is psyching yourself up to it.)

Holding the blade horizontally, start your cut between two nodes. Cut *up* into the stem at about a 45° angle, about one-third of the way through. *Don't be kind.* If your cut isn't deep enough, it will heal, and the effort will be wasted.

Set half a toothpick into the wound to keep it open (or fit in a bit of damp long-haired sphagnum moss).

Take handfuls of wrung-out *damp* sphagnum and wrap them as a collar around the wound, extending 3 inches above and below, and about 1 inch thick around the wound area.

Hold the moss in place with a piece of heavyish clear plastic held in place by twist-ties wrapped around the stem. (The work is easier if you tie the bottom of the plastic on before putting on the moss.) The plastic must be virtually airtight.

After some weeks or months, roots will be formed and you can cut off the top (below the roots) and pot it up.

Keep the top well misted for the first few weeks.

How do I know what to root in an open prop box and what to root in a closed prop box?

As a rule of thumb, plants with succulent leaves or stems get rooted in an open propagation box; plants with thinner leaves get rooted in a closed prop box.

If we are propagating small individual leaves of succulents, though, we will root those in a closed prop box.

Geraniums must be propagated in the open.

Begonias we prefer either open or in a closed prop box *with the top propped open a bit.*

The smaller the thing you are propagating (say, a bit of leaf or a chunk of rhizome), the more likely it is to need a closed box.

Can I air-layer my avocado?

Yes, as you can most tropical trees and shrubs, except palms.

What is the best medium for rooting African violet leaves?

For rooting most cuttings we have always recommended damp coarse vermiculite, but if coarse vermiculite is hard to get, you can mix fine vermiculite with coarse (horticultural grade) perlite. You can use perlite alone, too, but the water tends to fall out of the top and go to the bottom of a propagation box or pot—so you will have to mist the top from time to time. African violet leaves can also be propagated in Jiffy-7 peat pellets—though we prefer *not* to use ordinary peat moss for rooting them. Whatever you use, you will have to provide a high-humidity atmosphere, and be patient. Several months may pass before you get new plantlets.

Should I use Rootone on my cuttings?

Rootone and Hormoden are rooting stimulants—they are applied directly to the dampened base of a cutting, just before it is inserted into rooting medium.

Rooting hormone is interesting stuff. It does indeed stimulate quick formation of roots, but photos we've seen show that treated plants then make poorer subsequent root systems, so that the untreated cuttings soon catch up.

For most houseplant cuttings, rooting hormone is superfluous—they will root rather readily. For cuttings that are slow to root—such as houseplant shrubs (orange, gardenia, etc.), then by all means use a rooting hormone, but in a strong preparation: the grade recommended for woody plants.

If you do use it—avoid breathing it.

Every time I try to propagate my rex begonia by laying a whole leaf on vermiculite and cutting the veins, it rots on me.

It rots on us, too. We've had much more success by "wedging." Cut out a circle with a 1-inch diameter around the petiole (leaf stem). Cut the petiole to about 1 inch and insert this "hub" into your rooting medium as you would an African violet leaf. With the hole left by that "hub" cutting as the center, cut the remainder of the leaf into wedges. Insert the point of each wedge into medium. (First you'll have to make a hole in the medium with a pencil or a clean label.) Plantlets may show themselves within a few weeks. They'll need high humidity for some days after coming out of your high-humidity prop box.

If you still want to try the whole-leaf method, dust the cuts with flowers of sulfur from the drugstore.

We accidentally broke the top off our dumb cane in moving and just put it in water—about three years ago. It has lived and made roots, but the new leaves are coming in smaller and smaller. If we transplant it to soil, will the leaves grow to normal size?

If you transplant it to soil, it will probably die!

Those roots would be useless in soil—new ones would have to grow, and it's very unlikely the plant would survive that long. Keep it in water and enjoy it. Drop a few grains of a water-soluble plant food into the water—that may help.

My bromeliad pup died on me. It never rooted, though we followed your instructions. It just dried up and died. Why?

Yes, well, we have to take some of the blame for dying bromel pups. We said how easy it is (in *The Apartment Gardener*), and it is—*but not if you take them too young.* They must have some substance, some body, before they can strike roots and grow on their own. You can expect good results if the pup is about *half* the size of the parent plant.

Of course, some pups don't make it because of a pathogen. But, generally, the longer you wait before separating them from the mother plant, the more of your pups will succeed.

I just don't have any luck propagating pickaback; the leaves always rot on me. What do you suggest?

We have a friend who taught us a dynamite way to propagate *Tolmiea menziesii* (pickaback plant).

Take a leaf that has sprouted some young leaves. Cut it off with a few inches of leaf stem. Now, carefully peel away the old leaf. This leaves you with something looking quite odd: a 2-inch stem with a few small leaves on it.

Take a glass full of water and stand the stem (or stems, if you do more than one) in it, then cover the leaves and the top of the glass with a plastic bag, held in place with a rubber band. The roots should start forming near the leaves within a couple of weeks. When you have several roots about 2 inches long, cut off the stems, pot up several cuttings to a 6-inch pot, and you will have a brand-new lush plant in short order. Especially early on, keep the humidity high.

Similar cuttings can be made in damp vermiculite in a closed propagation box. Cut the leaf stem down to 1 inch and insert the stem into the vermiculite.

How can I propagate my dwarf banana tree?

After fruiting—or perhaps just when mature enough if you don't get fruiting—leafless offsets called "spears" are formed. These can be separated and potted and will develop roots and leaves.

Will *Costus malortieanus zebrinus* root in water?

The name is *Costus malortieanus* or *Costus zebrinus,* an alternate name.

Costus are large-growing tropical shrubs whose stems tend to grow in an elongated spiral. Not easy as a houseplant.

The stems will root in water, but we have had good success rooting them in an open pot of perlite, placed on our windowsill among other plants (and, so, partly shaded) and kept watered like a plant.

Can I get more than one plant from a columnea cutting?

Yes, several. In a high-humidity clear-plastic propagation box, lay the cutting down horizontally on the damp medium. Using hairpins (yes, hairpins), hold the cutting down to the medium at several places. It is important that the nodes of the cutting press firmly against the medium.

The columnea cutting will root at every node. When well rooted it can be cut between nodes and each piece potted separately. Or, the rooted cutting can be planted into a single pot, uncut, and it should make a plant with several stems. Many vining plants can be propagated similarly: for example, aeschynanthus, nematanthus, and *Hedera helix* (English ivy).

Will coleus propagate in water?

Yes, but don't let the roots get more than a couple of inches long or they will find it difficult to make the transition to soil.

When do you transplant a rooted cutting out of a closed propagation box and into potting soil?

Generally speaking, a cutting of 4 inches or less will be ready to pot when it shows roots about $1\frac{1}{2}$ inches long.

But that's not the end of it. Cuttings which come out of a closed propagation box need acclimatization to the real world (most especially in the winter when house humidity is so low). You can prop the top of the box open for several days, opening it farther the last few days before potting. Or, put the newly potted plant into a plastic bag right after potting. Punch a hole in the bag every day until it is more hole than bag. When the bag is in shreds, remove it, and the plant should be acclimated. If the plant droops, put it into another plastic bag and start making holes again, but more slowly.

How do you root geranium cuttings? In high humidity or low?

The same humidity as the rest of your plants. Take a tip cutting with some 3 or 4 inches of stem, cutting it off just below a node. Remove all flower buds and all but the youngest four or so leaves. Now, set the cutting aside for a few hours to allow the base of the cutting to callus. This helps prevent one of the major problems with geranium cuttings, rotting at the base.

Swell a Jiffy-7 peat pellet (available at most garden centers and plant stores), make a hole about ¾ inch deep in the open top with a clean pencil. Insert the cutting, perpendicular, and squeeze out the extra water as you firm in the cutting. Stand the Jiffy-7 in a 2-inch plastic flowerpot and place the pot among your other plants—in good light—and water it as you do them. The moderate humidity reduces the incidence of rot.

Since we began this method of propagating them, we've had just about 100 percent success.

If you have no peat pellets, try this alternate method that worked well for a box of scented-geranium cuttings. Pour about 1½ inches of coarse perlite into the bottom of a plastic shoebox. Dampen the perlite; make your cuttings and allow them to callus; then insert them almost to the bottom of the box and set them on a windowsill or under fluorescent lights. *But don't cover the shoebox.*

How do I propagate my streptocarpus?

How do you propagate your strep?

Let us count the ways . . .

From seed: on damp milled sphagnum moss, with a clear plastic top over the pot, but no moss covering the seed. This works best if the pot is then placed close under a single tube of fluorescent light.

By division: just turn the plant out of its pot and cut it up along the natural divisions.

By an entire leaf: insert the leaf stem (petiole) into a rooting medium (such as damp vermiculite), setting the whole into a large plastic bag. This method will take quite a while.

By leaf sections: lay the leaf on a paper towel; cut away the midrib (the thickened part that runs up the center) and discard it; cut what remains of the leaf into wedge shapes (with the points of the wedges pointing where the midrib used to be). You should now have a dozen or more pieces. Fill a small sterile flat with vermiculite and dampen it. With a clean plant label, cut deep short lines into the vermiculite to accommodate each wedge separately. Insert each wedge about a third of the way into the vermiculite and firm it gently in with the label. (Notice that your contaminating fingers have never touched the vermiculite.) Put the flat into a large plastic bag and place it under fluorescent light, or into a window with no direct sun but bright light. This method is slow, but can give you dozens of new streps.

Can snake plants really be propagated from a cross section of a leaf? I've tried it, but they always rot on me.

Sansevierias (snake plants) of all kinds can be propagated from leaf sections, so there is something faulty with your method.

Make your sections 2 inches or wider.

Keep track of which is the top and which is the bottom edge of your cutting.

Allow the bottoms to callus (dry and harden) for several hours before inserting them into your rooting medium.

Use a rooting medium with good aeration (sand, perlite, vermiculite), and keep it damp.

And propagate in the open air, not a closed prop box. Since you say yours rot, this may be where you go wrong.

Soil—and So Forth

Want to start a fight? Get up at a plant-society meeting and announce, "My soil mix can beat your soil mix!" Every advanced grower has a favorite soil mix (or soil*less* mix). We know one marvelous amateur-turned-professional who has a new favorite at least twice a year.

We are going to give you *our* current soil mix, our previous soil mix, and the one before that—just so that you won't feel we're holding out on you.

But first, what does soil do for a plant? Primarily, hold water. Food is usable by a plant only as chemical compounds dissolved from the soil (or dissolved in water and watered into the soil). Plants maintain their homeostasis (balance) largely through water they take up through their roots.

Next, it provides air. A plant must have a free exchange of gases between its roots and the soil to manufacture its food completely.

Then, soil provides support. Many plants do well only when well firmed into the soil, and all do better when their roots are holding on to something firmly than when they flop in the pot.

So, a good soil mix must hold both water and air and provide support for the roots.

Our current soil mix for houseplants is our homemade compost, pasteurized and mixed with enough perlite to allow it to drain well (see COMPOSTING). Into the compost (while it was making) we have added bone meal, eggshells (many soils are calcium-poor), cow manure, bat guano (high in phosphorus, unlike most manures which are high in nitrogen), wood ashes, and used houseplant soils which already have lighteners and some nutrients in them. Composted down in our indoor compost heap, it makes the best houseplant soil we've ever used: rich yet fluffy.

Prior to this, before we were composting, we were using a soil mix streamlined from an earlier mix.

1 quart topsoil (*not* potting soil)
1 quart sphagnum peat moss
1 quart coarse perlite
1 quart coarse vermiculite
1 tablespoon bone meal
1 handful dry cow manure

This is an excellent mix if you don't compost. (What! You don't have even one compost heap?) It will hold its nutrients for a long while, while staying aerated and providing excellent support.

Prior to this mix, we used a similar concoction, but with the addition of 1 quart of humus and a bit of limestone and perhaps a few ground-up eggshells. But humus got hard to find and we began to doubt the efficacy of the limestone.

All these mixes have been tested on literally thousands of plants, by us and by other growers.

One of the proudest things we can say about them is that they have inspired other growers to go out and find the soil mix best for them.

Soilless mixes (sometimes, and only sometimes accurately, known as Cornell mix) are growing in popularity. They are neat, clean, simple to put together. But they contain no nutrients and for our penny don't provide as firm support as we like. Also, some growers forget that a soilless mix has to be changed from time to time, and have plants just die on them from mineral buildup.

Soilless growing is sometimes called hydroponics—since the nutrients come only from water and not from soil. In these terms, any growing medium other than a soil mix becomes a soilless mix, not just the standard peat/perlite/vermiculite mix, but plain coarse perlite, or gravel.

Remember what we said about starting a fight? Well, if you want to start a *riot,* get up and say, "My soil mix can beat your soil*less* mix!"

For "soils" suited to ORCHIDACEAE, BROMELIACEAE, GESNERIACEAE, and POLYPODIACEAE—ferns—see those plant families.

To what does the term "one-one-one soil mix" refer?

Usually to a mix without any soil in it (a soilless mix) : 1 part peat moss plus 1 part coarse perlite plus 1 part vermiculite. It is popular among some fluorescent-light gardeners.

I've heard of 1-1-1 mix, but what is 1-1-1-1 mix?

Equal parts of peat moss, perlite, and vermiculite, plus an equal measure of topsoil.

1-1-1 is a soilless mix, but 1-1-1-1 has some of the virtues of a soilless mix (light weight, excellent drainage) , while providing some nutrition.

What potting mediums would you suggest for my gomesa orchid?

Fir bark or tree fern is fine, but why don't you consider mounting it on a plaque? Gomesas are epiphytic in nature, and virtually all epiphytes do better mounted.

We're not talking about cork bark, but branches of several kinds of wood you may find in your neighborhood woods. In general, you want wood that won't lose its bark (or that has already lost its bark) : sassafras, oak, cedar, or lake driftwood (no salt, you see) are all fine.

There's no need to sterilize the plaque. Choose a piece of branch with a little bit of shape.

Lay a bit of "decorator's sheet moss" (you can buy it packaged under that name) on the branch wherever you want to place the plant. Tie the moss on with some 4-pound-test fishing line or white nylon thread (you want a thread that won't rot out for a year) .

Put the base of the orchid in place, and lay another piece of "decorator's moss" over the roots (if there are any) or over the base of the plant and tie it in place with more line, firmly. The new roots will get damaged if the plant wiggles.

Soak the moss and allow it to drain.

Poke small holes in a plastic bag and cover the moss and base of the plant (leaving air holes) . You can rewater as the moss dries, soaking right through the holes in the bag. Remove the bag when new roots are well developed.

We are having some trouble finding the ingredients you recommend for bromeliad potting mix. Can't we just use your standard potting mix?

Nope. For terrestrial bromeliads you could use our standard mix for, say, 30 percent of the total, but the epiphytic bromels need an airier medium.

Can you get leaf mold? Some good bromeliad growers are potting into 60 percent or more leaf mold (mixed with sand, perhaps). If you gather your leaf mold from the woods, dampen it and bake it at 180°F. for half an hour to pasteurize it.

What would be a good potting mix for my geraniums? And how do I water them?

We grow geraniums in our standard mix, but we firm them in very well, and keep them in pots a size smaller than you'd think.

As for watering, they do best with moderate watering: feel the soil—when it is dry down to ½ inch below the surface, rewater well.

What is a good potting mix?

A good potting mix drains rapidly but provides support; it holds enough liquid for the plant to take from it food and water, and yet has enough air spaces to provide the roots with air; and it has a pH appropriate to the plants growing in it.

I was growing plants for a long while, then stopped for two years. I still have the soil that I saved from the pots. How can I recondition it to use again?

The basic question isn't difficult—the Israelis "reconditioned" the desert after thousands of years, simply by adding water.

On *your* scale, the best way to reclaim the soil is to compost it; add it to a compost heap and let the bacteria of the pile work on it. Mixing it with the other ingredients of the compost gives you an excellent potting soil. (See pages 158–163 for instructions on building an indoor compost heap.)

The compost should be pasteurized at 180° to 200°F. for half an hour before it's ready to use. If you have no compost heap, then mix the old soil with perlite (3 parts old soil to 1 part perlite) to aerate it, then dampen it and pasteurize it.

How do I tell if my potting soil is too acid or what?

Test it, of course. There are relatively inexpensive soil-test kits on the market (we've used one from Cornell that costs $3). Or your cooperative extension agent (everybody has one—even cities, now) will test it, either for a fee around $2 or for free. Contact your county agent and ask.

Finally, there are now electronic pH testers available, but they cost about $100. County agents are cheaper.

I used a layer of sand in the bottom of my pebble trays, and the plant roots have grown right into the sand! I tried to remove one plant and it seemed to have 2 feet of root in the sand. Everything seems to be growing well, but I want to repot a couple of the plants. What can I do?

Isn't sand the greatest rooting medium!

What you can do is to use saucers under your plants next time, as we recommend. As for now, don't let the sand go dry; probably your plants are taking the bulk of their water directly from the sand. It is not uncommon for a strong-rooting plant to send out roots several feet long in this kind of situation.

It may also be that you're not screening the bottoms of your pots adequately—though plants that are dry but "smell" water below will certainly send roots through screening.

As for repotting, you'll have no difficulty with the plants that have rooted just inches outside the pot. There will be some root damage but not enough, probably, to do serious harm. Do some top pruning on repotting day.

With those plants really rooted into the sand 2 feet, you are going to have serious root damage and trauma. Cut off some of that root (you wouldn't be able to fit it into a pot anyhow), and after repotting, put the whole plant into an inflated plastic bag for a few weeks.

During this time, don't water heavily, but don't let the soil dry out. Prayer helps—if not the plant, then you.

Can I grow foliage plants just in vermiculite?

We have had cane begonias and tradescantia, and epipremnum (formerly scindapsis) growing in vermiculite for three years, accidentally, because we never did pot them out of our open propagation box—be we don't recommend it.

If you really wanted to grow plants in vermiculite, you would have to feed, lightly, at almost every watering. You would also need to provide staking because the vermiculite doesn't support well.

And friends of ours have warned us of potassium buildup with some brands of vermiculite.

In measuring the parts for a peat-lite mix, do you measure the peat moss wet or dry?

You measure everything as it comes from the package. (Peat-lite is a 1-1 mix of perlite and peat moss.)

What is the difference between perlite and vermiculite?

Perlite is heat-expanded volcanic rock; vermiculite is heat-expanded mica.

Perlite holds water on the irregularities of its rough surfaces; vermiculite absorbs water into its accordionlike interior.

Perlite has a pH on the alkaline side, and no nutritive value.

Vermiculite has a neutral pH but contains potassium.

Perlite is white; vermiculite is tan.

Perlite is hard and holds its structure well, but in a soil mix tends to float to the surface. Vermiculite stays where you put it, but being soft and squishy must not be handled at all; so it has a shorter use life than perlite.

Don't breathe the dust of either, because both are irritants.

How should I sterilize used potting soil?

Don't sterilize it, pasteurize it. Dampen it (not sopping wet), put it into a deep roasting pan, set a meat thermometer into the thickest part, set it into the middle of your oven, and "roast" at very low temperature. It should cook at between 180° and 200° F. for thirty minutes (that is, stay at that temperature for about thirty minutes).

Temperature:
Growing Hot and Cold

The continuing oil "crisis" is a good thing for your plants—if you are running your indoor temperatures lower to conserve fuel, that is. Every houseplant you can think of grows better at a daytime temperature of 68°F. than at 74°F. And at night, a temperature drop of 10 or 15 degrees will benefit most plants—and not harm the others. In fact, many of your shrubby houseplants, jungle cacti, and other fall and winter bloomers won't set bud without that night drop.

Temperatures consistently over 74°F., on the other hand, unless accompanied by the strongest of bright light, will give you weak growth and premature bud drop.

Will the cold air from an air conditioner harm my plants?

One reads a lot about the importance of keeping plants out of "drafts." A draft is a blast of air with a sharply contrasting temperature. In our apartment, one window, opened a bit at the top, is the only winter temperature regulation (and air circulation) that we have. But the "sharply contrasting" outdoor air is very soon warmed as it enters through the opening. We have had an *Epiphyllum acker-mannii* (orchid cactus) spend the winter with a leaf sitting right in an open window. The plant flowered! And the one leaf was only slightly damaged. But orchid cacti are tough plants. We have seen a phalaenopsis (moth orchid) sitting inches from the front of a fan in a greenhouse in summer, shaken by the wind every few seconds as the fan oscillated. But orchids are sturdy plants. Air circulation is vitally important to most plants. But drafts can be damaging to warm-growers —or to plants habituated to warm temperatures.

To get back to your question: it is a poor practice to grow plants directly in the blast of an air conditioner. If you remove the plants even a little way, the air will be warmed and the force abated.

And some plants, like orchids and cacti, will be better able to withstand the draft than others.

I have long plastic windowbox-type planters on my terrace, and my tuberous begonias were coming along fine, but now the buds are dropping, unopened. I give them plenty of water, but they dry out very quickly. I'm using your standard potting mix with a little extra peat. Should I change their soil?

It's not the soil—it's the August heat. It sounds as if your plastic boxes are absorbing too much heat (or perhaps the surface of your terrace is—especially if it's black).

Tuberous begonias prefer coolish temperatures—especially at night—and if your terrace and/or boxes absorb a lot of heat during the day, not only do they dry the soil but they hold the heat into the usually cool nighttime.

Can you raise the boxes and paint or lay down a reflective surface?

Can you sink your planters into larger planters with a layer of wet peat moss between?

Both will help, as will hosing everything down a few times a day during the hottest weather.

At any rate, until you cool it (or the weather does) your buds will continue to blast.

All the plants in my south window are looking limp, yellow, and generally poor. The humidity in the room is about 50 percent (by a wet-bulb hygrometer) through most of the day. My soil drains well, and I keep the plants well watered. Could there be some kind of sickness in the window?

The sickness is called "heat." A south window is great for light, but it can be lousy for heat. The light rays coming through the glass are converted to heat. Some inches back from the glass, the heat dissipates, but close to the glass, the heat can be damaging, even in the winter.

This problem can be ameliorated by opening the window or by having a small circulating fan in the window.

By the way, it's obvious you didn't put your wet-bulb hygrometer right in the window, or the thermometer part would have indicated the high temperature; and the relative humidity would have registered very low in that heat—whatever the relative humidity in the rest of the room.

My African violets are sitting on a south window, but they look ratty—have stopped flowering. I thought they wanted lots of sun.

They do very well in moderately strong sun, but they suffer from *heat*. A south window can be a *hot* window—and that's what your problem sounds to be. Provide some air movement in the window (perhaps with a small electric fan). If necessary, put a lightweight curtain in the window, close the curtain at midday, and open it during the cooler parts of the day.

I have a room I call my indoor greenhouse, where I grow many plants under lights—but it gets so *hot!* Into the nineties when the lights are on. It seemed like such a good idea when I put in the shelves, but my growth is weak, and I'm sure it's from the heat. What can I do?

We agree with you: something must be done about the heat. First of all, you must vent the room: an exhaust fan in an open window, thermostatted to go on when the temperature goes over 75°F.; a small humidifier specifically in that room, on all hours that the lights are on (just plug it into the same timer that does your lights); and, if these measures are not enough, you may have to install a small air conditioner for that room.

If these seem like costly measures, you have a sizable investment in your "indoor greenhouse," in plants, labor, and emotions as well as the cost of your tubes and fixtures. (We never promised you a *cheap* rose garden.)

Can I grow plants on my radiators over the winter?

Yes, you can—provided your radiators are under windows and your plants get some light—but not unless you do something to keep the heat away from the plants. We recommend using pebble trays on top of the radiators and under the plants.

A pebble tray is any shallow waterproof container the size of your radiator or larger (not smaller—though two or three such containers put together work just as well). This container has a thick layer of gravel (or coarse perlite or sand or stones or broken-up bricks) put into its bottom. Water is added to just below the top of the gravel.

The plants are set on small saucers on top of the gravel. (The saucers are to keep the roots from growing into the gravel.)

You can have trays made to measure by a tinsmith—from aluminum or galvanized iron—you can recycle the drip trays or vegetable crispers from discarded refrigerators, or you can even use wooden trays painted inside with marine epoxy and/or lined with a sheet of heavy plastic.

The heat is dissipated by the water between the radiator and the plants while at the same time additional winter humidity is provided for the plants by evaporation.

My hanging tradescantia got frozen in my window last night. Is there anything I can do for it?

Probably not. If it looks watery, it is likely dead. As a last resort, cut it back to within an inch or so of the soil. But it's a faint hope.

I have just discovered the most horrendous thing. Last night, hearing it was to be the coldest night of the year, I went around putting newspapers inside the windows. But I missed one inside windowbox, and this morning I have frozen geraniums and English ivy. Is there anything I can do?

Dry your eyes. The two plants you mention should not be killed inside a window by cold weather. *Hedera helix* (English ivy) is fully hardy even outdoors (though it may lose some leaves).

We have had our pelargonium (geranium) leaves actually freeze to the inside of a window without apparent harm.

I bought a coleus at a florist on Christmas day. Within three hours of my getting it home, the leaves were droopy and then died. The plant was watered. What could have happened?

Winter happened—or perhaps you hadn't noticed. Almost all the plants we grow as houseplants are sensitive to cold. Buying a plant (perhaps it had already been out in front of the store for a while before you bought it) and carrying it around in subfreezing weather can kill it unless you protect it.

It should be wrapped in a couple of layers of paper—that will insulate it somewhat and protect it from the wind. It should be taken home under your coat—body heat is free.

And if the weather is too fierce and you have a long way to go—don't buy it at all.

I want to take a flowering plant to a friend who will be in the hospital over New Year's. What do you suggest?

There are still kalanchoe hybrids available in the shops, and we've fallen in love with them. They come in red, orange, pink, yellow, and white and are easy to care for, with long-lasting flowers. And when your friend comes out of the hospital, she or he will have an excellent chance to keep the plant alive.

Your real problem with any houseplant you buy in the cold weather is taking that tropical darling out of the warm store, through freezing streets, to your destination. A couple of layers of wrapping paper helps—but if you buy a really cold-sensitive plant, like an episcia, nothing less than an insulated picnic hamper will do if you have to walk any distance in the cold.

Watering
and Overwatering

While *when* to water varies from plant to plant and pot to pot, *how* to water is the same for most of your houseplants: water until the water comes out the bottom of the pot. A half-hour later, if there is still any water left in the saucer unsoaked up, throw it away.

This way, you soak the rootball, first by pouring through the soil, second by allowing the soil to soak up any more water it may need from below: a combination of top *and* bottom watering. Except for aquatics or semiaquatics (like colocasia), don't allow your plants to sit in water past that half-hour or so.

In the case of seriously overdried plants, soak the pot in a sink or pail of water until the surface is well wet. Then allow the plant to drain off, and discard any excess water.

Cold water will be a shock to roots and may discolor leaves. Plants can stand quite warm water, and we have spoken to a begonia grower experimenting successfully with hot water. Still, we prefer to use water at room temperature or a little warmer. You can't shock a plant with that.

There is no water so hard that it can't be given to plants—at least we've never heard of one. But mineral-rich water will leave deposits more quickly than will soft water.

Don't water only from the bottom. Bottom-watering causes fertilizer salts to rise to the surface of the soil, where they can deposit and damage stems.

If your way of watering has been working for you, don't suddenly change because of us or anybody else's advice. Plants *can* adjust to changes in watering style, but only if they are gradual.

I've heard you say that this plant or another is impossible to over-water—and I've got to tell you that sounds pretty silly.

You don't listen. What we've said is that it is impossible to overwater such plants as spathiphyllum or gardenias *in a well-drained soil*. If water sits on the surface of your soil before draining through, then it is *not* well drained. For a well-drained potting mix, see SOIL—AND SO FORTH.

Is there any way I can tell if it is time to water my plants—I mean without digging into the soil?

We assume you mean before the plant withers and dies from lack of water.

There are a number of ways. After watering, heft the pot: get to know what its weight is both watered and dry. Many professionals go by weight.

In clay pots, the pot will feel damp and cool where the soil is watered but dry and at room temperature where the soil is dry. This coolness can even be detected somewhat in plastic pots.

Finally, tap the pot. A watered pot has a different sound from one that needs watering. But it does take practice to tell the difference. In fact, all three of these methods take practice.

What have you got against putting your finger in the soil?

You say you have a thousand plants, but how can you take care of so many plants? I have forty-seven plants, and it takes me too long to water them. Don't you ever get bored with it or tired of it?

Tired? Yes. But bored? Never. It does take a long time to care for our plants—especially to water them. Usually we've been lucky, and when one of us gets too tired to water, the other one carries the buckets—and then we'll switch.

And sometimes a plant dies—from neglect or from being hidden behind another plant, or from any of a dozen other sad reasons.

But plants are plants and usually replaceable; they are not pets and they are not kids—thank goodness. And we have learned not to feel guilty about the death of a plant. It is not our ego on the line. If a plant has died because we didn't know how, then it's just an opportunity to learn how next time.

Besides, when we're watering or otherwise caring for our plants is when we really see them as individuals, not background, when we see what's new and really enjoy them. We are near enough to smell them—and near enough to find the new bug before it becomes a problem. Plants are for joy, and they are never such a joy as when proper care makes them thrive.

I have a large plant collection, and it seems I take *hours* to water my plants—they are just taking over my life. Aside from throwing them out, have you any suggestions?

Assuming that you're happy with your collection as it is, try hosing instead of carrying cans of water. This is not as bizarre as it sounds. In a hardware store you can buy the kind of fixture they put onto faucets for washing-machine hookups. Then, attach an appropriate length of garden hose with a good cutoff valve at the outlet end.

To use, turn the water on gently, with the outlet valve at "off," carry the hose over to your plants, and water all of them without filling a single can.

When not in use, leave the hose neatly coiled under the sink to which you've attached the fixture.

Remember, use a gentle stream, as you would from a small watering can.

There are watering wands available based on this principle, but we haven't tried them because they don't fit on our ancient sink fixtures.

Part III

Specialities

Balcony, Terrace, Rooftop

A balcony is a platform projecting from the side of a building, generally surrounded by a railing or parapet. It can be of any size, though it tends to be small, often hardly large enough to swing a cattail, and usually (except for the top floor) has another identical structure hanging over it. Our apartment is supposed to have a "balcony": it is 5 feet wide and 1½ feet deep. Large enough to stand on to wash the windows, but little else.

A terrace, though the term is often used synonymously with balcony, should have some terracing: that is, extend farther out than any structure above it. Terraces are usually larger than balconies, and they can have "interesting" shapes. One friend of ours lives in a penthouse that has a terrace that runs around the apartment for about 50 feet in all—but it's only 3 feet deep. We had a cousin who looked at the *plans* of a building going up and bought the apartment at the setback. She not only had a large terrace of her own to play with but got the rights to garden the top of the lower half of the building. Now *that* is a terrace.

A terrace does not have to be attached to an apartment building: it can be on ground level and part of a house.

Unlike balconies and terraces, which are usually put onto more expensive buildings, any building with a flat roof and access to it can have a rooftop garden. And rooftop gardens are often the most satisfying of all. The open areas allow you so much sun that you can, on a rooftop, grow any vegetable you wish—as long as you can provide enough water. Make certain your roof will support the weight of your garden (building specifications are always on file) .

That virtually all new apartment buildings are being constructed with balconies is very encouraging, but we do wish that more architects had enough imagination to alternate them rather than stack them. Stacking cuts off so much light. Not that you can't find excellent shade-tolerant plants, but the lack of sun eliminates roses—which are probably the perfect flowering city plant.

Sun or shade, your main balcony problem is going to be dirt. If you have an outdoor water faucet, great, but if you don't, we suggest you buy enough garden hose to run from inside to your garden. With a spraying attachment, you can easily water and wash off the leaves of your plant. City soot and dust can really keep light off of leaves and inhibit photosynthesis. A regular hosing-down of the undersides as well as the tops of leaves will wash away most of the dirt and keep bug problems under control too.

What perennial will flower in boxes of soil on my balcony? I get only morning sun.

Day lilies (hemerocallis) !

Day lilies are the queen of a balcony garden. By planting several varieties you can have bloom over many weeks.

Not as floriferous, but quite shade-tolerant, plantain lily (hosta) runs a close second.

Can I have rose plants on my east-facing balcony?

Absolutely! And they will be as hardy as roses in the ground, if you give them containers about 18 inches square.

The only special problem with roses in containers is that they dry out rapidly in hot weather.

Can I grow a blue spruce on my balcony?

Yes, but for a full-sized spruce you would need a box about 4 feet square. Will your balcony hold all that weight?

Dwarf evergreen shrubs are fully hardy on balcony or terrace and demand much less soil (a box 12 to 14 inches square) . They are much smaller and slower-growing too.

How do I prune the containered raspberries on my terrace? I don't seem to be getting much fruit.

Well, you can't just give your raspberries a crew cut and expect them to do well.

They flower and fruit on *year-old wood,* which means that the new branches must be allowed to mature (or ripen), while the old branches must be cut back after they bear—all the way back to the base. Poor pruning practices can reduce fruiting drastically.

And be careful—those thorns are rippers.

Can you recommend a couple of wind-resistant small trees (or big shrubs) for a very windy terrace?

We enjoyed one penthouse gardener's trees, all of which were pendulous. These weeping grafted trees cost more at the nursery, but have the additional wind resistance of staying relatively compact. Two of these beauties are Siberian pea tree (*Caragana arborescens*) and Camperdown elm (*Ulmus glabra camperdownii*).

Siberian pea is the ideal tree for a windy location. It will live happily in a 2-foot tub outdoors year round, bear yellow flowers in the spring, and then hold its brown pendant seed pods for a long while.

Camperdown elm is most handsome when in leaf, but of an interesting shape, too. And wind-resistant.

Russian olive (*Elaeagnus angustifolia*) has silvery-gray undersides to its narrow leaves, which makes it a most handsome plant. It, too, is very hardy and very wind-resistant.

What is a good shrub that will be attractive year round on a penthouse terrace?

Do you mean *all* year? If so, you want something evergreen. Though the traditional needle-leafed evergreens are *green* in the winter, we are loath to give them the space the rest of the year. Try a broad-leafed evergreen, such as *Rhododendron carolinianum.* Though not hardy in the far north, it is excellent in a large tub on a New York balcony, and will give you lots of flowers in only moderate sun.

If you will settle for something beautiful *most* of the year, mountain ash (sorbus) is a lovely deciduous tree that can be grown in a large tub. It has reddish berries into the winter, until the birds come along and eat them. Any sorbus will do because all have noticeable flowers, then berries, then gorgeous fall leaves, but *Sorbus decora* (showy mountain ash) has showier, larger fruit.

Pyracanthus (firethorn) will have orange or red berries all winter long, and will stay considerably smaller than the ash.

We are growing "Garden Delight," a genetic dwarf nectarine, in a 24-inch half-barrel, and even without a single leaf, the buds and branches are beautiful. (We are providing it with some winter wind protection.)

But probably the most beautiful of the containerable shrubs is plain old high-bush blueberry—which is a delight for most of the year. It flowers in early spring, then bears delicious fruit, makes a handsome summer shrub, and, in the fall, the leaves turn brilliant colors. And, in the winter, the bare branches make interesting patterns against the sky—if you go for that sort of thing.

My terrace dwarf apple tree is showing a chewing out of the leaf. I look for insects, but see none.

Well, something is chomping on your leaves, and if it's not a hungry child it's a bug—and if you don't see it during the day then it's a night feeder. Black vine weevils were around for a while, but they are so difficult to get rid of, let's sidestep that possibility for a moment.

Let's say the likelihood is that you have slugs. Look on your leaves and trunk for the shiny slime trails slugs leave (slime trails look like dried strips of airplane glue). If you are not eating the fruit, or the plant is too young to fruit, you can use a slugicide with metaldehyde in it. But we prefer a nonpoison method. Take jar lids of mayonnaise or similar size, sink them into the soil so that they are level with the soil, and fill with beer. The slugs die happy. To really find out what you have, go out late at night with a flashlight and shine the light on your plant. You should see the pests. Slugs can be picked off by hand.

Weevils are hard and small (about ¼ inch long) and can move rapidly. Sad to say, a plant with weevils should be thrown away—though you can try bare-rooting, discarding the soil, and potting afresh. This is very dangerous to the plant and an alternative only to discarding a favorite.

It is midsummer, but my 4-foot blue spruce (it is in a 14-inch cedar box on my balcony) is turning yellow. It started slowly but now seems to be getting worse.

Fourteen inches is not big for a 4-foot blue spruce (*Picea pungens* varieties). At this time of year, it will want a great deal of water. The container may just be too small to allow it enough water. If you are not watering frequently, water more often.

Consider repotting. And if you decide to repot, do it now—don't wait for the fall.

I have squirrels in my penthouse garden—I don't want to set traps. Is there anything I can do to keep them away?

Find their access routes and put rat guards over them (the kind they put over ropes on ships in port). Try putting up some chicken-wire fencing over the edge of the wall.

If these don't work, write us again and we'll send you a diagram for an electrified fence.

You had a guest on your radio show who spoke of having roses on his balcony as late as December (in Manhattan). What rose was it? My balcony roses are out of flower by the end of October.

Apparently you missed his point—he had a hot-water pipe running under a part of his balcony. Bottom heat, combined with burlap fencing protecting the plant from the wind, allowed the rose to stay in flower.

Though his case was extreme, you may have some luck of your own.

Take a thermometer and leave it in various places on your balcony, and you will discover there is quite a bit of variation. By gardening specific microclimates, you may be able to extend your own flowering season considerably.

Speaking of gardening microclimates, the United Nations garage is located under its rose garden, generating a lot of warmth—and in the open they cut their last roses at about Thanksgiving.

Do I have to bring my *Ficus carica* plant in from the terrace for the winter?

Kept in a protected corner, *Ficus carica* (edible fig) can stay outside with minimal protection as far north as Long Island.

Does mulching the tubs on my balcony do any good? I mean, does it provide any protection against the cold?

It does—and the deeper the mulch, the better the protection. In addition, for even more effective protection, you can wrap your tubs in heavy tar paper.

This year we moved to an apartment in Danbury, Connecticut. Can I keep my evergreens alive through the winter without spraying with an antidesiccant?

The enemy of evergreens in tubs on terrace or balcony is wind, not cold—as you seem to know. The wind blowing across the leaves dries them out, which causes the plant to draw more water up from the roots. If the soil is frozen solid, no water is available and the leaves dry and die. The antidesiccant (antidrying agent) deposits a thin film of plastic on the leaves, and very little water is lost through evaporation. Rains wash the plastic off, and so it must be reapplied in mid-winter.

Anything that keeps the wind off the leaves—such as burlap woven through a fence or wrapped around the plant—acts in a similarly protective manner.

I'm afraid that my roof will not support large tubs of soil. Can you suggest a solution?

Yes, you can use a soilless mix. Soilless mixes are *much* lighter than soil mixes. But, remember, you'll have to feed at one-eighth strength with every watering.

I want to build flower boxes for my terrace. What wood would you suggest?

Cypress lasts very well. Redwood is durable, too, but those redwood trees are becoming an endangered species. Oak is handsome and tough.

What kind of containers would you suggest for a terrace?

We like well-cleaned half- or quarter-barrels, with holes drilled into the bottoms for drainage, and casters for easier moving. They are durable (and used to be cheap).

In case you've never come across the phrase before, half-barrels are large barrels cut in half horizontally; quarter-barrels are about half as deep (we suppose the center is just thrown away).

The casters are wheels that are placed under or screwed into the bottom and are sold separately.

I have a balcony that is overhung by the balcony upstairs. It does get an hour or so of sun in the afternoon. Is there any shrub I can grow there? I mean to leave out all year.

Hydrangea macrophylla (snowball, *boule de neige*) sounds perfect for your situation. It should flower for you—if not as profusely as if grown in full sun outdoors—and will survive even severe winters with a little protection. Grow it in a 16-inch tub in an acid soil, and don't keep it sopping—but don't allow it to go dry.

Can I grow an elm tree on my rooftop garden?

We have a friend who has had great success with Camperdown elm (*Ulmus glabra camperdownii*) in a half-barrel (with drainage holes drilled into the bottom). The tree, which is compact, lives outside on a New York rooftop all year.

I would like to grow an evergreen shrub on my shady terrace; can you recommend one?

Try yew (taxus) and arborvitae (thuja) for narrow-leafed evergreens, and rhododendron as a broad-leafed evergreen. Yew is dioecious: male and female flowers are borne on separate plants. This means you need plants of both sexes to make berries—not that either berries or flowers are going to be plentiful in a place as shady as yours.

My wife and I are thinking of putting up a plastic greenhouse on our apartment-building rooftop—what problems are we likely to run into?

A stubborn landlord, for one.

Also, rooftops are hot, so lots of watering and hosing down will be necessary.

Some small plastic greenhouses are unvented; that is, they make no provision for air circulation or the release of the heat built up by the sun (from the greenhouse effect).

Finally, soot. This greasy stuff will not hose off with water alone. A hose nozzle which accepts pellets of detergent is on the market; though sold for car-washing, no one will tell if you use it to wash your greenhouse.

The tomato ("Patio" type) on my terrace dropped its flowers this summer. I keep it well watered. What happened?

When temperatures go over 90°F., tomato buds will just drop from the heat. Balconies and terraces will often be even hotter than the rest of the world if the building absorbs heat or the terrace is floored in black.

If you have a hot terrace, make certain your tomatoes are in white (reflective) pots, or sink the pot into another pot, filling the space between with damp peat moss—this will keep the roots cooler.

Could I put some gravel for drainage in the bottom of my windowbox instead of drilling holes?

Drill holes. Otherwise, rain will gather in the bottom and perhaps rot you out. Drill.

Bonsai:
Plant Martial Art

It bothers us that young bonsai plants are sold to beginners for as much as $80 with just the sketchiest of advice (often wrong) and no book on bonsai or bonsai course. Which gives these little plants a life expectancy of three to ten weeks.

Would you practice brain surgery without knowing which end the brain was in? Plant roots are not brains and surgery on them is not as delicate—but bonsai does require at least a minimum of good instruction or reading for success.

We have a lot to learn from the practitioners of this art. Their concepts of the relationship of plant to container, of leaf surface to root length, can teach us a great deal about growing all houseplants.

If you have wondered about the desirability of this form of artistic expression (the only one that requires "cooperation" between "artist" and "subject"), and you have regarded it as a form of torture for the plant, perhaps you don't know that the longest-lived plants in cultivation are bonsai plants: there are many that have been in collections for well over a hundred years.

Can I grow my bonsai serissa indoors all winter, or must I keep it cold?

Serissa foetida is a tender plant, makes a tender bonsai, and should certainly be grown *indoors* year round. It will want frequent watering, perhaps twice daily in the summer, and it must not be allowed to go dry even in winter.

Give it your brightest window year round . . . and take a bonsai course at a nearby botanical or horticultural institution.

I have a juniper bonsai plant that is losing its leaves. Is it supposed to die in the wintertime?

No, junipers are evergreen. When you got the plant did anyone tell you that it might require daily watering—except in hot weather, when it might require twice-daily watering? And did anyone tell you that in winter it should be kept at about 40°F.?

Hardy bonsai plants all demand frequent summer watering and special winter care, and are not really appropriate for the inexperienced indoor grower.

Instead, we would like to recommend *shrubby houseplants* as bonsai: they take well to root pruning, they require no more watering (and no less) than hardy bonsai, and since they are in growth year round, they demand no special winter care.

Think it over.

In bonsai class, I worked on a dwarf Japanese holly (*Ilex crenata convexa*); I have followed directions, but after a day and a half the leaves began falling. Help!

In a way, the bonsai treatment of any plant (root pruning, especially) is a real blow and trauma to the plant. A root-pruned plant will often need "emergency-tent" treatment, which means high humidity and bright light without direct sun. A plastic bag will do, or you can put it into an existing terrarium.

But why didn't you call your teacher? At any rate, hardy bonsai plants are difficult in a heated winter house or apartment without special instructions.

A new kind of bonsai being taught is houseplant bonsai (tender bonsai) . This is much better for the average grower because the plants require no winter dormancy or special equipment beyond the tools needed to make the bonsai.

The Brooklyn Botanic Garden at 1000 Washington Avenue, Brooklyn, NY 11225 (probably the greatest center for bonsai study in the Occident) sells three booklets ($1.75 each) on bonsai, two for hardy bonsai and one for tender bonsai.

✐ ✐ ✐ ✐

Edibles

Eating something you've grown yourself is a marvelous experience, especially for kids. And especially for us city dwellers—after all, we are kids when it comes to knowing and understanding the problems of food production.

There is no location that is incapable of growing something edible, from tomatoes in a sunny bay window to bean sprouts in a closet.

That is not to say that every indoor situation will yield a large crop; however, the federal government is lending urban gardeners a helping hoe. Congress has passed an appropriation for the USDA of about $3 million providing for county agents where there were none, and for the establishment and furtherance of an Urban Gardening Program all over the country. If you have a community group that would like to participate in this program, call your county agent (county agents are usually discovered by calling Cooperative Extension under your state listing) .

You know, there are reasons other than education and amusement for growing your own edibles. When you grow it yourself, you know what it has been raised on and you know if it has been sprayed. Besides, often, the best-tasting vegetables are not the best travelers or the best keepers. Agribusiness grows for shelf-life and traveling, not flavor.

Can we grow cucumbers on our windowsill?

You can grow them outside a sunny windowsill, if you're satisfied with a crop of one or two cukes. Cucumbers are *gross* feeders and big drinkers. We have seen them grown successfully right on a rooftop compost heap. We grew them one year on our tiny balcony in large wooden boxes (too large, really, for a windowsill) full of ultrarich soil. But the crop was not worth the space or the manure.

Are there really any strawberries that I can grow on my windowsill? I mean everbearers, to harvest all summer?

We have a friend who swears by the strawberry variety named "Baron Solemacher." This past year she picked berries every morning into late November, taking, from half a dozen plants in 6-inch pots, enough berries for breakfast every morning. And when we were looking for an almost foolproof plant for a beginner, our favorite herb grower recommended "Baron Solemacher."

Give it as much bright sun as you can, and don't allow it to dry out.

I got a ginger root from a Chinese grocery on impulse. Can I grow it in a pot? Can I then eat it? Can I flower it? I have some friends in Majorca who sent me pictures of their beautiful ginger plants—but they grow them in the ground.

What your friends are growing is probably ornamental ginger (though some of the ornamental gingers are also edible).

What you bought is *Zingiber officinale* (common ginger). Even in the tropics, where it can be grown outdoors year round, common ginger does only make tall, thin, plain green reedlike growth.

But, sure, you can grow it in a pot, and even expect some increase in the tubers—if you're lucky. And you can eat your crop or replant it for still more ginger. Also, you can snip the leaves into a salad or just munch on them. They have some of the ginger taste, but little of the ginger snap.

To grow it, bury a tuber about 1 inch under a porous soil and keep it moist and warm. It should soon sprout, at which time you move it into the sun. It is unlikely to flower.

While we are mentioning the ginger family (Zingiberaceae), there is one family member you should try as a houseplant if you have enough space and a sense of adventure: costus. Plants of this genus generally grow *in a spiral,* and may be sold as "spiral ginger." The leaves of this tender shrub are often striped.

Can I grow ginger in a container on my balcony?

Yes, and in a large enough container you'll get not only the green tops (which can be cut into a salad or nibbled) but also a spreading and multiplication of the tubers.

Ginger is not winter-hardy, so a crop can be taken in the fall and all the tubers lifted. Either save some for replanting or buy fresh roots for spring planting.

How do I "blanch" my chives for freezing?

Chives needn't be blanched. Just put them into small plastic bags and freeze. Then you defrost a packet at a time, as you need chives.

What is an "onion set"?

A very immature onion. Onions can take quite long from seed (in some areas, more growing time than weather permits).

Commercial growers start the onions from seed, grow them for a couple of months, then take them up when less than an inch across and store them over the fall for sale. You buy the sets, plant them, and take up a full-grown onion at the end of the season (when the green foliage browns and dies down).

Some short-season onions are available from seed, but the more desirable globe type are almost exclusively grown from sets—in most of the country.

Are onions practical for a windowsill gardener?

Not really. In a windowbox, perhaps, but not in a pot. Even in a windowbox, they take up space. If you have enough sun for onions, you can get a much bigger crop of tomatoes from the same space.

Can I grow garlic and shallots on a shaded windowsill?

Your bulb crops (garlic, shallots, onions) need sun to build the bulb. But if you are growing the garlic and shallots for the greens (the young tops are excellent clipped into salads), you don't need sun.

Can I grow Jerusalem artichokes on my terrace?

You certainly can. *Helianthus tuberosus* (Jerusalem artichoke) is a fine, low-calorie food, and lowest in calories when freshest. It is a close relative of *Helianthus annuus* (sunflower).

Heli-anthus means literally "sun flower," in a combination of Greek and Latin. This vegetable is called "Jerusalem" artichoke probably as a corruption of its Italian name *girasole:* "turn to the sun." So there you have it in Greek, Latin, and Italian. Plant these vigorous vegetables only in the fullest of full sun.

Plant the tubers as early as you can chop a hole into the soil (say, March—they like a long season), four tubers in a large container—a half-barrel or a large box. Allow to go part dry between waterings, and grow in compost or some other very rich soil.

Store the tubers cold (in the fridge).

You can find American or Jerusalem artichokes in health-food stores, in some small greengrocers, and in A & P stores, where they are called "sunchokes."

I want to make a manure tea to feed my terrace vegetables. I have dried manure; what proportions do I use?

About 1 cup of dry manure to 1 gallon of water, left to soak overnight. You want a color that really looks like tea. If it's too dark-looking, thin it out; if it looks too weak, make it stronger next time.

We hope there is bone meal in your soil (or ground phosphate rock) to provide phosphorus along with the nitrogen provided by the manure.

(We love to find organic terrace and indoor growers.)

Can I grow radishes on my windowsill?

Yes, but why bother? A single radish plant, which yields a single radish, will grow in a 4-inch pot. That's a lot of space for a little return. You can grow enough mustard greens or curly cress for half a salad in the same sunny space.

What's the fastest vegetable crop I can have under lights?

The fastest vegetable crop of all is bean sprouts. In springtime, mung beans grown in a covered dish—in the light or out of it—barely dampened two or three times a day, will be edible in three days. In the winter, it may take five days.

We soak the beans overnight (2 ounces of beans in 2 cups of water), then discard the excess water. Continue to wash and discard the excess water twice a day until the beans have tails about 1 inch to 1½ inches long. We keep our dish covered to eliminate dust and bugs.

Do vegetables in pots get fed like houseplants?

No, they generally require *more* food than houseplants. Tomatoes, for instance, are gross feeders; cucumbers are *very* gross feeders. Tomatoes get fed 15–30–15 plant food at full label strength. Cucumbers get the same, plus having dry manure in their soil.

Green peppers must have ample root room and, like tomatoes, need a food high in phosphorus.

Leafy crops, like lettuce and spinach, should get a high-nitrogen food such as fish emulsion (at label strength) or manure tea, every two weeks.

Herbs are exceptions to this heavy feeding schedule. Give herbs a monthly half-strength feeding—and easy on the nitrogen.

Quick crops like cress and mustard greens—crops that will be in the pot a month or less—need not be fed at all.

Under four tubes of fluorescent light my "Atomic" tomato has flowered very well all winter, but it won't set fruit. Why?

Indoors, tomatoes just won't self-pollinate readily. You can take one open flower and poke its face at other open flowers, or you can blow into every open flower, or you can just give the plant a shake every couple of days while in flower (gently but firmly).

As soon as the windows open, the breeze will pollinate for you.

How often do I water tomatoes on my windowsill?

Tomatoes should never be allowed to go dry. As soon as the surface of the soil dries at all, water well. This may be twice a day in really hot weather.

Can the tomato seed from a tomato I buy in the market be grown into a plant in a pot if I have enough sun?

Tomatoes can of course be grown from the seeds taken from your market tomato. But it won't necessarily be the same tomato. The tomatoes we buy are often F1 hybrids, and don't necessarily come true from seed.

Also, the tomatoes grown for market are not grown for taste: for color, for shipping, for self-life—but not for flavor. Of course, they are free, once you've bought the tomato. To take the tomato seeds, simply squeeze some seeds from the tomato onto a paper towel. Spread them over the towel thinly, hang the towel, and allow it to dry. Just peel off the seeds when you are ready to plant them.

My windowbox tomato flowers are dropping off. I keep them well watered and fed. Why do they fall?

They fall because they are not pollinated. Perhaps the weather had a cold snap or a hot spell—either would hinder pollination. The flowers that open in more temperate temperatures should set fruit readily.

Can you grow a really good tomato plant indoors in a pot?

Absolutely. If you have bright sun. Give it a large pot (12 inches or more), plenty of water, plenty of food, pollinate it (by shaking it or blowing at it) when in bloom, and you can have a dynamite tomato plant. But, as you may have noticed, this takes a commitment of time and effort.

What tomato grows best on a balcony? Do I have to grow miniatures?

Not at all. In fact, any tomato that a vegetable-patch gardener can grow in the ground can be grown in a tub of soil (say 12 inches to 18 inches square). "Patio" is a superior compact plant with smallish fruit; "Better Boy" is an excellent beefsteak type; get "Roma" for plum-type tomatoes; "Ramapo" is a long-season tomato, but fine if you have a sunny protected place for late-season growth. There are many great tomato varieties, and new ones coming out every year.

No, by no means must you stick to miniatures.

Do tomato plants in pots have to be fed?

Yes, and quite heavily, at full strength according to label instructions (all vegetables in pots have to be fed regularly), with a plant food of the proportions 5–10–5 or even 6–18–6.

Even if you use a rich potting soil (say, your own compost) and a large pot—both of which are desirable for tomatoes—you will want to feed your potted tomato with a food rich in potassium and low in nitrogen. A food high in nitrogen and low in potassium will inhibit the flowering and fruiting of your tomatoes.

I'm growing "Tiny Tim" tomatoes in a large box on my balcony. I give the plant plenty of sun and water, but the lower leaves are dropping. It is making tomatoes, but if this goes on, I'll soon have a tomato-palm! What can I do?

Your tomatoes are suffering (probably) from verticillium wilt (a fungus disease). There is no cure, but there is something you can do: discard the soil and next season grow a tomato that is verticillium-resistant. In the catalogs, tomato offerings are sometimes followed by the letters "VFN" or "VF." This means that that particular variety of tomato is resistant to verticillium wilt, fusarium wilt (another fungus disease), and nematodes; or just verticillium and fusarium wilts.

Now, why are you growing "Tiny Tim"? This is a tomato for those of us with little space; it is a tomato for a windowsill or for a light garden. In a large box on a balcony you can grow a full-sized tomato. Or, if you want a compact plant, try "Patio," which is VFN-resistant and gives you tomatoes twice as large as "Tiny Tim."

My "Tiny Tim" tomato has been in flower and making tomatoes on my east windowsill for a year and a half. Did you ever hear of this kind of "perennial tomato"?

Tomato *is* a tender perennial, and, given the sun, food, water, and soil, it will grow on and on (though two years is the oldest we've heard of). Don't be afraid to cut it back somewhat when it gets leggy. And then root the cuttings (they root readily). It's the cold weather, not flowering, that ends the life of the tomatoes in the outdoor garden.

I am growing "Ramapo" tomato on my balcony this summer in your standard potting mix (you recommended "Ramapo" on TV), but the plant looks leggy and so far I've got all of two flowers. Could they be suffering from a vitamin deficiency?

What it sounds like is *sunlight deficiency*. Tomatoes need sun. Is your balcony sunny enough for tomatoes?

And do feed: they need plenty of food—15–30–15 food or any tomato food at full label strength.

Can I grow a "Pixie" hybrid tomato in a bright southern window this summer?

Absolutely.

Give it a 10-inch or 12-inch pot, plentiful water and plant food (follow the label directions—tomatoes are heavy feeders), and provide air circulation, either by opening the window or with a circulating fan. A southern window is a *hot* window. On a summer day, the heat can easily go up to 120°F.: enough to shrivel leaves and cause bud drop.

And don't forget, if the air is still, you'll have to hand-pollinate the flowers, either by shaking the plant gently when the flowers are open or by transferring pollen on a cotton swab, toothpick, or brush.

Garbage Gardening

Here is your chance to practice the lost art of alchemy: you can make something beautiful out of garbage.

Plants grown from your leftovers are free, and often they are as beautiful as anything you can buy. Citrus foliage is among the handsomest in the world, and the plant is as lovely grown from your own leftover seed as it is bought from a florist.

Remember that citrus seeds (and the seeds of many other tropical fruits) are most likely to germinate if fresh and moist. If you allow your citrus seeds (or mango or litchi or pomegranate seeds) to dry out, your chances of sprouting them are much reduced. If you can't plant them as soon as you take them from the fruit, keep them in water until you can plant them.

Many of the houseplants we grow from our leftovers are long-lasting, but some, like that sweet-potato top and that avocado, may last only from a few months to a couple of years.

Can I grow avocado outside of my window?

Yes, but avocados are quite tender to cold—they can't take any frost in a pot. So, unless you live in a frost-free area, you must bring them inside for the winter.

240 ·

We started one seed in bright sun and grew it there for the warmer months, and it was the most densely leafed avocado we've ever seen.

Be careful moving indoor-grown avocados into outdoor sun: you have to acclimate the plant to the sun over a period of a week or so, or you'll get sunburned leaves.

I planted a yam in water and it grew very well for months: made lovely vines and lots of roots in a jar of water. But now the leaves are yellowing. Should I transplant it into soil?

Don't bother. It's very unlikely to survive a transplant. Think of it as a temporary plant and plant another.

If you really want to grow one, start it in a large pot of soil and give it a sunny window.

How do you start a mango seed?

First, eat the mango. Next remove the fibrous and hard outer jacket of the seed.

Plant the seed horizontally under about an inch or so of damp rich soil. Keep damp until the seed sprouts.

If you can't plant your mango seed immediately, keep the seed in water until you can plant it. Drying reduces your chances of germination considerably.

I am growing a mango plant from seed, and it seems to be a dwarf. Will it stay this way?

In a pot, mangoes can be quite slow-growing. Give it good care (bright sun, ample water, moderate humidity), and prune it to keep it shrubby and compact. In the tropics, they are quite tall trees.

Can I grow papaya from the black seeds?

Certainly, *Carica papaya* (papaw or papaya) will come readily from seed, but first you must scrape away or at least break through the fleshy outer covering of the seed.

Dump the seeds in a large wire strainer and scrape against the mesh, then wash well and plant in a pasteurized soil mix.

Papaw doesn't make much of a houseplant. The leaves are large and showy, but the plant will drop its lower leaves, giving it an unsightly appearance.

Give your seedlings full sun and lots of water when you get them into individual pots.

In the tropics, they can grow into quite tall trees.

Can I start my pineapple top in water?

We've heard of it being done, but we've never done it, or known anyone personally who has.

Pineapples are bromeliads, and we treat them as such, because bromeliads need to be held firmly in their pots to root well.

Twist off the top, then scrape away any soft pineapple left on it. Prepare a terrestrial bromeliad mix (see BROMELIACEAE), dampened.

Set the base of the pineapple top into the mix, and prepare your tapes. Take three strips of cloth tape or electrician's tape, and fold each in half lengthwise, all except the ends. Take one strip, stick an end to the rim of the pot, pass the strip close to the stem (over a few lower leaves), and stick the other end to the other side of the rim (180° away). Repeat with the other two strips so that the tapes are more or less equidistant around the rim, and the top is held firmly in place. Immobilizing the top in this way encourages rapid and vigorous rooting.

Water the base weekly, do not feed, sprinkle the top with water frequently, and keep in moderate sun (full sun often burns it unless the plant has high humidity, too).

A normal pineapple plant can grow two feet across rather rapidly, and you should be prepared for that.

Also, it is best to start with a spineless variety whose leaves will stay spineless rather than with a spiny type which will play "gotcha" with you all the time.

Following your advice, we went to Chinatown and got fresh instead of dried litchi nuts, and one has sprouted for us. Now how should we care for it?

Congratulations! Your *Litchi chinensis* (litchi) plant wants a good-size pot with a rich soil that drains well. Give it bright sun year round, and don't allow it to dry out. Yours is unlikely to flower or fruit, and it is not a fast-growing tree, but it is *very* handsome.

Litchi is, of course, not winter-hardy, but it does better with cool temperatures in the winter.

I never am able to sprout date seeds. Is there a trick to it?

There are two tricks. The first trick is to buy unpasteurized dates. Pasteurization kills the seed. And the second trick is to have patience. Some date seed can take months to sprout.

Keep the soil damp, and keep the temperatures in the middle seventies.

I have recently successfully sprouted a date seed. Can I ever look forward to its bearing fruit?

Certainly, provided it grows to about 15 feet tall, gets moved to Florida, and meets a date palm of the opposite sex. Even then you will have to hand-pollinate.

Kind of gives you something to look forward to, doesn't it?

Can I realistically expect my potted avocado to flower?

A year ago we would have said no chance, and certainly we've never seen a potted avocado flower, but recently the *New York Times* showed a photo of a young grower's avocado, only two or three months old, but in flower.

And one of our viewers sent us a photo of her four-month-old avocado, only about 8 inches tall, but covered with dozens of tiny deformed flowers—and no leaves! Now, those are freaks—but they did happen.

However, don't hold your breath.

Can I propagate my avocado from tip cuttings?

Not really, but you could try air-layering, described in the PROPAGATION section; you've got a much better chance of success with air-layering than with cuttings.

I get white spots on the surface of my avocado leaf. They won't brush off, but they do wash away and then come back a few weeks later. The plant is doing great, but the spots worry me. I've looked at the spots through a magnifying glass, and they don't look alive. What do you think it is?

It sounds like some sort of mineral deposit. Is your water hard? Hard water can leave a deposit if misted onto and allowed to dry on leaves. Insecticides leave similar deposits.

But if the spots are really white and well defined, let us ask *you* a question: how long has it been since your ceiling was painted? *Old ceilings* can give up calcium deposits to the leaves. They don't actually harm the leaves, but they do block the light and, if not washed away, they will cause yellow spots.

I started an avocado seed in water and it had several leaves—it was doing really well, looked so beautiful, with a lot of roots. And then I was told to pinch the top. I pinched it and left the seed in the water, and now all the leaves are browning around the edges. Is there anything I can do?

Look, we don't recommend pinching young avocados, and we never recommend growing them in water.

We pinch out avocados only when they are mature, and then only to *shape* them, not to make them branch on bare stem. But your problem isn't the pinching. Your problem is growing your avocado in water—or trying to.

We start our avocados in soil: bury the seed half to two-thirds of the way into the soil in a 6-inch pot. And keep the pot in good light. An avocado is a tree; you can't really grow a tree in a glass of water.

The only thing you can do with your damaged avocado is to plant it in a 10-inch pot of damp soil that drains well. Be very careful of the roots: they damage most easily. Put the plant into a clear plastic bag and keep it in moderate light (move to full sun when you remove the bag).

But we give it little chance.

Start a new seed in soil. You'll find avocados make much stronger plants with thicker stems if they grow in soil.

How do I start an avocado pit?

We start them in damp soil, with about half the pit exposed (the indented end goes down, the pointed end up). We keep it among our plants so as not to forget to water it. When it sprouts, we *do not* split or chop off the stem.

We're sorry so much wrong advice has been making the rounds. Certainly, pinch out a begonia or other juicy plant the day you pot it up. But it doesn't work that way with trees. Your avocado has a tendency to grow as a single stem until it matures, when it will often branch spontaneously. (Starting your seed in soil encourages early branching.) Allow the plant its first few months to make healthy leaf growth, then prune or pinch to shape the plant and encourage branching.

We move our avocados into 10-inch pots at about the same time. Strong tree roots need room to spread.

I have an 8-foot avocado that is six years old, and now, for the first time, the leaves are dropping as if it were autumn. Why? I haven't changed its care, and it's already in as big a pot as I can manage.

Unfortunately, the avocado doesn't know that, and it sounds as if it's ready for replanting—into the soil south of Fort Lauderdale.

It gets very difficult to maintain a large avocado because of the amount of root room it needs.

And now, a home truth—one should not put all one's affection onto one avocado. One should always have new plants coming along. With avocados, heartbreak is always around the corner, because most die when less than a year old.

However, before you garbage your plant, try these last-ditch chances: prune the roots and the top, both, by about 25 percent. This may stimulate new growth and give your avocado a second wind.

Why do the leaves of my avocado point down? I don't mean just when the plant goes dry—all the time.

It's been our observation that if avocados are allowed to dry thoroughly between waterings, eventually their leaves will not return to an upright position. They will live, and grow, but their leaves will always *look* droopy.

Now that you know what big drinkers avocados are, maybe you want to start a new one that will be handsomer for having had a more robust childhood.

I started an avocado seed under fluorescent lights, and when it grew too big, I moved it to a corner with a grow bulb—and all the leaves turned brown and fell off. All I've got now is a bare green stem. What should I do?

Start a new seed.

You can cut the stem back to within a few inches of the soil and it may resprout (and it may not), but your best bet for an attractive tree is to start a new seed.

As for what happened, our guess is that the grow bulb (which we assume was incandescent) was too close and gave off too much heat while providing much less light than the avocado was used to.

Next time, put the avocado in your brightest window; then, if that isn't bright enough, you can provide some supplementary light (either with fluorescent tubes or with a spotlight kept about 4 feet from the foliage).

The bottom leaves of my avocado are spotting. What should I do?

Water the plant, turn it out of its pot, and check the roots. We think your avocado wants repotting.

How long will it take my avocado to sprout in a pot of damp soil (as you suggest)?

Avocados can take quite a while to sprout in soil. There are many variables: ripeness of the fruit, temperature, time of year, variety of fruit. We have had seeds take two months to sprout, but as long as the seed is plump and pink, keep watering, and you should be rewarded with a plant.

Herbs—
Sniffin' and Chewin'

Herbs are the best plants we grow. Not only are they decorative and scented (and tasted) , but they are also, by definition, useful.

Where many indoor gardens are not suited to a real food crop, they often have enough light or space for a few pots of herbs.

Herbs do very well in pots, many of them thriving in the restricted root room. Also, since many herbs are light feeders, the person who spends *nothing* on fertilizer may do best with them.

With herbs, we don't have to give you long lectures on the desirability of pinching and shaping your plants. You'll be in there frequently, snipping away leaves and bits of stem to use as the plant grows.

Whether you grow many pots of a favorite herb or pots of several different herbs, your herb corner will become, as you brush by it or come in to remove a leaf or two, one of the happiest spots in your life.

I bought a plant of thyme, but it doesn't have much scent. Could you say why?

We could guess that it's one of two things. If the plant was scented when you bought it, but no longer is, perhaps you are growing in a soil that is too nitrogen-rich. If the plant lacked scent when you bought it, it could be that you have bought a creeping thyme

(*Thymus serpyllum*) instead of the culinary common thyme (*Thymus vulgaris*). The creeping thymes may have much fainter scents.

Many books say that herbs give less scent in rich soil, but we had a recent conversation with a great herb gardener who grows in good soil and his herbs do marvelously well. He says it is not "rich" soil, but "*nitrogen*-rich" soil you have to watch out for. Bone meal is better for your herbs than manure.

My windowsill basil is very attractive to whitefly. I want to keep it (the basil, not the whitefly), but not if it endangers the rest of my plants. Is there anything I can do?

We'll tell you what you cannot do, and that is to spray any edible herb with a poison. Try taking the plant to the sink and washing the backs of the leaves thoroughly every few days; that will get rid of the adults and the young as they mature, but not the eggs. That's why you repeat the treatment. Take your other plants to the sink, too, and wash them periodically, just to make certain no whiteflies are hiding.

The leaves on a small bay-leaf tree I recently bought turned brown, and the damned thing looks dead. What can I do?

Use the leaves for cooking and compost the rest. It *is* dead. *Laurus nobilis* (bay) is not an easy windowsill plant. Keep it cool, sunny, well watered, and humid (and if you can do all that, you can grow orchids instead of bay), and pinch out the tip to make it branch.

Bay is slow to propagate, so you have to be certain of your seller—only well-rooted plants will thrive.

We are growing two beautiful plants now—under fluorescent lights.

I grew some tarragon from seed—but it doesn't have any flavor. I have it in the same potting mix as my other herbs, which are doing fine. Does tarragon require something special?

We're sorry to say you've got the wrong plant. You have Russian tarragon (*Artemisia redowski*), and what you want is French tarragon (*A. dracunculus*). No, we're not mind readers: Russian tarragon is grown from seed; the French (which has the flavor) is propagated from divisions of the succulent roots or tip cuttings—in other words, vegetative propagation only.

The sellers should really make the difference clear.

Can I grow herbs in a strawberry jar on my windowsill?

Only plants of similar cultural needs should be grown together in any combined planting. Most herbs want full sun, and so your jar would only work with these if it were outdoors on a sunny terrace or rooftop. On a shady balcony, try several kinds of mint. Indoors, forget it.

My garden rosemary (in my vegetable patch) does just fine over the summer, but as soon as I try to grow a plant in a pot, it does poorly. Can rosemary be grown in a pot?

It certainly can, and will make a handsome pot-shrub if given good care. Give it plenty of sun (or bright fluorescent light), plenty of water (more water than it got while in the ground), a rather large pot, a very well-drained neutral pH soil, and a relative humidity of 40 percent or better. If your normal potting soil is on the acid side, as so many are (and should be), this, or too little water, is likely to be your problem.

Is there a species of rosemary that will make a hanging basket?

Only one species of rosemary is recognized in cultivation, *Rosmarinus officinalis* (common rosemary), but it does have several varieties with several *habits* (including prostrate and pendulous, as well as the familiar upright forms): *R. o. humilis* has shorter dense leaves and will grow straight down; *R. o. foresteri* has longer leaves and is less pendant—but still appropriate for a basket. Turn the basket frequently, give it plenty of sun, and pinch the growing tips frequently.

How would I make my rosemary into a standard?

["Standard" refers to an upright form of a plant, where the top is bushy (usually clipped into a sphere) and the lower stem has no leaves.]

First of all, make certain you have an upright grower: some rosemarys are droopers or prostrate growers.

As the plant grows upright, remove the major side shoots (just pinch them or cut them off very close to the main stem) and pinch out the top to encourage branching.

Bright sun (or four tubes of fluorescent light) is important at this stage, because you want as stocky and strong a main stem as you can grow. Keep pinching the growing tips as the plant grows, until you have reached the globular shape you wish (or the shape the plant is determined to take).

Now remove the minor branches and the individual leaves along the stem.

Probably it will take a year or more to reach a standard of 12 to 18 inches, so this is a process that needs patience.

Keep your rosemary in a rather large pot (about as wide as the top of the plant), in very well-drained soil, in bright sun, and well watered.

Once you have reached your desired shape, you must work to keep it in shape.

Probably you will need a stake to keep the plant upright (rosemary doesn't "normally" grow in this shape). We suggest a thin metal "hyacinth" stake. These are painted green and will be almost invisible.

I would like some foliage plants for scent in my house. I already have rose-scented geranium and pineapple sage, but are there any others? I don't really have enough sun for flowering plants.

If the only scented geranium you have is rose, you've not even scratched the surface. There are lime- and nutmeg- and lemon- and apple-scented geraniums, just to mention some. The only one that takes any special care is the "Prince Rupert" geranium (curly lemon leaves), which demands bright sun.

And then there are the mints—many of those, and all marvelously scented—though they do need a good deal of water.

And we'll bet you do have enough light to flower *Spathiphyllum clevelandii,* which does have a slightly fragrant flower.

Can I start lavender from seed?

Yes, but while lavender can be started from seed, it is so slow to germinate that we have always preferred to buy plants.

On the other hand, if you have the patience to carry the project through, the survivors from your seed packet might make excellent plants for your conditions. Generally, lavender is difficult to adapt to indoor conditions. Do give your plants full sun—that's one condition that lavender must have.

Can I grow coriander in my windowbox? I mean, can I expect to harvest some seeds.

Coriander sativum (coriander) is an excellent herb for a *sunny* windowbox or outdoor tub. It is an annual and quite fast-growing and quick to flower. Start it from seeds in early springtime.

It may even self-seed in your windowbox.

I have a sunny windowsill, and I want to grow basil. I saw this very large-leafed kind growing outside an Italian restaurant, but they couldn't tell me what kind it is. Can you tell me what to order?

There are lots of different kinds of basil around, but you are looking for *Ocimum crispum* (lettuce-leaf basil) .

We prefer *Ocimum basilicum* (sweet basil) for flavor. Also, it tends to be less rangy in a pot. *Ocimum basilicum minimum* (little-leaf basil) is a delightful plant with tiny leaves but good basil flavor and scent; and it can be kept quite small and bushy with frequent pinchings.

Give your basil plenty of water, and pinch, pinch, pinch.

Which herbs do I grow to make that great chicken soup my husband's grandmother made?

First of all, some of the vegetables used in a real European chicken soup are not literally classed as herbs, but they are important: carrots and carrot tops, turnips and parsnips, and celery.

But, after those, all the following herbs *can* go into a chicken soup: parsley, dill, marjoram, sage, thyme (a pinch or two at most) , fennel seed.

Fennel and dill are rather tall-growing and not well suited to small-container culture—certainly not in a small window.

Parsley is a biennial, but you can begin to crop it the first year. Harvest the oldest leaves: the outside leaves.

Marjoram, sage, and thyme are all possible on a sunny windowsill.

If you use only the vegetables, your seasonings, and MARJORAM and SAGE, your husband will forget about his grandmother and start talking about *your* chicken soup.

I bought a small plant of lemon verbena for $5 and it died. It has such a lovely lemon scent that I'd like to try again. How should I care for it?

Five dollars seems a lot for a small plant of this super-smelling herb; it is slow-growing, and cuttings are slow to root—still, you should get a second-year plant for that money.

Lemon verbena (*Lippia citriodora*) will not winter outdoors where there is cold weather, but try it cut back in the fall (before it drops its leaves) , on your very brightest window, quite cool, but protected from freezing.

In other words, treat it like a geranium.

This isn't the easiest plant to grow, but those lemon leaves are so grand in drinks!

Is summer savory a different plant from winter savory? I like the flavor and would like to grow one year round.

They are different species of the same genus: *Satureja hortensis,* summer savory, is an annual; *Satureja montana,* winter savory, is a perennial.

Kept cut back and cool over the winter, winter savory will grow in a sunny window year round. Your best bet with summer savory is to grow it as an annual in a very sunny location. Without sun, you will probably not succeed with either herb.

I have a terrace tub full of dill, and it is being a great success. The feathery leaves are a delight, and it is beginning to flower. Now what? I have used very little of the plants, which are over 2 feet tall, and I'd like to have some of the herb for the winter.

You're really asking us two different questions. If you want to know how to get dill seeds, allow the flowers to mature. They will be pollinated, and, later in the season, seed pods will ripen and open, spilling out dill seed. You must harvest the seed before it spills upon the ground.

As for drying the foliage to have dill weed (as it is called), that can be done right now. Cut the plants down to the ground and strip off the leaves and stems from the thick main stalks. As you strip them, throw them into the bottom of a clean paper shopping bag. Put both handles of the shopping bag over a doorknob and leave it there for a few days. After a few days, and every few days thereafter, give the dill a turn in the bag—until the leaves are dry enough to crumble readily. Bottle in airtight jars, and you have it.

The paper bag allows air circulation, important in drying herbs, but keeps out bugs and dust.

I was doing poorly with my balcony tubs, and so I had the soil tested, and I came out neutral! Are there any herbs I can grow in this kind of soil?

Most vegetables prefer a soil that approaches neutral.

As for herbs, there are indeed several: all the thymes will tolerate your soil, as will the lavenders and santolina (though santolina is more decorative than specifically useful); rosemary will probably prefer it.

I have a 4-inch pot of apple mint, and it's not doing at all well. I remember it used to grow like a weed for my mother outside. But for me it seems weak and wilted half the time, and it has lost leaves. I give it shade; does it require a special soil?

Mints are among the most soil-tolerant plants you can grow. As for keeping it in the shade, that is probably a mistake. Though a shade-lover outdoors, mint will want bright windowsill light indoors—with a touch of sun.

But the poor growth and leaf loss are probably caused by lack of water. Mints are *drinkers,* and in a small pot they may not be able to get enough water. Move it to a sunnier location, pinch it back, and increase your watering. If the plant perks up, repot it to a larger pot and see if that doesn't solve your problem.

As you suggested, I sent away for the seed catalogs, and you're right, they are terrific winter reading. I want to start some herbs from seed, but I have no experience. What are the easiest herbs from seed? How soon can I start them? I'm eager to begin, but I have no greenhouse.

For us, the easiest and quickest herbs from seed have always been sage and basil—they are both almost foolproof. And you can start them as soon as you get them from the seedsman. No greenhouse is necessary, just a bright windowsill and a plastic flowerpot.

Fill a 3-inch pot with your damp potting soil, then sprinkle a layer of dampened milled sphagnum moss over the surface so that no soil is seen. Sprinkle the seed thinly over the surface (reserve half your seed for safety), then sprinkle on enough additional damp moss to just cover them. Cover the top of the pot with a piece of clear plastic, held on with a rubber band. Put the pot in bright light, but no sun. You should see sprouting within a few days to a week. Use a different pot for each herb. You will probably get enough seed for several pots of each.

We don't have room to keep plants indoors over the winter, but we would like a few pots of herbs on our windowsill for the summer months. It is sunny, but not wide. Do you know any herbs we can grow like that just as annuals?

Actually, almost any of the herbs *can* be grown as annuals, if you are willing to discard them over the winter. But for a few that will grow very well in pots on your windowsill, try summer savory, marjoram, and basil (*Ocimum basilicum minimum*—little-leaf basil)—all will stay within bounds. Parsley is a biennial, but it will give you good growth the first year. Hardy sages and thymes will also grow nicely in pots if you give them plenty of water (basil needs lots of water, too).

I bought a pot of chives in the supermarket. They look very crowded. Can I divide them and grow them on?

Perhaps, but not definitely. Those pots of chives are so overgrown, so potbound, that they don't take well to repotting. Unpot them and break them apart into three or four clumps. Discard any dead or dying material: this is very important because rot can easily spread. Use fresh soil, and put them into full sun.

When autumn comes, if they've survived, cut them back to within an inch or so of the soil, keep in a bright sunny place, and you may have fresh chives all winter.

Can all herbs be grown from seeds? Are they easy enough to be a good class project with my fourth graders this fall?

"Herb" is a compote category, descriptive, not botanical, and includes annuals, biennials, and perennials, shrubs and herbaceous plants, small and large, and both tender and winter-hardy plants. Many of the herbaceous plants and some of the woody ones come readily from seed.

Some of the shrubby herbs, such as lavender and thyme, are slow from seed, and you may want to start them at home a month before your project begins.

French tarragon is *not* possible from seed, but only from vegetative propagation (divisions and cuttings). There are seeds of Russian tarragon sold, but it has no fragrance. Bay is so slow-growing that it is impractical from seed.

Our favorite of the shrubby herbs is sage, which is very easy from seed, and very fast to make a plant.

Do include coriander. It is an annual, fast-growing, and may well make its own seeds for your next class.

Dill and fennel require big pots and lots of sun, but if you have those big schoolroom windows, that should be no difficulty.

Do try: parsley (the seed is slow to germinate if you don't soak it in water for 24 hours before planting); basil (our favorite culinary herb—we couldn't cook without it); summer savory; borage, chervil; chives (will grow about a foot tall, form bulbs, and spread); lemon balm; and marjoram.

Your main problems will be slow germination in the fall months (the seeds "know" it isn't spring), the potential destructiveness of radiator heat at the windowsill (something wet should be put between the plants and the heat: we use pebble trays), and watering over the weekend (seedlings should be kept in plastic bags over the weekends, because even slight drying will kill them; plants like basil and mint are *big* drinkers and should be kept in largish pots or else have some arrangement made for watering them) .

Do check that your humidity goes no lower than about 30 percent in the winter and rejoice that your budget-conscious maintenance man turns the furnace down when school is out. With coolish (not freezing) nights, your class herbs will do better than herbs grown in keep-it-warm-all-the-time houses.

As a last thought, we suggest that you grow nasturtiums. Though usually not included as an herb (in the sense that you asked in your question) , the leaves and flowers are edible, it is fast-growing and quick to germinate, the seeds are large and easily handled, even by the clumsiest kid, and it will flower for you in almost any conditions.

✐ ✐ ✐ ✐

Indoors—Outdoors

The time when you could say of people that this one is an indoor grower and that one an outdoor grower is, thank goodness, passing. City dwellers grow on the outside of their windows as well as inside. New buildings all have balconies. And no neighborhood is too crowded to have some outdoor community vegetable garden.

On the other hand, even dyed-in-the-wool suburbanites and full-time farmers have ornamental houseplants indoors.

Great!

But while the differences among people are getting less, plants have not yet given up some of *their* differences.

Most of what we grow as houseplants in the great indoors are native to the tropics or hybridized from tropical plants. Our hardy or half-hardy outdoor plants are native to temperate regions. However, none of that is rigid. Outdoor plants can be brought in, and indoor plants can be taken out for a while—*IF YOU KNOW WHAT YOU ARE DOING.*

Do my houseplants need any special care before going outside in the spring?

We don't put our houseplants outside for spring and summer—except for the bright-sun-lovers like succulents, and our potted lilies or other bulbs that have already flowered. It just leads to trauma, leaf loss, and bug problems when we come to bring them inside in the fall.

But if you must move your plants outside, at least acclimate them to the bright sun and cooler nighttime temperatures. Even cacti can sunburn if they are thrust right out into the sun.

And don't stand your plants directly on soil—set them on bricks, benches, or stands, or hang them. And be sure you water them adequately; houseplants outdoors drink more water than indoors.

All right, you told us to write you in the fall about bringing plants back inside. How about it?

Very funny.

Your plants outdoors have spent the season growing leaves, accumulating bugs, and getting used to the outdoors. And now comes early September and the day of reckoning.

First of all, your plants must be examined and may need to be treated with both insecticide and miticide. But, if you start early, and you are lucky, perhaps a few thorough washings will be all you'll need.

Then, all plants which lend themselves to it must be cut back, or they will drop leaves as if they were deciduous when they come in.

Finally, they must be acclimated to indoor temperatures, indoor humidity, and indoor light. They can be brought in for a while each day, or brought in at night and left out for most of the day—but they must begin getting used to the great indoors before your heat goes on and lowers the humidity to a dangerous level for your plants and you.

And, after going through all this trouble, and having your plants give you difficulty as they make the transition back indoors, perhaps next time you'll leave your indoor plants indoors for the warm times.

Floss, can you help me with a plant project for my first-grade class? I used a sweet potato in water last year and it was good for a while, but I think they would prefer something edible or that flowers.

Here's a simple project using recycled egg cartons and marigold seeds.

Tear the top off the egg carton and put it below as a "saucer." If the carton is plastic, punch a small hole in the bottom of each compartment for drainage. If the container is cardboard, you don't need the holes.

Almost fill each compartment with potting soil, and in each plant one 'Petite' marigold seed. (See APPENDIX for mail-order sources.) Water, and set in a bright warm place.

When the seedlings are an inch high, repot each one into a 2-inch pot.

The plants will eventually move to 3-inch pots and be 7 inches tall. Right now, we are looking at a ½-inch orange flower on a 3-inch plant that is just 5 weeks old. A darling!

We recommend "Petite" because marigolds come in so many sizes now, including 4-inch flowers on 3-foot plants: not really suited to a crowded school windowsill—not thirty of them.

If it's the spring term, let the kids take them home for outdoor planting. If it's the winter, make sure they keep the plants under their coats as they travel home.

Remember to keep your seedlings well watered.

Can insect-eating plants be grown successfully indoors?

Not by us, but we've spoken with people who've grown them in a very bright and very wet terrarium (in long-haired sphagnum moss), in which they eat things like fungus gnats.

These plants are mostly sunny-bog plants, and most of us try to grow them too dry and to dim.

In a small town we passed a plant shop the other day, and there was a beautiful terrarium of several kinds of insectivorous plants, all in very good shape. We rushed in, to find out what he knew that we didn't, and asked how long the plants had been in the terrarium. Answer? Two days!

Postscript About Insectivores

We attended a country fair in the South and had an interesting experience. We stopped by a booth selling insectivorous plants and other bog plants, and as we often do, we struck up a conversation about the plants. The man knew nothing about growing the plants, and it surprised us because he had a great deal of plant material in front of him. We asked him if he grew them himself. He got a cagey look on his face and then asked *us* if we'd like to make a few bucks. Obviously he didn't know our faces, and perhaps we were dressed a bit casually—well suited actually to tromping around after horses at a fair.

His proposition was that he would tell us where to find the plants, we would go out and gather them, and he would pay us for them. Apparently he supplied quite a few plants to commercial sellers— many more than he showed on the table.

We thanked him and moved on.

These plants are protected as endangered species, but he was gathering them and rather openly recruiting other gatherers. It's a shame that a niche in the plant world can be raped and the plants destroyed to provide novelties for people who can't grow them and profits for people who just don't give a damn.

Can I grow garden annuals, like marigolds and petunias, in pots on my windowsills over the winter?

Of course—if you have enough sun. Dwarf or 'Petite' marigolds will do well in 4- to 6-inch pots, petunias want to be potted up and up as they grow. Pinch for branching, keep well watered, and feed with a 15–30–15 plant food as long as they are in vigorous growth.

Watch out for bugs—annuals in pots are susceptible. And if you keep your house sweater-cool all winter, your annuals will be stronger and less buggy than they will be in overheated rooms.

Just recently, October 1, I got twelve hyacinth bulbs from Holland as a present. I live in an apartment, and there is no way of putting them outdoors. Is there any way that I can have them in flower in the spring?

Yes, if you're willing to give over the bottom of your frost-free refrigerator.

Using no crock or screening in the bottom, plant your bulbs in three 6-inch plastic pots (four bulbs to the pot) with the tips just covered by a light and porous soil mix. Fix low kraft-paper or aluminum-foil collars so that they extend a few inches above the rims. (Hold them on with rubber bands or string.) Fill the collars with some mulch: peat moss, broken-up peanut shells, ground-up leaves. Water the bulbs well, allow the soil to drain well, and set into the bottom of the fridge for about thirteen weeks or until several roots grow out the bottom of the pots.

Don't allow the pots to go dry—heft them and judge their dryness from their weight. But allow them to drain well before putting them back in.

If mold forms (one of the reasons you use plastic pots), scrape it off.

When well rooted, with some top growth, bring the pots out one at a time into the real world as you would bulbs that were forced outdoors or on a windowsill: keep them as cool as you can, and don't put into bright sun before the new growth gets dark green.

Once the buds show, the cooler you keep your bulbs, the longer the flowers last.

If you don't have a frost-free fridge, you may find fungus a serious problem.

Can my husband and I force crocus on a windowsill?

Inside a windowsill, no, but outside a windowsill, yes. That is, you can have your crocus about two weeks earlier than they would bloom outdoors. Here's how. As soon as you can buy the corms, take a 4-inch plastic azalea pot and set a piece of screening in the bottom so that all holes are covered. Fill to the neck with a very well-draining soil, on the dry side. Place six crocus corms on the surface and press in to their own depth gently but firmly, then cover the top with a bit more soil. (If the soil is not light and porous, this pressing can damage the corms.

Take a strip of ordinary aluminum foil long enough to go around the pot with a bit of overlap. (If you want a formula for the length of your aluminum strip, try this—the circumference of a circle is calculated as πd or 3.17 $\times$ the diameter of your pot, in this case 4 inches = 12.68 inches plus 2 inches for overlap, or about 15 inches of foil for a 4-inch pot.) Fold the strip lengthwise in half, wrap it around the pot so that most of the strip stands above the pot (like a soufflé collar, for you cooks) , and hold it on with a rubber band or a piece of string. Fill the collar with damp peat moss, pressed down just a bit, and water the whole pot well. Make out a label with variety and date, and stick it under the rubber band. Now, place the pot *just outside* a window that can be easily opened during the winter. Since the pot is close to the window, the heat that radiates through the glass during the winter will keep the corms from being completely frozen hard. The pot must be watered every two weeks or so during the winter. In late winter, you will see the thin foliage start to push above the peat moss. Water more frequently. In a few weeks more, the buds will start to show; at this point, you can bring them inside. Take off the collar and the peat moss, and keep for a couple of days in a cool and not too bright location. The cooler you can keep the pot, the longer the flowers will last—though crocus don't last as long as hyacinths.

Note: This method is unlikely to work in areas with really severe winters, or if your winter has weather alternately quite warm and then quite cold.

How do you feel about crocus in a tree pit?

Love them. Just love them—almost anywhere.

Crocus are shallow-rooted enough so that they won't compete with the tree roots.

In the fall, work some bone meal into the tree pit soil (some organic material like compost or leaf mold, too, if you can), and plant each crocus so that the flattish base is buried to a depth of about 3 inches. If you can keep the dogs and cats from overfertilizing the tree pit, you should have crocus for several years without additional care beyond an annual application of bone meal—provided your soil is well drained.

We are now using some other minor bulbs for tree pits, also: ornithogalum, muscari, and scilla.

Can you recommend some specific crocuses for windowsill forcing?

We suspect that there are no bad ones. Among others, we've grown "Al Jolson," "Pickwick," "Yellow Mammoth," and "Remembrance." "Yellow Mammoth" is very early. Potted in November, the bulbs flowered in the middle of January (in New York City).

Can you force tuberoses indoors?

You can't "force" them, but you can have them. That is, you pot them as soon as they are available, and they bloom in their normal summer time. They need a large pot and a lot of soil, though.

Take a standard-shape 8-inch pot. Put a piece of screening in the bottom and fill about halfway with a rich well-drained soil. Firm somewhat, set in one tuber, pointy end up, and fill to the pot's neck with soil. Water well and place in bright sun (outside the window, where weather permits). Keep outdoors, watered and fed, and you will get a tall stalk with buds. When they start to open, bring inside and enjoy an enormously powerful sweet scent. Single-flowered tuberoses have a stronger scent than the double-flowered ones.

Floss, I heard you say on the radio: "Anyone who says money can't buy happiness has never planted bulbs." I laughed when you said it, but I live in an apartment. Can I have bulbs too?

We live in an apartment and we have forced bulbs every spring, as anyone can who has the bottom of a refrigerator or the outside of a windowsill to spare.

But these special forcing procedures apply only to hardy spring-flowering bulbs. Among the summer-flowering and winter-flowering bulbs there is a wealth of beauty (and we do mean *wealth:* our current catalogs quote $3 each for lycoris bulbs).

In the Amaryllis family we are currently flowering *Lycoris squamigera* in pots, and if this year is like every other year we will have amaryllis (really hippeastrum) near Christmas. And we have had good success with true lilies in pots, as well. Not enough members of the Amaryllis family are available in stores, but by mail-order you can get *Lycoris squamigera, L. radiata* (skinny red petals instead of pink) , *L. aurea* (yellow) , and *L. straminea* (white) (see APPENDIX) .

Can I plant tulips in my windowbox?

Absolutely. Plant them in November in a 10-inch or deeper window-box, and, when the soil freezes, cover the soil with as thick a mulch as you can manage. If your box is protected from the rain, you'll have to water when the ground is unfrozen. Your tulips should come up just a bit earlier than the same variety in the outdoor garden.

How should I dig wild flowers to grow in a pot?

You shouldn't. Many of them are protected by law (or by common sense, where the law lags) , they seldom make good pot plants, and they live in a special relationship to tiny fungi in the soil which makes them often just peter out even if they seem to take the transplant successfully.

Have you tried all the *good* houseplants yet?

Can rhododendrons be grown in pots?

Outside, not inside. They won't winter well even on a sun porch, but in a 14- to 16-inch tub, with a very acid soil, they will winter quite well on a terrace or balcony.

Of course, since rhododendrons are evergreen, you will have to provide some protection against the wind. (Try wrapping the plants in burlap.)

Can I grow a dwarf juniper indoors on my windowsill?

It's possible, but not realistic. The summer sun would be too little and the winter temperature would be too high.

If you have a cool southern window, and can keep it open year round, it might just work.

Pets 'n' Plants

Your pets can hurt your plants and your plants can hurt your pets—even though they have, in nature, been in harmony for quite a while.

Pet wastes are good fertilizer—if composted and diluted. Undiluted (such as a "deposit" on the surface of the soil of your favorite plant) they are too much of a good thing. Undiluted pet excreta act as a poison, and like most poisons to your plants, they work their way up the midrib (turning it yellow) and then to the edges of the leaves (turning them yellow, then brown, then dead).

The reverse problems, the ones pets have with plants, are mostly self-inflicted—like the listener who scoffed when we suggested she grow cacti. She had tried it, but her kamikaze cat had insisted on swatting and chewing the spines, damaging both cat and cactus.

My cat has about chewed the life out of my Boston fern and spider plant. Is there something I can spray to stop him?

We advise you to stay away from pet repellents. They do the plants no good. But there are lots of other things you can try, and probably the most effective is growing something especially for the cat. Cats need a little green in their diet, and most city cats get no chance at grass-chewing at all. A pot of wheat grass is very attractive to felines.

Fill a 6-inch pot with any soil mix, and sprinkle wheat seed (sold in health-food stores as "wheat berries") over the damp surface. After about two weeks the sprouts are long enough to attract tabby. Make a new planting every two weeks as your cat will chew it to death.

Cats are bright, and they will understand a "chomp here but not there" distinction.

There are other solutions, more or less effective.

Hang your plant out of cat reach.

Grow only spiny plants: cacti or bromeliads.

Explain your displeasure clearly (perhaps with a rolled-up newspaper).

Mix a garlic and hot-pepper spray. (Boil garlic and hot red peppers for one-half hour, drain, cool, strain, then spray on the leaves.) Cats are sensitive to strong smells, but you may be also.

Your best bet, really, is to grow something specifically for the cat.

Barring all these, bury the cat up to its neckline in a well-drained soil . . . (joke—honest).

My cat is using the pot of my biggest avocado for a litterbox. Is there anything I can do to keep her out? I think it may be hurting the plant.

We would be most surprised if it were *not* hurting the plant.

We've had good results sprinkling red pepper over the soil (that keeps bugs away, too).

Or, you can try cutting a hardware-cloth cover for the pot—one that fits around the stem. But this is an ugly thing to look at all the time.

It could also be that your cat resents the plant and is expressing its opinion in this way. If so, it may persevere through both pepper and hardware cloth. Have you considered a cat shrink?

I have this heartleaf philo with vines hanging down to the ground. I saw my dog nibbling on a leaf of it, and while the plant can afford to lose a few leaves, I worried that the leaves could be poisonous. Can you help me?

Philodendron is in the Arum family and many of the Araceae are poisonous. For the chronic nibbler, the worst plant in the family is dieffenbachia. Philodendron itself has the reputation of being somewhat poisonous. However, our own pups nibbled on philo leaves when they were quite small, without ill effect.

In general, it is by far best to discourage animals from eating any plant that is not specifically edible.

Street Trees

Street trees are not just handsome things to look at. They clean the air and provide oxygen for us. And they speak for us city dwellers, too. They say, "Though we live in the city, we are not alienated from growing things." Planting a tree in a city is making a political statement, taking a stand for a better, less automated and polluted life.

Communities in New York have begun to take responsibility for the trees on their blocks. Not only are they pruning, watering, and feeding the tree itself, but they are also planting into that bit of soil at the base of the tree: the tree pit.

On a walk from our apartment to the studio, we can see everything growing in tree pits from wax begonias (they did flower) to sweet corn (it did not ripen).

We have also seen many kinds of protectors built around the trees, from low fences to keep out the dogs to steel guards to keep away the cars. Most of them are quite unlovely. But we are learning, and that's the important part—though it would be better if we could learn quite soon that low fences provide little protection and can be dangerous to pedestrians.

We saw a marvelous solution to the tree-pit problem in the NBC neighborhood—an area of terribly heavy auto and pedestrian traffic. The bottom of the tree was surrounded by a dwarf evergreen shrub:

yew (taxus), though prostrate cotoneaster would have done as well. No fence was used and none was needed: no sane dog would have tried to get into that prickly and densely planted area, and the tree was set far enough back from the curb that cars were not a threat. The yew was a perfect choice: shallow-rooted, and so not competitive for deep water; tolerant of shade, so that the leafy tree doesn't shade it to death; prickly enough so that vandals and dogs are discouraged; high enough so that pedestrians don't trip and hurt themselves. A fine solution.

One of the biggest failures we have seen in street trees is the use of full-size trees in huge above-ground tubs. The trees die. You see, rain is not enough, and it seems that once the trees are planted, no one is responsible for them. Tubs filled with roses or holly or other evergreen shrubs do fine. This shrubby stuff has shallower roots. But trees don't survive. A terrible solution.

Our block association has managed to secure matching funds for twenty trees. What tree should we plant?

Terrific! But don't think of it in terms of planting *one kind of tree*. That kind of monoculture can lead to problems. Diseases are spread most easily between trees of the same genus. Look at Dutch elm disease, and current London plane tree problems.

Alternate: a Greenspire Linden (*Tilia cordata* 'Greenspire'), a Shademaster Honeylocust (*Gleditsia triacanthos inermis* 'Shademaster'), a Bradford Callery Pear (*Pyrus calleryana* 'Bradford'), a Korean Mountain Ash (*Sorbus alnifolia*) —then start over. This kind of arrangement is handsome, interesting, and will prove more disease-resistant.

Can you recommend a really decorative street tree?

The Japanese Tree Lilac (*Syringa amurensis*) flowers handsomely in the spring, and its shiny bark is nice year round.

The Bradford Callery Pear (*Pyrus calleryana* 'Bradford') holds its fruit well and is most handsome, with white flowers in the spring and red foliage in the fall.

A car backed into the ginkgo in front of our building and broke it off about 1 foot from the ground. Is there anything I can do?

Not with any real hope for reviving it. Cut it off evenly and paint the cut with wound paint. There is a small chance of a side shoot sprouting. Your best bet is to redig the pit and plant a new tree.

We hope that future city plantings will have sidewalk trees set well back from the curb—now that we're out of the horse-and-buggy era.

About how much water does a good-size street tree need?

About 12 gallons any week there isn't an inch of rain. The younger the tree, the more necessary is supplementary watering. Mature trees have deep roots which give them better access to the water table.

There are several street trees on our block that have broken and/or dead branches. My block association would like to prune them. What do we take off and how?

First, all cutting and pruning should be done as close to the major branch or trunk as possible.

Cut away all dead or dying branches of whatever size. Cut off stumps close to the trunk. Cut away cracked branches. Cut away branches that interfere with pedestrians or which provide a temptation for kids.

Do as little ladder-climbing as possible, and when up on a ladder have someone foot it. Do not climb in the tree at all.

Be careful of passing pedestrians. There should be someone on the ground to handle traffic.

When you make your final cuts, saw downward, roughly parallel to the trunk, but always tilting slightly *down,* so as not to have water collect on the wound.

In my town they put in street trees with burlap around the trunk held on with plastic stretch ties. Are these better than string?

Better and worse. If the burlap is held on with a strand or two of burlap, that's better than plastic, because the burlap strings decompose at the same rate as the rest of the burlap, and so fall off when the burlap is ready to come off. Also, it is weak and will be torn by the widening of the trunk as the tree grows. Strong string is worse than plastic, because it is slow to decompose and will strangle the tree, cutting into the vital cambium layer. Plastic stretches a bit, but still cuts into the trunk. Eventually, it too may strangle.

When the rest of the burlap has rotted and fallen off it is time to cut away the tapes.

When you can see a bulge on either side of the plastic tape, it should have been removed months ago.

One of the stakes supporting a two-year-old tree on our block has pulled out, and I noticed that the remaining stake is causing the tree to whip against the wire. Should I try to restake it?

No, cut off the wire or remove the other stake. The tree sounds mature enough to stand on its own, and the likelihood of your successfully restaking it is small.

The people on our block use the metal car guards around the bottom of the trees as garbage cans. They dump in paper and bottles and everything. I can't believe this doesn't hurt the trees.

Well, it doesn't do them any good. Those car guards are little protection—and if they are left on too long (as we've often seen), they can cut right into the tree as it grows. Why don't you make a recommendation to your block association: remove those guards and put up guards made of iron pipes sunk into the ground. These don't enclose the tree, just stand between it and the curb.

ℐ ℐ ℐ ℐ

Terrariums:
A View of the World

If you live in a dark, hot, dry apartment and cannot afford to humidify it or light all of it and you aren't home enough to take care of your plants anyhow . . . why not try a terrarium?

If you live in a perfectly lovely, bright house, with plants growing in every corner, but need something to accent an otherwise dull spot . . . why not try a terrarium?

Terrariums can solve so many problems, and they can require less care than your cacti.

With two fluorescent tubes above it and a clear cover over it, a terrarium comes close to being a closed system. Little of the water evaporates, the humidity stays high, plants thrive; even those leaves that die and fall off are quickly rotted and reincorporated into the soil.

Speaking of soil, we use our basic soil mix for our terrariums, but we don't add any cow manure to it. We don't feed terrariums either. The plants in a terrarium should grow slowly, or your design quickly becomes a jumbled jungle.

We make more demands of a terrarium than we do of a plant growing in a pot. Plants in pots, aside from pruning and shaping, are allowed to grow as they will. But we demand that our terrariums grow the way *we* want them to. Parts are clipped to size, pinned to shape, and pulled out and replaced if they don't shape up.

Cruel? We don't really think you can be cruel to plants. At any rate, a terrarium is above all a design: a picture of a created world. And, as the creators, we are allowed to play god to that extent. We take pride in our terrariums, and our terrariums must be things we can be proud of, not just the week we make them but for months afterward, too.

To this end, as we said, we don't feed. We also make certain that the terrariums we plant have room for growth. They may look sparse tonight (though they have to look sparsely handsome), but in a few weeks, wow!

We seem to spend a lot of time talking in negatives about terrariums: Don't do this, don't use that. It's because everybody, whether he knows anything about plants or not, considers himself an expert when it comes to terrariums. And so many bad ideas go around.

Worst must be the plants being used and sold as "terrarium plants" —everything from hardy woodland material to seedlings of 75-foot trees. So here we go again. Please don't plant into your terrariums plants that need a winter dormancy (they can't survive the warmth); don't put in trees or palms or large-growing shrubs or deiffenbachias or dizygotheca or philodendrons or . . .

Grow true miniatures, plants that will stay small and healthy in your beautiful terrarium.

I listened to your program on terrariums last Saturday, and I was surprised that you said there should be no soil showing in the front. The plants need soil for their roots. You can't grow a miniature palm in a thin layer of soil, for instance.

What we said is that we dislike a *thick layer of soil* showing at the front of a fishtank terrarium. The soil is distracting and unattractive. What we have recommended is that the soil be very low in front and then built up to as thick a layer as you wish in the back. This thick layer of soil can stand on its own or be held in by handsome stones or interesting pieces of driftwood.

Also, we wish the professional suppliers would stop putting miniature palms in terrariums. They are not suited to terrarium life and soon outgrow one if healthy (though most don't stay healthy in the tank). Also inappropriate for a terrarium are *Araucaria excelsa* (Norfolk Island pine), young podocarpus (Japanese yew), and pittosporum. They all would outgrow a terrarium if they were healthy (which is unlikely), and develop such deep and intertwined root systems that the competition would be fierce, and separation (when they grew) impossible without severe root damage.

Additionally, no really deep layer of soil should ever be necessary in a terrarium except in design terms. *The best terrarium plants* (the handsomest, freest-flowering, most care-free, and best adapted to terrarium life) *are shallow-rooted plants:* begonias, gesneriads, ferns, calatheas, mosses, selaginellas, pileas, some peperomias, pellionia, etc.

We didn't mean to be nasty, but poor ideas seem to be easier to perpetuate than good ones, so we have to keep slugging.

How do you feel about sand painting as the base for a terrarium?

We hate it a lot.

There's nothing wrong with sand painting—as sand painting we have nothing against it, and some of it can be attractive. But a terrarium is a "story" about plants (with rocks as a subplot, perhaps). The sand painting of the terrarium base detracts from both the plants and the painting.

At any rate, there should be as little soil as possible visible at the front of your terrarium.

Can you recommend a small terrarium foliage plant? Something with variegations?

Peperomia prostrata is a small-leafed peperomia, of creeping habit and subtle variegations. It is slow-growing and will propagate from short cuttings pinned to the soil of your terrarium.

Chamaeranthemum venosum (the plant is smaller than the name) is an unusual and rare plant, small-growing, variegated with silver veining (which is where the "venosum" part of the name comes from). And it makes spikes of small white flowers quite freely—which self-seed in your terrarium.

Can I put my terrarium (ferns, mosses, prayer plant) outside for the summer?

You could, if it was well shaded—direct sun would cook your plants under glass. But why would you want to? Terrariums bring a little bit of the outside world in. Besides, outside it would be open to all sorts of garden pests: things difficult to get rid of in a terrarium.

Don't.

What should I feed my terrarium?

Very little: if anything. If it's planted with soil, a few drops of water-soluble fertilizer every few months—when you water (if you water). If your terrarium is planted with a soilless mix, you can give it just a bit more food.

Would you recommend some miniature sinningias for a small terrarium?

Love to. There are no lovelier flowering miniatures for terrariums.

Sinningia pusilla is about 1½ inches across as a mature plant. Its lilac-colored flowers are about 1 inch long and should be produced several at a time. It is likely to self-seed, giving you a miniature surrounded by its young mini-minis.

Sinningia 'White Sprite' is a white mutation of *S. pusilla,* and is exactly the same, except for flower color.

Sinningia 'Bright Eyes' is a slightly larger plant with slightly larger flowers—also lilac.

Sinningia 'Wood Nymph' is a bit larger still (understand, it is still under 3 inches across as a mature plant), and its flowers, purple and white, are spotted in purple.

Sinningia 'Cindy' will readily grow 6 inches across and produce a dozen large purple and white (purple above and white below) flowers with purple spots. Beautiful and showy. Don't hesitate to cut back all the top growth if the plant goes leggy.

We know you only asked for miniature sinningias, but our favorite terrarium gesneriad is *Koellikeria erinoides.* Individual mature plants are only about 4 inches across, but they multiply and will readily fill a terrarium. Individual flowers are small, but are borne by the dozens on tall spikes. And the heart-shaped leaves are spotted with silver and streaked with red. Super! Its only drawback is that it is a *seasonal,* not a *continuous,* bloomer (as are the sinningias). But it is a long season.

If disaster strikes, don't panic: cut all your miniature sinningias back to the ground, save the tiny potatolike tuber, and start over again.

My terrariums always get so crowded so fast: can I prune inside a terrarium?

Yes, you can groom and prune in a terrarium, as you would out of it.

But it sounds as if you are planting your terrariums too densely to begin with. A terrarium should take months to grow to its fullness.

Use more space. A good open space in a terrarium can be as effective as an accent plant. Don't be afraid of space. This is one of the major flaws in the terrariums we have seen and judged over the years—an unwillingness to trust an empty space.

And don't feed. If you feed your plants, they will grow.

I have gray mold in my new bottle garden—how can I get rid of it? And where does it come from?

If your bottle is a wine bottle, then perhaps you didn't clean it properly. There is sugar in many wines, and sugar is a terrific medium for molds.

Wine bottles should be washed out thoroughly with hot water and detergent and then with a solution of 9 parts hot water to 1 part chlorine bleach—and then rinsed very thoroughly with hot water to get rid of the bleach residue. Give the bottle a sniff—if you smell bleach, give it another hot rinse.

Mold can also be the result of a too wet soil. In a bottle garden the soil should be barely damp.

Now, you cannot spray the inside of your bottle with a fungicide— there is no place for it to go; it stays in the system and becomes a problem itself.

However, there are two approaches you can try. We have occasionally had success just scraping off what mold we could and stirring the rest into the soil. Sometimes the miniature environment inside the bottle achieves a balance after several scrapings and stirrings. Or, you can take the plants out of the bottle, treat them individually for the fungus (perhaps with a spray of Benomyl 50%), dump the soil, resterilize the bottle, and do the whole thing over with a cleaner bottle and more careful water balance.

However, with certain types of molds and fungus you don't have much of a chance of coming out of it successfully. They just take over too quickly. If you've already lost the battle, give in gracefully. Dump everything but the bottle, sterilize that as described, and start from scratch.

Better luck next time.

Is it true that maidenhair ferns will grow only indoors in a terrarium?

No, it is not. Some adiantums (maidenhair ferns) will not *even* grow indoors in a terrarium. Some of them require moist air, moderately dry feet, and cool temperatures. How do you provide that unless you live on the Pacific Palisades?

I have made the 50-gallon fern terrarium we spoke about, and it is great (two cool-white fluorescent tubes). Where I could never grow a fern before, I have dozens thriving. Except for one. I have twice tried a *Pellaea rotundifolia*, and twice it has got leggy and just not grown well. I have moved it close to the tubes, but that doesn't seem to help. Besides, can it need more sun than my maidenhair?

We don't think it is a light problem. We think it is a soil problem. *Pellaea rotundifolia* (button fern) needs a more alkaline soil than most other ferns. This makes it difficult to grow for any time in combinations with other, acid-loving, ferns.

Create a little pocket of neutral to slightly alkaline soil (pH 6.9 to 7) by adding a little ground dolomitic limestone to a small bit of soil near the bottom of the tank; that should help. And congratulations.

How do I water cacti in an open terrarium?

The same way porcupines make love: very carefully.

We really hate cacti in a terrarium a lot. If you are at all careless with the watering, the plants will rot.

Cacti don't need a terrarium.

If you want to make a "picture of the world" showing cacti, make a shallow dish garden instead of a terrarium. You can use the same elements of design, but in a dish with drainage holes and without those glass or plastic sides that just get in your way and provide extra, unwanted, humidity.

Which is the real fittonia—the one with the red veins or the one with the white veins?

Will the real fittonia please stand up? (It can't, it's a prostrate grower—a creeper.)

They are both the "real" fittonia. The red-veined plant is *Fittonia verschaffeltii,* and the white-veined plant is *Fittonia verschaffeltii argyroneura.* Their culture is identical.

Give both the high humidity of a terrarium, constant moisture at their roots, and bright light without direct sun.

They are excellent spreaders in a protected environment. In fact, we have seen a lovely terrarium made up of only these two fittonias.

Why should I go to the expense of fluorescent lights for my terrarium when I have a perfectly good sunny window?

Because your good sunny window will cook your good terrarium plants. Sunlight passes through glass, and in the passing its wavelength is changed so that some of that light is changed to heat. (This, the so-called greenhouse effect, is why greenhouses are so hot on a sunny winter day, whatever the temperature outside.) The heat builds up and the plants are literally cooked.

Fluorescent light doesn't build up heat in the same way, and so it is safer for our terrariums.

How about a couple of unusual plants for my terrarium? All you seem to talk about are miniature gesneriads and begonias.

How about some miniature gesneriads or begonias? No?

Barring those, you might try *Pellionia daveauana* (or *Pellionia pulchra*—they are quite similar), an excellent colorful-leafed creeper that thrives so in a terrarium that you must keep cutting it back to keep it from taking over, or *Caladium humboldtii*, a truly miniature caladium, green-leafed with silver spots, quite beautiful as a small accent plant.

Are you sure we can't interest you in a miniature begonia?

Stan, you say a terrarium needs truly miniature plants, not just young plants. How do you feel about miniature geraniums and miniature roses in a terrarium?

All terrarium plants should be miniatures, but not all miniatures can be terrarium plants. Miniature roses are among the most adaptable of plants (hardy outdoors, but excellent houseplants) and miniature geraniums (pelargoniums) are wonderful on windowsills, but neither one will survive inside a terrarium. Both would likely succumb to fungus.

I have twice collected hardy woods plants for terrariums, but these wild flowers have died. Is there some trick to it? Can you help me?

Woodland plants live in a special relationship with the microorganisms in their soil. They can seldom be transplanted successfully, even to an outdoor garden; they are almost always a disaster in a terrarium. Add to this the heat of the average indoor environment and the need these plants have for a cold winter, and you have futility piled on pillage—many woodland plants are threatened by extinction because of collectors and construction.

But we will help you—to be a more responsible person: *buy* your "wild" plants from reputable nurseries, who propagate them themselves, rather than stealing them from the woods, then keep your terrarium below 64°F. (See APPENDIX.)

I suppose it's like asking how you get a ship into a bottle, but how do you get plants into a bottle? Do you start with seeds?

No, you couldn't start with seeds for most plants: terrarium light isn't strong enough to keep seedlings thrifty. (Though some of the nicest plants you get in a bottle garden are "volunteer" ferns and mosses, which come from spores.)

You get plants into a bottle in exactly the same way that you get a ship into a bottle: with care and small parts (plants) and with special tools. If you can get a small rootball through the bottleneck, you can often gently roll the leaves to get them through. Once through, they open and look too large ever to have come in through the opening.

Settle an argument, please. If I grow one plant in a container, is that a terrarium?

Not to us. It is a "protected environment," but for us a terrarium has to have *design*. It must be a *picture* of the world.

But "terrarium" is only a word, and creepers like episcia, fittonia, and pellionia do beautifully as single plants in a protected environment. Why let a word stop you from doing something beautiful?

What begonias would you recommend for an all-begonia terrarium?

There are so many!

Begonia prismatocarpa is special in a couple of ways, but especially because of its profusion of yellow flowers. It's in constant bloom and covers the bottom of a container well, too. A hybrid of it, *Begonia* 'Buttercup,' grows larger and has larger flowers, but we prefer the original.

Begonia 'Peridot' is a miniature rex begonia with dark, silver-spotted leaves that are almost round.

Begonia 'Rajah' and *B. versicolor* and *B.* 'Universe' all have exquisite foliage, are all high-humidity plants, and will grow only in a terrarium for us. But they tend to grow a little larger than the miniatures.

Begonia 'Chantilly Lace,' *B.* 'China Doll,' *B.* 'Robert Schatzer,' and *B. bowerae nigra-marga* are all small to tiny and will stay small.

Will button fern grow outside of a terrarium? How about table ferns?

For us, *Pellaea rotundifolia* needs the high humidity. It also needs a soil that tests out near neutral, not acid.

Table ferns (pteris ferns), however, may do well outside a terrarium; they are fairly sturdy in normal home conditions. In fact, we no longer grow ours in a terrarium, because it insisted on growing its fertile fronds out the top.

On the radio you often talk about plants I never see in plant catalogs. I don't think that's fair, do you, really?

Yes, really, because we weren't born with those plants. You can get them the same way we did. By joining plant societies—even if you live too far away from a chapter to go to meetings, most of the plant societies have seed funds (or, in the case of the American Fern Society, a spore bank) for rare and valuable plants. From the plant societies, you make plant friends, with whom you exchange cuttings and seeds.

Go to botanical garden-plant sales; they often sell off divisions of extremely desirable plants.

Finally, there are more catalogs in heaven and earth than you have sent for—yet. Spend a little! Some of the best catalogs cost anywhere from a few cents to a few dollars.

All right, now you know our secret.

APPENDIXES ✍ ✍ ✍ ✍
Plant Societies

African Violet Society of America, Inc.
Box 1326
Knoxville, TN 37901
$6/year includes *African Violet Magazine* (5 times/year)

American Begonia Society, Inc.
8302 Kittyhawk Ave.
Los Angeles, CA 90045
$5/year ($5.50 foreign) includes *The Begonian* (monthly)

American Bonsai Society, Inc.
228 Rosemont Ave.
Erie, PA 16505
$10/year includes *Bonsai Journal* (quarterly) and *Abstracts* (newsletter)

The American Camellia Society
Box 212
Fort Valley, GA 31030
$10/year includes yearbook and *The Camellia Journal* (quarterly)

American Fern Society
Biological Sciences Group
University of Connecticut
Storrs, CT 06268
$5/year includes *American Fern Journal* (quarterly)

The American Gloxinia and Gesneriad Society, Inc.
PO Box 174
New Milford, CT 06776
$7/year includes *The Gloxinian* (bimonthly)

The American Hibiscus Society
PO Box 491F, Rt. 1
Fort Myers, FL 33909
$5/year includes *Seed Pod* (quarterly)

American Ivy Society
National Center for American Horticulture
Mount Vernon, VA 22121
$7.50/year includes *The Alepole, American Ivy Society* (quarterly)

American Orchid Society, Inc.
Botanical Museum of Harvard University
Cambridge, MA 02138
$15/year includes *American Orchid Society Bulletin* (monthly)

The American Plant Life Society (amaryllis)
PO Box 150
La Jolla, CA 92038
$7/year includes *Plantlife-Amaryllis Yearbook*

American Rhododendron Society
617 Fairway Drive
Aberdeen, WA 98520
$12/year includes *The Quarterly Bulletin of the American Rhododendron Society*

American Rose Society
PO Box 30,000
Shreveport, LA 71130
$15.50/year includes *The American Rose* (monthly)

Bonsai Clubs International
445 Blake St.
Menlo Park, CA 94025
$7.50/year includes *Bonsai Magazine* (10 issues)

The Bonsai Society of Greater New York, Inc.
PO Box 343
New Hyde Park, NY 11040
From $9/year includes *Bonsai Bulletin* (quarterly)

The Bromeliad Society, Inc.
PO Box 3279
Santa Monica, CA 90403
$10/year includes *Bromeliad Journal* (6 issues)

Cactus and Succulent Society of America, Inc.
PO Box 3010
Santa Barbara, CA 93105
$12.50/year includes *Cactus and Succulent Journal* (bimonthly)

Epiphyllum Society of America
PO Box 1395
Monrovia, CA 91016
$3/year includes *Epiphyllum Bulletin* (7 times/year)

Gesneriad Society International
PO Box 549
Knoxville, TN 37901
$6/year includes *Gesneriad Saintpaulia News* (bimonthly)

The Herb Society of America
300 Massachusetts Ave.
Boston, MA 02115
The Herbarist (annually)

The Indoor Light Gardening Society of America, Inc.
423 Powell Drive
Bay Village, OH 44140
$5/year includes *Light Garden* (bimonthly)

International Cactus and Succulent Society
PO Box 1452
San Angelo, TX 76901
$7.50/year includes *Newsletter* (4 issues/year)

International Geranium Society
6501 Yosemite Drive
Buena Park, CA 90620
$5/year includes *Geraniums Around the World* (quarterly)

Los Angeles International Fern Society
2423 Burritt Ave.
Redondo Beach, CA 90278
$5.50/year includes fern lessons and monthly magazine

The North American Lily Society, Inc.
c/o Earl A. Holl, Exec. Secy.
Box 40134
Indianapolis, IN 46240
$7.50/year includes *Yearbook* and *Quarterly Bulletin*

The Palm Society, Inc.
1320 South Venetian Way
Miami, FL 33139
From $12.50/year includes *Princepes* (quarterly)

Saintpaulia International
PO Box 549
Knoxville, TN 37901
$6/year includes *Gesneriad Saintpaulia News* (bimonthly)

The Terrarium Association
57 Wolfpit Ave.
Norwalk, CT 06851
$7/year includes *Terrarium Topics* (4 issues/year) and *Terrarium Plant Lists* (handbook)

Mail-Order Sources

ABC Herb Nursery
Rt. 1, Box 313
Lecoma, MO 65540
Houseplants, herbs. **F**

Alberts & Merkel Bros., Inc.
2210 S. Federal Highway
Boynton Beach, FL 33435
Bromeliads, orchids. Tropical foliage **C** $1.50; orchid **L** $1.50

Arthur Eames Allgrove
North Wilmington, MA 01887
Bonsai plants, live sphagnum moss. **L** 25¢

Alpine Gardens
280 S.E. Fir-Villa Rd.
Dallas, OR 97338
Sempervivums, sedums. 25¢

Annalee Violetry
29–50 214th Place
Bayside, NY 11360
African violets only. **S L**

Antonelli Brothers
2545 Capitola Rd.
Santa Cruz, CA 95062
Tuberous begonias, gesneriads, houseplants. **N** 50¢

Applewood Seed Co.
833 Parfet St.
Lakewood, CO 80215
Wildflower & houseplant seed. **F L**

Baldsiefen Nursery
Box 88
Bellvale, NY 10912
Rhododendrons only. **C D N** $2

The Banana Tree
245 N. Ninth St.
Allentown, PA 18102
*Banana plants and "bulbs," tropical
  nuts.* **L** 25¢

Beach Garden Nursery
2131 Portola Drive
Santa Cruz, CA 95062
Bromeliads. **L X** 25¢

The Beall Company
PO Box 467
Vashon Island, WA 98070
Orchids only. **F**

Black River Orchids, Inc.
77th St., Box 110
South Haven, MI 49090
Orchids, supplies. **F**

Bolduc's Greenhill Nursery
2131 Vallejo St.
St. Helena, CA 94574
Ferns. **L S**

Bonavista
807 Van Buren St.
Douglas, WY 82633
Interesting flower & vegetable seed. **F**

The Bonsai Farm
Rt. 1, Box 156
Adkins, TX 78101
Bonsai plants, supplies. **D** $1

Bountiful Ridge Nurseries, Inc.
Princess Anne, MD 21853
Fruit & nut trees, berries, shrubs. **F**

The Bovees Nursery
1737 S.W. Coronado
Portland, OR 97219
Rhododendrons, etc. 50¢

Frank Bowman
771 Williams Ave.
Brooklyn, NY 11207
Rare & unusual succulents. **L P** or **S**

Brittingham Plant Farms
Ocean City Rd.
Salisbury, MD 21801
Berries, grapes, asparagus. **F**

Brown's Omaha Plant Farms, Inc.
PO Box 787
Omaha, TX 75571
Vegetable plants, onions. **C F**

John Brudy's Rare Plant House
PO Box 1348
Cocoa Beach, FL 32931
*Tropical tree & shrub seed (includ-
  ing coccoloba).* **C D** $1

Brussel's Bonsai Nursery
305 Colonial Rd.
Memphis, TN 38177
Bonsai starter plants. **L** 25¢

Buell's Greenhouses, Inc.
PO Box 218L6
Weeks Rd.
Eastford, CT 06242
Gesneriad plants & seed. **L** 25¢

Burpee Seed Co.
Warminster, PA 18974
Wide variety of seeds & plants. **C F**

D.V. Burrell Seed Growers Co.
Rocky Ford, CO 81067
Vegetable & flower seed. **F**

California Epi Center
PO Box 2474
Van Nuys, CA 91404
Epiphyllums. **D** $1

Capriland's Herb Farm
Silver St.
Coventry, CT 06238
Herb seed & plants. **L F**

Carlsons Gardens
Box 305
South Salem, NY 10590
Azaleas & rhododendrons. **D** $1

Carobil Farm
Church Rd., RD 1
Brunswick, ME 04011
Geraniums, including mini and scented. 35¢

Common Fields Nursery
Town Farm Rd.
Ipswich, MA 01938
Blueberries, flowering shrubs, evergreens. **L F**

Conley's Garden Center
Boothbay Harbor, ME 04538
Wildflower plants, herb & wildflower seed. 35¢

Cook's Geraniums
712 North Grand
Lyons, KS 67554
Geraniums only. 35¢

Cornelison's Bromeliads
225 San Bernardino St.
North Fort Myers, FL 33903
Bromeliads. **P**

Country Hills Greenhouse
Rt. 1
Corning, OH 43730
Interesting variety of houseplants. $1.50

DeGiorgi Company, Inc.
Council Bluffs, IA 51501
Large selection of general seed. **X** 50¢

J.A. Demonchaux
827 North Kansas
Topeka, KS 66608
Vegetable & herb seed. 25¢

DoDe's Gardens
1490 Saturn St.
Merritt Island, FL 32952
African violets & supplies. **P**

Emlong Nurseries
Stevensville, MI 49127
Nursery stock, including fruits and berries. **F**

Farmer Seed and Nursery Co.
Fairbault, MN 55021
Varied vegetable seed, fruit trees, supplies. **C F**

Far North Gardens
15621 Auburndale Ave.
Livonia, MI 48154
Rare flower seed. 50¢

Faubus Berry Nursery
Star Route 4
Elkins, AR 72727
Berry plants. **L F**

Fennel Orchid Co., Inc.
26715 S.W. 157th Ave.
Homestead, FL 33030
Orchids, ferns, supplies. **F**

Fernwood Plants
PO Box 268
Topanga, CA 90290
Rare cacti & other succulents. 50¢

Finck Floral Co.
9849 Keniker Lane
St. Louis, MO 63127
Orchids. **L F**

Fischer Greenhouses
Linwood, NJ 08221
African violets, other gesneriads, supplies. **C** 15¢; supplies 25¢

Jim Fobel
598 Kipuka Place (598-AG)
Kailua, HI 96734
Tropical seeds & plants. $1 for 3 packets tropical seed

Fort Caroline Orchids
13142 Fort Caroline Rd.
Jacksonville, FL 32225
Orchids only. $2.50

Dean Foster Nurseries
Hartford, MI 49057
Berries, fruit trees, vegetable plants. **C F**

Fountains's Sierra Bug Co.
Box 114
Rough-and-Ready, CA 95975
Ladybugs only. **L F**

Four Winds Growers
42186 Palm Ave.
PO Box 3538, Mission San Jose Dist.
Fremont, CA 94538
True dwarf citrus. **X** 25¢

Arthur Freed Orchids, Inc.
5731 South Bonsall Drive
Malibu, CA 90265
Orchids. **C F**

Garden Place
6780 Heisley Rd.
Mentor, OH 44060
Perennials only. **F**

Geiger Orchids
PO Box 245
Wellborn, FL 32094
Orchids. **L F**

The D.S. George Nurseries
Fairport, NY 14450
Clematis. **L** 20¢

Gilson Gardens, Incorporated
U.S. Rt. 20
Perry, OH 44081
Groundcovers, vines (including sil-verlace). **F**

Girard Nurseries
PO Box 428
Geneva, OH 44041
Ornamental trees & shrubs, including dwarves & grafted weepers. **L F**

Gladside Gardens
61 Main St.
Northfield, MA 01360
Tender bulbs. **L F**

Gleckers Seedsmen
Metamora, OH 43540
Unusual vegetable seed. **L F**

Grace's Gardens
Autumn Lane
Hackettstown, NJ 07840
Unusual vegetables. **C F**

Greenbrier Orchids
4711 Palm Beach Blvd.
Fort Myers, FL 33905
Orchids & ferns. **L S**

Greenland Flower Shop
RD 1, Box 52
Port Matilda, PA 16870
Houseplants. **L** 25¢

Greenlife Gardens Greenhouses
164 Meadovista Rd.
Griffin, GA 30223
Houseplants (many unusual). 50¢

Green of the Earth
1295 Lownes Pl.
Pomona, CA 91766
Begonias & other houseplants. 50¢

Greer Gardens
1280 Goodpasture Island Rd.
Eugene, OR 97401
Hardy & houseplant rhododendrons. **C** $1

Bernard D. Greeson
3548 N. Cramer St.
Milwaukee, WI 53211
Labels & other supplies. **D** 50¢

Ben Haines
Box 1111
Lawrence, KS 66044
Hardy cactus **L** 53¢; *tender succulents* **L** $1.10

Robert B. Hamm
2951 Elliott
Wichita Falls, TX 76308
Begonias & gesneriads. **L** & 2 supplements $1

Hana Gardenland
PO Box 177
Hana, HI 96713
Tropical seeds & plants. **L P**

Hardy & Fouquette Orchids
East Heaney Circle
Santee, CA 92071
Orchids. **L** 25¢

Joseph Harris Company, Inc.
Moreton Farm
Rochester, NY 14624
Vegetable and flower seed (good varieties). **C F**

Heatherbloom Farm
Rt. 1, Box 230A
Lakeville, CT 06039
Coleus, impatiens, fluorescent-light fixtures. **D** $1

Henrietta's Nursery
1345 N. Brawley
Fresno, CA 93711
Cacti & other succulents. 35¢

The Herb Garden
Haynes Road
Deerfield, NH 03037
Wide variety of herb plants. **L F**

Herb Shop
PO Box 362
Fairfield, CT 06430
Herb seed. 50¢

Hidden Springs Nursery
Rt. 1, Box 186-1A
Cookeville, TN 38501
Fuchsias only. **L** 25¢

Hilltop Herb Farm
PO Box 1734
Cleveland, TX 77327
Herb plants & seed. **D** 50¢

Jerry Horne
10195 S.W. 70th St.
Miami, FL 33173
Polyscias, palms, other tropicals. **L S P**

Hortica Gardens
PO Box 308
Placerville, CA 95667
Nursery stock for bonsai. **D** 25¢

House Plant Corner, Ltd.
Box 5000
Cambridge, MD 21613
*Indoor gardening supplies, house-
plants.* **F**

J.L. Hudson, Seedsman
PO Box 1058
Redwood City, CA 94064
Many rare and interesting seed. $1

Hurov's Tropical Seeds
PO Box 10387
Honolulu, HI 96816
Tropical seeds. **L F**

Inter-State Nurseries
Hamburg, IA 51644
*Roses, trees, shrubs, bulbs, peren-
nials.* **F**

Jackson & Perkins Co.
Medford, OR 97501
*Roses, general seeds (separate cata-
logues).* **F**

Le Jardin du Gourmet
West Danville, VT 05873
*Herb plants & seed, shallots, Egyp-
tian onions.* **L** 25¢

Johnny's Selected Seeds
Albion, ME 04910
Organically raised vegetable seed. **D**
50¢

Johnson Cactus Sales Co.
1571 E. Parkway Loop
Tustin, CA 92680
Desert & jungle cacti. **C L** 25¢

Jones and Scully, Inc.
2200 Northwest 33rd Ave.
Miami, FL 33142
Orchids. **C** $4 (worth it)

Jungle-Gems, Inc.
PO Box 95
BelAir, MD 21014
Orchids. **F**

J.W. Jung Seed Co.
Randolph, WI 53956
*Flower & vegetable seed, some sup-
plies, houseplants.* **C F**

Kartuz Greenhouses
92 Chestnut St.
Wilmington, MA 01887
Begonias & gesneriads. **C** $1

Kelly Bros. Nurseries, Inc.
Dansville, NY 14437
Trees, shrubs, fruit trees. **C F**

Kelly's Epiphyllum Collection
141 Quail Drive
Encinitas, CA 92024
Epiphyllums only. **C** $1

Klinkel's African Violets
1553 Harding
Enumclaw, WA 98022
African violets & episcias. **L** 25¢

Krider Nurseries, Inc.
Middlebury, IN 46540
Shrubs, vines, nursery stock. **C F**

Kuaola Farms, Ltd.
PO Box 4038
Hilo, HI 96720
Anthuriums. **L F**

Lakeland Nurseries Sales
Hanover, PA 17331
Unusual fruits & nursery stock, lady-bugs. **C F**

Lauray of Salisbury
Undermountain Rd., Rt. 41
Salisbury, CT 06068
Houseplants. 75¢

Orol Ledden & Sons
Sewell, NJ 08080
Vegetable & flower seed, supplies. **F**

Little Lake Nursery
Rt. 2, Box 2503E
Auburn, CA 95603
Magnolias. **F**

Loehman's Cactus Patch
8014 Howe St.
Paramount, CA 90723
Cacti & other succulents. **L F**

Louise's Greenhouse
55 North Street
Danielson, CT 06239
Hoyas and bougainvilleas. **L** 50¢

Lousise's Greenhouse
PO Box 767
Sour Lake, TX 77659
African violet leaves only. **L** 25¢

Loyce's Flowers
Rt. 2, Box 11
Cranbury, TX 76048
Hoyas and Bougainvilleas. **L** 50¢

Lyndon Lyon
Dolgeville, NY 13329
African violets, miniature roses. **L F**

Cathryn Mangold
PO Box 1998
Rancho Sante Fe, CA 92067
Lithops seed. **L S**

Ann Mann's Orchids
Rt. 3, Box 202
Orlando, FL 32811
Orchids & potting medium. 50¢

Marz Bromeliads
10782 Citrus Drive
Moor Park, CA 93021
Bromeliads & hoyas. **L** 35¢

Earl May Seed & Nursery Co.
Shenandoah, IA 51603
General seed & nursery stock. **C F**

Rod McLellan Co.
1450 El Camino Real
South San Francisco, CA 94080
Orchids, supplies. **C F**

McComb Greenhouses
Rt. 1
New Straitsville, OH 43766
Unusual houseplants. **Y** 35¢

McDaniel's Miniature Roses
7523 Zemso St.
Lemon Grove, CA 92045
Mini roses only. **L F**

Mellinger's
2310 West South Range
North Lima, OH 44452
Supplies, nursery stock, houseplant seed. **F**

Merry Gardens
Camden, ME 04843
Houseplants. **L** $1.50; 50¢

The Meyer Seed Company
600 S. Caroline St.
Baltimore, MD 27231
Vegetable & flower seed, supplies. **F**

J.E. Miller Nurseries, Inc.
Canandaigua, NY 14424
Fruits, berries. **C F**

Mincemoyer Nursery
County Line Rd., "Rt. 526"
Jackson, NJ 08527
Perennials, wildflowers, hardy ferns. 25¢

Mini-Roses
PO Box 4255, Sta. A
Dallas, TX 75208
Mini roses only. **L F**

Moore Miniature Roses
2519 E. Noble Ave.
Visalia, CA 93277
Mini roses only. **F**

Cactus by Mueller
10411 Rosedale Highway
Bakersfield, CA 93308
Cacti & other succulents. **L** 30¢

Metro Myster Farms
Rt. 1, Box 285
Northampton, PA 18067
*Vegetable & herb seed, bulbous veg-
etables, Jerusalem artichokes.* **C F**

E.B. Nauman
324 Avalon Drive
Brighton, NY 14618
*Rhododendrons & other broadleafed
evergreens.* **F**

Nichols Garden Nursery
1190 North Pacific Highway
Albany, OR 97321
*Herb & vegetable seed, sedums &
sempervivums.* **F**

Nor'east Miniature Roses
58 Hammond St.
Rowley, MA 01969
Mini roses only. **F**

Nourse Farms, Inc.
Box 485
RFD South Deerfield, MA 01373
Strawberries, asparagus. **F N**

L.L. Olds Seed Co.
PO Box 7790
Madison, WI 53707
Vegetable & flower seed, supplies. **F**

Orchard Nursery
6955 Howells Ferry Rd.
Mobile, AL 36608
Azaleas, camellias. **D** 25¢

Orchid Gardens
6700 Splithand Rd.
Grand Rapids, MN 55744
Wildflowers, including native orchids.
50¢

Orchids Bountiful
826 West 3800 South
Bountiful, UT 84010
Orchids & supplies. **L P**

Orinda Nursery
Bridgeville, DL 19933
Camellias, rhododendrons. **C** 50¢

Palette Gardens
26 West Zion Hill Rd.
Quakertown, PA 18951
Dwarf evergreens, perennials. **D** 50¢

Paradise Gardens, Inc.
14 May St.
Whitman, MA 02382
Water plants & supplies. **D** $1

Geo. W. Park Seed Co., Inc.
Greenwood, SC 29647
Vegetable, flower, houseplant seed.
C F

Peekskill Nurseries
Shrub Oak, NY 10588
Ground covers. **L F**

Penn Valley Orchids
239 Old Gulph Rd.
Wynnewood, PA 19096
Orchids (largely paphiopedilums). **C**
$1

Phipps African Violets and Supplies
RR 1
Paris, Ontario N3L 3E1
Canada
African violets & supplies. **S** 25¢

Pixie Treasures
4121 Prospect Ave.
Yorba Linda, CA 92686
Mini roses only. 25¢

Plant Master
PO Box 2486
Allentown, PA 18105
Houseplants. **F**

The Plant Room
6373 Trafalgar Rd.
Hornby, Ontario LOP 1EO
Canada
Gesneriads & other houseplants. **L** $1

Ponzer Nursery
Lecoma Star Route
Rolla, MO 65401
*Flowering shrubs, fruits, Jerusalem
artichokes.* **L P**

Rakestraw's Perennial Gardens &
Nurseries
G-3094 S. Term St.
Burton, MI 48529
Dwarf conifers. **L** 50¢

Rayner Bros., Inc.
Salisbury, MD 21801
Berries. **F**

Redwood City Seed Co.
PO Box 361
Redwood City, CA 94064
Vegetable & tropical fruit seed. 25¢

Rex Bulb Farms
Box 145
Newberg, OR 97132
Lily bulbs & seed only. **C** 10¢

Romanoff Greenhouses
Canterbury, CT 06331
Phalaenopsis & paphiopedilum orchids. **L F**

Routh's Greenhouse
Louisberg, MO 65685
Begonias and African violets. **L F**

Rutland of Kentucky
3 Bon Haven
Maysville, KY 41056
Herbs. **D** $1.50

Savage Farms Nurseries
PO Box 125 ML
McMinnville, TN 37110
Fruit trees, nursery stock. **C F**

Savory's Greenhouses
5300 Whiting Ave.
Edina, MN 55435
Hosta (about 100 varieties). **L P**

Schmelling's African Violets
5133 Peck Hill Rd.
Jamesville, NY 13078
African violet leaves & supplies. **L**
    50¢

Sea Breeze Orchids, Inc.
PO Box 1416
Bayville, NY 11709
Species orchids. **L F**

Shadow Lawn Nursery
637 Holly Lane
Plantation, FL 33317
Unusual houseplants. 35¢

The Shrinking Violet
28 Sawin St.
Natick, MA 01760
Mini African violets only. **L S**

R.H. Shumway Seedsman
Rockford, IL 61101
General vegetable & flower seed. **F**

Slocum Water Gardens
1101 Cypress Gardens Rd.
Winter Haven, FL 33880
Water plants. **C** $1

Louis Smirnow & Son
85 Linden Lane
Brookville, NY 11545
Leading peony hybridizer, amaryllis.
    C $1 (but $2 credit allowed);
    amaryllis **L F**

Stark Bros. Nurseries
Louisiana, MO 63353
Fruit trees. **C F**

Steele Plant Company
Gleason, TN 38229
Vegetable plants. **F**

Stern's Nurseries, Inc.
Geneva, NY 14456
General nursery stock, bulbs, berries.
    C F (if you mention us)

Fred A. Stewart, Inc.
PO Box 307
San Gabriel, CA 91778
Orchids. **C D** $1.39

St. Louis Violet Nurseries
2662 Smoke View Drive
Maryland Heights, MO 63043
African violet plants & seed. **L S** or
    25¢

Stokes Seeds, Inc.
737 Main St.
Box 548
Buffalo, NY 14240
*Broad variety of vegetable & flower
    seed.* **F**

Ed Storms
4223 Pershing
Fort Worth, TX 76107
Lithops & other succulents. 50¢

Sunnybrook Farms Nursery
PO Box 6
9448 Mayfield Rd.
Chesterland, OH 44026
*Herbs, houseplants, scented & dwarf
    geraniums.* **D** 50¢

Geo. Tait & Sons, Inc.
900 Tidewater Drive
Norfolk, VA 23504
Vegetable & flower seed. **F**

Talnadge Fern Gardens
354 "G" Street
Chula Vista, CA 92010
Bromeliads (no *ferns*) . **L D** $1

Thompson & Morgan, Inc.
PO Box 100
Farmingdale, NJ 07727
Interesting vegetable & flower seed.
  C F

Three Springs Fisheries
Lilypons, MD 21717
Water plants & accessories & fish.
  C N $1

Tinari Greenhouses
Box 190
2325 Valley Rd.
Huntingdon Valley, PA 19006
African violets & supplies. **C** 25¢

William Tricker, Inc.
74 Allendale Ave.
Saddle River, NJ 07458
Water plants, water-garden supplies.
  C 25¢

Tropical Plant Gardens
PO Box 16472
Jacksonville, FL 32216
Tropical houseplants. **S**

Tropical Plants
Box 2186
Harlingen, TX 78550
Tropical houseplants. $2

Otis S. Twilley
Salisbury, MD 21801
General vegetable & flower seed. **F**

Utopia Greenhouses
PO 313—US 64
Hayesville, NC 28904
African violets. **L P**

Vesey's Seeds, Ltd.
York, Prince Edward Island, Canada
*Vegetable & flower seed, "Seeds for
  short season areas."* **F**

The Violet Farm
306 Woodlawn Ave.
Willow Grove, PA 19090
African violet plants & leaves. **L** 25¢

Volkmann Bros. Greenhouses
2714 Minert St.
Dallas, TX 75219
African violets, supplies, plant stands.
  F

Walther's
RD 3, Box 30
9W Highway
Catskill, NY 12414
Bromeliads & supplies. **P**

The Wayside Gardens Co.
Hodges, SC 29695
Bulbs, perennials, shrubs. **C** $1

Bob Wells Nursery
PO Box 606
Lindale, TX 75771
Fruit & nut trees, berries. **F**

Mrs. R.C. Welsh
Rt. 3, Box 181
Madison, FL 32340
Jasmines, daylilies, houseplants. **L** 15¢

White Flower Farm
Litchfield, CT 06759
Perennials, bulbs, etc. **C N D** (from
  $20 order) $5

Gilbert H. Wild & Son, Inc.
Sarcoxie, MO 64862
Daylilies & peonies. **C D** $1

Wileywood Nursery
17414 Bothell Way S.E.
Bothell, WA 98011
Fuchsias only. **F N**

Wilson Bros. Floral Co., Inc.
Roachdale, IN 46172
Houseplants. **C F**

The Whole Herb & Spice Shoppe
38 Miller Ave.
Mill Valley, CA 94941
Herb seed. 35¢

Wood's African Violets
Proton Station
Ontario, Canada NOC 1LO
African violets. **L** 25¢

Yankee Peddler Herb Farm
Dept. D, Hwy. 36N
Brenham, TX 77833
Large selection of herb plants & seeds.
   D $1

Index